POWDER RIVER

Let 'er Buck

Books by

STRUTHERS BURT

Prose

JOHN O'MAY AND OTHER STORIES
CHANCE ENCOUNTERS
THE INTERPRETER'S HOUSE
THE DIARY OF A DUDE WRANGLER
THE DELECTABLE MOUNTAINS
THEY COULD NOT SLEEP
THE OTHER SIDE
FESTIVAL
ENTERTAINING THE ISLANDERS
ESCAPE FROM AMERICA
POWDER RIVER: LET 'ER BUCK

Verse

IN THE HIGH HILLS
SONGS AND PORTRAITS
WHEN I GREW UP TO MIDDLE AGE

THE
RIVERS OF AMERICA

Editor

CONSTANCE LINDSAY SKINNER

Assistant Editor

ELIZABETH L. GILMAN

Art Editor

RUTH E. ANDERSON

POWDER RIVER

Let 'er Buck

by

STRUTHERS BURT

Illustrated by

Ross Santee

FARRAR & RINEHART

INCORPORATED

New York   *Toronto*

TO

HARRY HARRISON

horseman, cattleman, gentle and
courageous gentleman, who em-
bodies the best traditions of the
Far West, and to his wife, Ethel.

Contents

PART ONE. THE SIOUX RIDE

PART TWO. RED NOON

YOU MOUNT YOUR HORSES FROM THE RIGHT; INDIANS
MOUNT FROM THE RIGHT

ix

PART THREE. RED SUNSET

PART FOUR. CATTLE COUNTRY

YOU MOUNT YOUR HORSES FROM THE LEFT; WHITE
MEN MOUNT FROM THE LEFT

PART FIVE. NEXT-DOOR NEIGHBORS

"HERE'S TALK OF THE TURK AND THE POPE, BUT IT'S
MY NEXT DOOR NEIGHBOR WHO DOES ME HARM."
THOMAS FULLER, *Gnomologia*, 1608-1661

CONTENTS

CHAPTER ONE

· Grass

THIS story of Powder River is—in reality—the story of grass. The search for it. The fight for it. The slow disappearance of it. Grass, that strange green thing which covers the earth and without which man cannot live, and the color of which, the secret of life itself, is still as much of a mystery to man as when he first saw it.

Bluestem, buffalo grass, slough grass, bunch grass; miles and miles of it, up to a horse's withers!

As is always the case, however, in great movements of mankind, the people—red man; after him, white man—who followed the grass into the Powder River country were only dimly aware of what they were doing. They went where the country looked good. They would have been astonished had you put their search in such grandiloquent terms.

The Sioux followed the buffalo, the buffalo followed the grass, across the greatest grasslands this country has ever known. The high immense plateaus of what

3

are now the Dakotas on to the high immense plateau of
the Powder in what is now eastern Wyoming. The
Sioux came out of the forests of the South, the forests
of the lower Mississippi. They were canoemen. They
followed the Mississippi north through the forests of
Wisconsin and Minnesota where they fought the Chippewa, or Ojibway, and then a part of their nation, the
Teton Sioux, turned west and came out into the great
grass. The great grass that rippled to the horizon like
a green ocean. There they found the horses that were
to make them "the finest natural cavalry the world
has ever seen," as General George Crook and Captain
Frederick Benteen called them.

Mounted they became the terror of the northern
plains. The Sioux, more properly the Dakotas. The
Otchenti Chakowin, or Seven Council Fires. The
Brulés and Oglalas, and Miniconjous. The Sans Arcs
and Two Kettles. The Blackfoot Sioux. The fierce
Hunkpapas, Sitting Bull's people! That part of the
Sioux nation, the Teton Sioux, which came west. The
Santee Sioux remained in Minnesota.

The Teton Sioux came as far as the Big Horns
which, curving from the west back again to the west,
cut northern Wyoming in half like a huge shining
scimitar, tempered with the blue of streams and the
dark green-blue of forests. The Sioux drove the Absarokas, the Crows, from the Powder back across the
Big Horns into the Big Horn Basin, and for over seventy
years held the Powder River country. It was their country. They fought the Crows in constant raid and
counterraid, they fought the white man by treaty,
always broken by the white man, and by war, prolonged
and formal, and formally declared. No isolated bands
or raiding Apaches here! And then the white man won
and the Sioux were sent east along the trails they had

come to the reservations in the Dakotas where they now are.

There was a great wailing among the Sioux when they went.

Up from the south, from southern Wyoming, across the dead line of the North Platte, came other seekers of the grass: the cattlemen who had been waiting for the Sioux to be driven out; Texans most of them, who had been held up for over ten years in their gigantic, dust-blown trek from the Red and the Canadian and the shores of the Gulf itself. They moved into the Powder River country with their longhorns, and their horses, and their families, and their cowboys. They had found their home . . . this sweet grass country, with the mountain streams coming down from the pines and firs and aspens of the Big Horns, and the grass spreading eastward until it began to thin near the banks of the Powder River. Twenty-five, thirty, thirty-five miles the grass spread toward the rising sun, until finally, beyond the river, it was lost in the ocher plateaus and tumbled buttes of the arid badlands that in their turn lost themselves far beyond the morning horizon.

But time moved faster when the cattlemen came; was collapsed. Modern man had met the Stone Age man in final combat and had conquered, but modern man brought the shortness of modern time with him.

For almost eight decades the Sioux and the buffalo had kept inviolate the green strip of country, a hundred and fifty miles long from north to south, twenty-five to fifty miles wide from east to west, between the Big Horns and the Powder; between the North Platte in Wyoming and the Rosebud in Montana. The great cattlemen in the eastern shadows of the mountains were lords as far as they could look for only a decade. For only a decade, for less than a decade did they permit themselves to live a feudal, pastoral life such as has been equaled nowhere else save in Mexico, Texas, the Argentine and Southern California.

This was partly their own fault, they lived too largely and too carelessly. News of their easy profits spread too far. The Powder River country was opened up to white settlement in 1878; within five years the grass was crowded.

Blizzards took their toll. Speculation ruined others. Rustlers working on the flanks of the herds, like wolves on the flanks of the vanished dark pools of buffalo, grew powerful. Overgrazing narrowed and killed the range. The "nester" appeared . . . the tragic, too big-familied, running-nosed figure of the homesteader. The sheepman came. The farmer followed, plowing up the light soil and the grasses that held it down, stirring the alkali to the surface, spreading it by irrigation. Still the cattleman survived. He alone, besides the sheepman and the horseman, was where he should have been.

With the turn of the century, speculation struck again, this time in the form of land instead of cattle, sweeping across the mountains and the meadows and the plains, as ruthless as a blizzard and more devastating. After the war, all through the hard-eyed, loose-lipped twenties, this recurrent menace, as old as the first fool, battened and grew taller. Drought came, even deadlier than blizzard. Erosion was helped along by its greatest friend, man. Still the cattleman, his ranks thinned somewhat, survived.

He is there today, perhaps on the edge of greater security than he has ever known. He has had to ask himself many questions; his friends and his enemies have had to ask themselves questions, too. And the land and the cattleman have found new allies, even if in many instances this is still unrecognized. Science is a new ally. Nature has been a Spartan schoolteacher. The government has at last awakened. The spirit of the times has changed. And a new form of ranching, an addition to whatever form of ranching the rancher has been engaged in, has appeared to offer a further source of income and a round, hard, cash dollar backlog. And the men engaged in this business are in favor of the West as it has been and always will be if good sense is used.

Twenty-five years ago the West laughed at the ladies in "queer pants" and their male companions who wore neck handkerchiefs wrongly. The West also regarded with suspicion those ranchers who encouraged these aliens to ruin horses and frighten steers. Now all this is changed. Today most Americans know the West and, being Americans, most of them love the West and find there something indigenous, and American and revivifying; and comforting, and magnificent.

The "wild West" as it persists in fiction and the movies, for the refreshment of city dwellers who never leave their eastern towns, is based on actuality however distorted and foreshortened and heightened. It is merely ten years of history, let us say, condensed into two weeks of impossible living. The real West, as it actually was—and still is—yields tales that need no heightening; that are beyond the imaginings of scenarists.

How could it be otherwise in a vast and thinly settled country peopled for the most part by adventurous men and women, there because they want to be? In that air, that altitude, with those horizons, there is the deepest sort of laughter, quick drama, and plenty of grimness for those who feel that the East alone is reality.

Nor can the "real West" die; not so long as there

are cattle and the herding of them is a business and a way of life. Not so long as there are thousands of miles of loneliness; of plains, of mountains, of forests, and of deserts.

And this, the whole of it, is just a simple fact, apart from "blurbs," denials, "dudes," highways, or anything else you care to mention.

To those who deeply know the West, from the Rio Grande to the Arctic Circle, from eastern Oregon to western Nebraska, the West is a fact, a tradition, an intention, a point of view, a blood stream, a way of doing things, and a devotion.

CHAPTER TWO

A Mile Wide and an Inch Deep

SOME rivers are feminine, those that run through green reaches and trim meadows, but the river it is my exciting task to attempt to describe is purely masculine, with every masculine virtue and most masculine vices.

A purely American river, too. Not a trace of any other land about it. It heads in the very heart of the United States, just east of the continent's backbone, and not a breath of the Atlantic nor the Pacific blows upon it. The non-Americans who settled near it, many of whom are still there, became American, and in a local and solid fashion, or else failed to survive. The country they encountered, its way of living, its atmosphere, were too direct, too stark, too clear, too American for prolonged hesitation.

But not much of a river to look at. Too lean and sun-baked. Too many dislocated bones in the shape of buttes and mesas and abrupt arroyos.

A buckaroo among rivers. A bow-legged, broken-nosed buckaroo, secretive, sardonically humorous, minding its own business; casual, insouciant, but swift and deadly in action, a jaunty twist to its battered Stetson. That's the Powder!

A remarkable and dramatic river, but an odd one to be so important, if you consider the shortness of its history, its lack of size, and the fact that it begins nowhere in particular and ends in much the same fashion. In reality, of course, it ends in the Gulf of Mexico after

9

debouching abruptly into the Yellowstone up in Montana, and afterwards, if any trace of its personality is left, into the Missouri, and thence into the Mississippi. Thousands of miles from where it starts it flows past the Creoles of New Orleans, who know little of it and care less.

"A mile wide and an inch deep" is the acidly affectionate description used by those who are its intimates, and although the Powder is by no means a mile wide, and although it is considerably over an inch deep, the phrase possesses the exaggerated truth common to folk descriptions; an exaggerated truth conveying a picture clearer than exactness.

A narrow, yellow, winding little river, twisting often between cut banks of sand or clay, high or low, sheered off as by a knife, with every now and then groves of cottonwoods affording the only shade. A small river, fierce in the spring floods, coiling torpid and slow in the summer heat like a rattlesnake. A river spotted with the horrid blackness of quicksands, whose muddy waters the cowboys working on roundups used to clear by dropping a halved cactus into the bucket.

A river starting hardly at all in the arid east where creeks with such sinister names as Salt and Dry enter it. Doing better toward the south and southwest where the South and Middle Forks join at the end of a lovely, endless, rolling country that dips north from the too-famous Teapot Dome Divide to the foothills of the Big Horns. A river heading in the west, as righteous rivers should, in jubilant mountain creek after creek that come down from the Big Horns; creeks, however, that speedily lose their mountain exhilaration as they wind out across the plains. And finally a river that, having gathered together its principal subsidiaries, almost at once plunges into a hundred miles or so—counting coils—of badlands as if deliberately and insolently turning its back on men.

Badlands, yellow, ocher, pink, russet, gray; at dusk a tender exquisite violet, where, in occasional folds, are a few cattle and sheep ranches whose only access to the civilized country and paved roads of Buffalo and Sheridan, thirty-five miles or so to the west, are narrow cart tracks almost impassable in bad weather.

Neither a broad river then, nor a pretty one, nor a long one. Only about three hundred miles in length, and a lot of these due to tortuousness. None of the more complimentary fluvial adjectives apply to it. Self-respecting fish do not live in it. Two summers ago, on a day that burned your saddle horn, I tried to find a place in which to swim, but could discover no pool where a wise man would trust a sinking foot.

Strahorn, one of the most enthusiastic of the early commentators (Strahorn is still alive) and the author of Wyoming's first guidebook, an excellent guidebook, and one that bears the comprehensive title, *The Hand-Book of Wyoming and Guide to the Black Hills and Big Horn Regions. A Glimpse at the Prominent Resources of the Territory, with special articles on Stock raising, Mining, Lumbering, Agriculture, Manufacturing, Climate, Game, Fish, etc., and full descriptions of the Big Horn, Black Hills and Yellowstone Regions, for Citizen, Emigrant and Tourist, by Robert E. Strahorn, Cheyenne, Wyoming, 1877,* was at a loss for anything more complimentary than this:

In briefly describing some of these prominent streams and valleys, we may be frank in commencing by declaring that we have nothing good to say of Powder River, the southern boundary of the Big Horn region. Its waters are darkly mysterious and villainously alkalied; its southern tribu-

taries ditto; and it is far from a fitting gateway to the land
of beauty and plenty just outlined.

Nor could Brigadier General F. W. Raynolds, then
a captain and brevet colonel, in his report of his expedition of 1859, the first official report of the Powder
River country, think of anything better. In the language the government seems to prefer, he wrote:

Its valley [that of the Powder], which is barren and
yields but little grass and an abundance of artemisia [wild
marjoram, i.e., sagebrush], averages a mile in width throughout its entire length, until within fifty miles from its mouth,
it becomes narrower and the bluffs more ragged and broken.
Travelling in it is greatly impeded by deep and almost impassable ravines which cross it at nearly right angles, and
are concealed by the sage until their very edge is reached.
These gullies are caused by the action of the water upon the
light soil, and are among the most disagreeable features of
the country. The bed of the river is mainly a treacherous
quicksand, and great care is necessary in selecting fords. The
depth of the water is not, however, such as to offer any obstruction, except during freshets. The bluffs bordering the
valley are throughout the much-dreaded and barren "bad
lands," and this stream must ever remain of little or no value
to the country.

Brevet Colonel Raynolds, like most of his con-
temporaries, knew little of those sparse-looking but
nutritious herbs, the western range grasses, which fool
the ignorant but never fool a steer. You remember,
perhaps, the Easterner who, being told by a ranchman
that western cattle lived on bunch grass, was thought-
ful for a moment, and then asked, "Yes . . . but what
do they live on in between the bunches?"

And, indeed, in some ways Strahorn and Brevet
Colonel Raynolds were right. The Powder has never

been an obviously useful stream as so many other ugly rivers are. It has few apparent solid virtues to make up for its lack of pulchritude. It was never, like its big brother to the north, the Missouri, a liquid trace into the unknown. It runs in the wrong direction, south to north. It is not now, and never has been, a green arrow of civilization pointed at the wilderness.

It was not, like the Sweetwater to the south—the Sweetwater that bisects Wyoming from west to east and finally joins the North Platte which comes up from the south and the Medicine Bow—a hard-working and kindly river, as its name implies, furnishing water to the explorer and immigrant and plainly indicating where great trails such as the Oregon and Overland should go. For a long while the Powder was merely a crossing, a ford, a trading post in a dimly known and forbidden country, used by only a handful of trappers and prospectors, and these did not linger. Beaver did not build in its bitter waters and "pay dirt" did not glint in the miner's pan.

We do not even know how the Powder got its name.

Probably the casual guesses of old-timers who speak Sioux, or Cheyenne, or Crow, or all three, are correct as casual explanations often are. In all three languages, naturally, are words that mean powdered earth, or sandy soil.

How, then, did this river, short, ugly, unvirtuous, almost anonymous, born to every handicap, become the most famous river in a state filled with lovely rivers? More famous even than the Snake, the mighty Snake that is the main tributary of the Columbia. More famous even than the Yellowstone, that is the main tributary of the Missouri. More famous than the Green, that is the main tributary of the Colorado. Heading all three within fifty miles of each other in the mountains of western Wyoming and emptying, the first, into the Pacific; the second, into the Gulf of Mexico; the third, into the Gulf of California.

The most famous river in Wyoming? The Powder is the most famous river in the Northwest. Famous now all over the country, its name familiar to thousands who haven't the faintest idea where the river is, or whether it's an actual river or merely an exclamation. A river spoken of with contempt by all who first saw it, whose name has become a battle cry. A shout of encouragement. A cry of derision. A password to a secret society. And above all a symbol of an American way of living which, despite all the varied drama of American life, took hold of the American imagination, and still holds it, as an epitome of perhaps the deepest and most universal expression of this continent's wish.

The expression of some longing, some vision, some desire for loneliness in crowds, some inherited horizon line, some nostalgic hope, as close to the American heart as the old life of the South or the lost quiet elms and spare democracy of New England.

"Powder River! Let 'er buck! A Mile Wide and an Inch Deep!"

Nor, lest it seem to contradict my former statement, does the feminine in "Let 'er buck!" refer to the river but to the large generic fact of bucking. Powder River is completely masculine.

During the last war the Wyoming troops fought under this gonfalon of words, usually just the two words "Powder River!" Short, sharp, shrill, like the cowboy yell, which is the Confederate yell brought up the Texas Trail with the longhorns, the echo of the coyote added, the last note pitched high and held so that it will carry a long distance. Presently almost the entire United States Army in France knew the battle cry.

Wherever men ride bad horses, either for amusement or for money, "Powder River!" greets them as man and horse turn loose, in wholehearted admiration if the ride is good, or edged with ridicule, the admiration reserved for the horse, if the rider is thrown.

The two words possess all the gradations of meaning of the Spanish used by bull ring aficionados.

In the most unexpected places they spring out at you. A brand. An open-sesame. A voucher. A visiting card. To repeat . . . a password. In the East. In Europe. In South America. In the Orient. That's all a man has to say to you and the roaring stampedes of cities are soundless for a moment. And you are surprised, and pleased.

In Wyoming, in Montana, in Idaho, all over the Northwest, men and women out riding, when they shake their reins loose for a gallop, are likely to shout the words as the joy of swiftness begins to brush their foreheads.

Wherever cowboys live, north of the Rio Grande; wherever cattle are branded in western fashion; wherever rodeos, those recent developments, travel, and they travel nowadays even as far as London; wherever old-timers foregather, or new-timers for that matter, the phrase "Powder River!" means something secret, profound, the inner significance of which is known only to the initiated.

Something large, vague; definite, concrete; symbolic, exciting.

And primarily, to those who live in it, it means that far-flung principality, Wyoming.

You might suspect "main strength and awkwardness," to use far western phraseology as the basis for this phenomenal success story until you look into it, and then quite clearly you perceive why Powder River is famous.

Epic is a large word, overused in American writing. One of two moods seems to seize upon American writers when they sit down to write about their country: either they become epic or else they become abusive, and both moods are difficult to sustain. No land, however large, can support properly more than one epic river. The Mississippi is enough for the United States. The Powder would become embarrassed if you called it "epic." But along its banks and in the country it drains, three great national epics have been enacted, one of which—the epic of grass—has not yet reached its conclusion. Powder River is still asking the question of what shall happen to the great grazing highlands of America.

As for the other two epics, they are quite clear. To begin with, are the Sioux. Their rise to power, their might, their downfall. To end with, there is the northwestern cattle business. The northern cowboy. The epic of the open range.

To the American, although most of them don't know it, the Powder River country deserves to be as memorable as Marathon is to the Greeks, the walls of Vienna to the Austrians, Charles Martel at Tours to western Europe.

Powder River witnessed the end of over two hundred years of Indian fighting. There finally the Indian lance was shivered; there white clay overlaid red earth. There the rifle conquered the bow and arrow. In the shadow of the Big Horns the tepee fires were put out and the tepees folded. Not that there wasn't plenty of Indian fighting afterwards; there was. The Nez Percés, the Utes, the Apaches; the tragic Messiah Craze—the Ghost Dancing—of the early nineties. Half a dozen other outbreaks. But with the final defeat of the Sioux the Indian everywhere knew he was beaten, and for good. The mounted warrior was done. The pride of the proudest and most arrogant Americans this continent has ever seen was broken by other Americans, less proud but more dogged. On the Powder was finished what had been begun ten generations before in the forests of the Atlantic seaboard. The whole wide continent was safe from everyone but the white man himself.

Into the still rising sunset dust of the retreating Sioux rode the waiting cattleman. And there began the second great epic of the Powder.

The story of the northwestern cattle business, the truly American cattle business, not half Spanish as was the cattle business of Texas and the Southwest, began on the Powder. And with it the companion epic of the northwestern open range. I don't mean the unfenced range. There are millions of acres of unfenced range today, government controlled. I mean the old open range where a man turned his cattle loose and saw them maybe only twice a year, at the spring and fall round-ups, and where in blizzards the stock drifted a hundred to three hundred miles.

Because the Powder was the greatest grass country in the Northwest, save for the Dakotas and south-eastern Wyoming, because it lay right in the path of the advancing Texans, it became an epitome of the indigenous American cattle business and of that new figure, never before known in the Northwest, the purely American cowboy. The Powder, partially settled by Texans, instructed by them, taught all the Northwest the lore of the range. The Powder changed the great northern Rocky Mountain states from gold countries to cattle countries, just as awhile before the gold miners had changed them from fur states to gold states.

Powder River deserves clear title to its password and rallying cry.

CHAPTER THREE

The Shining Mountains "dont la pierre luit jour et nuit"

THE "Senator" was especially interested in the altitude of his adopted state. The Senator had come up the Texas Trail before Wyoming was a state, and I can see him now, tall, slim, walking with the quick, catlike, slightly rolling gait of the cowpuncher, his voice soft, and yet edged with the soft and dangerous edge of the Texas drawl.

The Senator, of course—no need to tell Wyoming men or women—was that epitome of the Far West, the late John B. Kendrick.

"We're mountaineers!" he was fond of saying. "The mountaineers of America. We've got all the virtues and all the vices of mountaineers." And the Senator was right.

The history of Wyoming, its character, has been conditioned primarily by one soaring fact, Wyoming's immense height above the level of the sea. And this primary fact produced two other conditioning factors.

The shortness of the Wyoming mountain ranges; the width of the main valleys between. Wyoming, as a matter of fact, is a mountaintop. All of it. And its mountain ranges are merely the tips of a single mountain. And Wyoming is the only place in the country where this happens.

If you will look at a map of Wyoming you will see that it is a huge square laid down upon the principal height of land of the United States, with Yellowstone Park, another square, up in its northwestern corner like a misplaced postage stamp.

To give you some idea of the size of Wyoming, this postage stamp, relatively about the size of a postage stamp on an ordinary envelope, is a little over one-fourth the size of Holland, much bigger than Delaware.

Wyoming is twice the size of New York, that large eastern state, and thirty-eight times larger than Rhode Island, and in this huge territory live only a little over two hundred thousand people; two and a half persons to the square mile. No wonder Wyoming is more of a secret society than a state, where everyone knows everyone else, at least by reputation, and there is a special handshake and an implicit acknowledgment. And yet Wyoming is only half as large as Montana, its neighbor to the north.

If you visualized Wyoming you would see it as a mammoth mesa. You have to climb to get to the mesa. Going west you climb steadily from the Mississippi; coming east you climb more abruptly from the glimmering stretches of the Salt Lake deserts where you are already fairly high. In either case you have climbed so imperceptibly that you are hardly aware that you have reached the southern plains of the mesa, its highest part, except for the startling wideness of the sky, the sunlit air that softly warms your lungs, and the strange luminosity of lights at dusk.

This mesa, except where it is broken by mountain ranges running north and south, like the Big Horns, in the north central section, and the Wind Rivers and Absarokas, and the Tetons, and the other great ranges in the northwest, slopes steadily from the south to the north.

And because Wyoming is so high no one yet has been able to get at its minerals, if there are any. That is another conditioning factor. Most Wyoming mountain ranges are huge, overlapping faults. You would have to pry off the top layer to find anything. And so Wyoming, surrounded by great mineral-bearing states —Montana, Idaho, Utah, Colorado—has remained a grazing state pure and simple. There have been plenty of rumors of gold in Wyoming, and a few gold rushes, especially in the Big Horns and in the South Pass country at the base of the Wind Rivers, and all Wyoming streams and rivers carry flour gold. You can pan a dollar or so a day—perhaps. At all events, with every depression prospectors appear again, haunting the lonely creeks, nowadays even girl prospectors with matted sunburned hair, but gold in paying quantities has never been found. There is some oil, however, and a little low-grade coal. But still Wyoming is grass country.

Like the Big Horns, the majority of the Wyoming ranges arise out of nothing and die away into nothing, and all the Wyoming ranges are short and most of them do not run out of the state. That's because, as I have said, the entire state is in reality a mountain and its ranges are merely the peaks of the mountain. One hour you are traveling through hot plains, the next you are in the cool recesses of incredible hills. Thousands of people cross southern Wyoming every year convinced that it is a semidesert state. They do not know that to the north and south of them . . . all around them . . . are green valleys and greener forests and luminous uplands. In July wildflowers tapestry Wyoming like the handiwork of proud and lovely ladies.

If you are adroitly stupid enough, and plenty of Americans are, you can dodge in and out around Wyoming hardly aware that there are any mountains at all. The big ones hide themselves.

It was because you can dodge around and through the Wyoming ranges, it was because southern Wyoming is so high that the mountains level out and afford an easy gateway, as if the earth were content to rest and lie down having climbed so high, it was because Wyoming is the only place in the United States where this happens, except far to the south in New Mexico and Arizona, that Wyoming became the great northern route to the coast. It was suddenly discovered in the 1840's that you could take wagons straight across southern Wyoming to the Pacific.

But for the same reason, until the late sixties and the coming of the cowmen and the railways, Wyoming remained no more than a rather dangerous way station on the road to Oregon and California. No one thought of really living there.

All mountains, of course, at certain times, in the wrong light, at the wrong time of day, look dull and huddled and foreshortened, but if you see the Rockies at just the right moment they are astonishing. They have a translucent quality under the sun; a glimmering quality at night; an inner fire. They are among the few mountains in the world that retain color after dark.

Who were the first people to see them, to live on their flanks? We do not know. When the first white men history records drifted into the present states of Montana and Wyoming, the Crows, the Absarokas, lived, and had long lived, in the fastnesses of the Big Horns. They were the first discernible inhabitants.

But at the northern tip of the Big Horns is a relic of peoples older than any we know: the famous Medicine Wheel. Famous, that is, to all those who live in Wyoming, but not especially famous to anyone else. A relic which, if the United States were England, would be as famous as Stonehenge. Some dim forgotten tribe long before the Crows, or the Sioux, or the Blackfeet, or the Cheyennes, some very early Americans, worshiped at this huge circle of stone with its radiating spokes of carefully laid boulders.

We have no definite knowledge of the first white men in the region, though, like the vague silver of the moonlight that haunts the Powder on August nights, the tradition of the Spaniard haunts the Big Horns and eastern Wyoming as it haunts so many other parts of the Northwest. No one knows just how far north the Spaniards got during the greatness of their seventeenth century. Too many records were destroyed when the Indian insurrection of the 1680's blazed along the New Mexican Spanish frontier. That the Spaniards got as far north as Colorado we know. For a couple of decades at least, in the middle sixteen hundreds, Spanish pack trains laden with gold and furs were coming down from the north to the settlements near Santa Fe, and undoubtedly this continued up to the insurrection. But probably the Spaniards never got as far as Wyoming.

When a couple of generations later the French voyageurs and fur traders began to push west along the Canadian line in their search for the Pacific and the Columbia, they constantly ran into relayed Indian stories of "tall men in armor, feathers on their heads,"

tall men who had mysteriously appeared as far afield
as eastern Oregon and had as mysteriously disappeared.
And we know that the earliest American trappers
called the Green River in western Wyoming the "Spanish River," whatever their reasons may have been. Perhaps because the Green River ran straight down to the
Spanish possessions in the Southwest.

A hundred miles or so southeast of the Powder,
where Niobrara and Platte and Goshen counties come
together, are the so-called "Spanish Diggings," huge
abandoned quarries covering an area of ten by forty
miles. Archaeologists have decided, in contradiction of
the name given these and the popular belief, that they
are neolithic mine pits and factory sites. But there are
other vague traditions.

In 1865 members of General Connor's "Powder
River Expedition," the first hostile military expedition
to enter the Powder River country, reported the finding of the ruins of stone houses on the shores of Lake
De Smet at the eastern base of the Big Horns. A year
later the supposed remains of a Spanish arrastra, a tool
for crushing quartz, was found in the same vicinity.
In 1874 Colonel Mill's expedition to the Big Horns also
reported the ruins of stone houses. In 1866, miners
coming out of the Rosebud country in Montana which
is just north of the Powder River Basin, their hair flying back of them because of Indians, brought word of
an ancient mining ditch they had come across. A ditch,
and traces of iron tools and of mining on a fairly large
scale. But these remains, Iberian or not, have disappeared, all save the "Spanish Diggings."

Whatever the Spaniard in Colorado may have
called the "Shining Mountains," the first American
called them the "Stonies," and subsequently the Rockies.
The Indians dwelling in what is now the province of

Alberta in northwestern Canada knew the luminous quality of the Rockies and had their descriptive name for them. In 1729 that great Canadian explorer, Pierre Gaultier de Varennes de la Vérendrye, Sieur de Varennes de la Vérendrye, at his post on the Nipigon River, wrote in his journal what he had heard from a Cree hunter of these glowing peaks, "dont la pierre luit jour et nuit." And the Sieur de Varennes de la Vérendrye copied a map which the Cree had made for him of the course and the headwaters of the Saskatchewan, a river still unknown to him, and in the extreme left corner of the map he marked the Rockies, naming them "Les montagnes de pierres brillantes." A legend, a shining dream; for it is probable that no Vérendrye was ever to see the main cordillera of the Rockies.

But two of Pierre's sons, the Chevalier Louis Joseph and his younger brother, François, with two white companions, in 1742, came near to seeing them. They had come down from the Mandan villages on the Missouri to the Cheyenne River and were journeying slowly in a general westerly direction seeking for the Western Sea, or the river flowing into it, the goal of explorers for over a century. A huge concourse of Indians, chiefly Arikaras, traveled with them, bent on war with their foes on the western border of the present Wyoming. On January 1st they saw mountains, so the Chevalier Louis Joseph tells us in his narrative.

Several pioneer historians have thought that these mountains were the Big Horns and that the four Canadians saw them from the north; the Big Horns sticking up there off to themselves with the vast rolling country of Montana spreading out from them. A sight, indeed, for wandering explorers. A sight for anyone, then and now. The Big Horns, startling and shaggy as a buffalo bull on that cold pellucid New Year morning in the thin clear air of those winter altitudes that tastes like chilled wine, the blue of the forests dark above the glistening white of the snow. But recent research has shortened the Vérendryes' trail considerably and it seems likely that they got no farther west than the Black Hills, which at that time were held by the Kiowas, the "Gens du Serpent," who were the dread of the plains before the Teton Sioux arrived some thirty years later to conquer them, make allies of them and usurp their title of "snakes" or "enemies"—the sign manual of the Plains tribes is the same for both words. The Arikaras accompanying the Canadian explorers were afraid of the Kiowas, so the four white men were forced to turn back without climbing a high peak to look westward as they had desired; perhaps Harney Peak, the highest of the Black Hills, from which they might have glimpsed the Big Horn section of that vast range along the west, shining by night and day.

At Fort Pierre in South Dakota, where the Bad and the Missouri meet, there was found in 1913 a leaden tablet, six inches by eight, one of those taken with them by the Vérendryes to mark their journeys. On one side, carefully stamped, are these words in Latin, "In 1741, the twenty-sixth year of our most illustrious Seigneur Louis XV, in the time of his Viceroy, Monseigneur the Marquis de Beauharnais, Petrus Gaultier de Laverendrie, deposited." But Pierre himself was not on this journey and did not deposit this tablet. One of his sons scratched on the lead surface of the other side, with his knife probably, the date, March 30th, and four names, his own and his brother's and two others which seem to be Louy la Londette, or Laudette, and A Miotte. The names, unfortunately, are not clear on the tablet and are not mentioned in the Vérendrye journals.

CHAPTER FOUR

Painted Ponies

Iɴ the summer storms of the Powder, of all the high country of the West, little dust whirls gather, spin, die down; gather again; come together as the great wind grows.

Until the end of the eighteenth century, the Powder slept in its age-old calm, broken only by occasional raids of the Blackfeet down into this country of their enemies the Crows. Then, up over the horizon from where the sun rises, there appeared small war parties of another nation.

The Seven Council Fires were on the move.

Through the country not yet named for them, up to the Black Hills, discovering the horse among the Arikaras on the banks of the Missouri, and trading for him the fusils and ammunition they had got from the French in Minnesota, fighting at first that small but deadly tribe the Kiowas, then making allies of them, following the buffalo, came the Dakotas, the Sioux. The "Dakotas," as the Minnesota Sioux call themselves. The Yanktons say, "Nakota"; or, if you go among the Oglalas, it is "Lakota." The word with its various pronunciations means "friend." When two Sioux meet they greet each other so.

As for "Sioux," it is the last syllable of the Ojibway name for the Dakotas "Nadawessiwag," corrupted by the French into "Nadiousioux," and similar spellings. It means "serpents" or "enemies." The Algonkins of

Wisconsin called the Dakotas "Chah" in La Salle's time
(1679) and the Pawnees today call them "Chah-ra-
rat," which also seems to contain the root of the Pawnee
word for enemy.

The Cheyenne name for the Sioux is "O'ho-
omo-ío" or some dialect variant of it and possibly
means "enemy," which seems to have been a general
designation for these truculent newcomers.

At first the Cheyennes fought these strangers;
then like the Kiowas they, too, became allies, the best
the Sioux ever had.

Southwest from Minnesota, across the plains, up
to the Black Hills, raiding, hunting, trading, exploring; across the Black Hills into southeastern Montana;
southward up the Powder into Wyoming, came the
Seven Council Fires.

Blue and green and gold in the summer, the "Shining Mountains" faced them. Everywhere the Dakotas
looked, when they looked to the west, were the Big
Horns; a great forested wall near at hand, a blue thin
cloud in the distance. A fortress holding the farther
sunset marches. A place of streams and lakes and thick-
grassed mountain meadows where the tall trees, their
endless tops like infinitely larger meadows, rose to bare
rock peaks and ringed the feeding buffalo and mountain
sheep. The Big Horns, one hundred and twenty-five
miles long, their greatest mountain, Cloud Peak, rising
thirteen thousand feet into the air! The Big Horns, coming up out of nothing, out of rolling prairie country to
the south, and ending in the same abrupt fashion just
over the Montana line in the north! Thick as most
eastern counties and truly called after the Indian
word, "Ah-sah-ta," which means mountain sheep. For,
whether their shape was recognized or whether the Big
Horns were merely given their name because of the

mountain sheep that once inhabited them, they bend from west to east and then west again in a long slow curve like the horns of a gigantic sheep.

Garrisoning the Big Horns during the summer, retreating west into the Big Horn Basin during the winters, raiding down upon the Sioux whenever the inclination seized them or they thought they could do it, stealing Sioux horses, driving the small Sioux war parties back at first, and then, as the Sioux returned in increasing numbers, retiring reluctantly and more definitely across the Big Horns into the Big Horn Basin, were the Crows.

The Crows—Les Corbeaux, as the French-Canadian trappers called them—the Absarokas, which means "crow." A big dark tribe, tall men and women, and clever . . . the Mountain Crows, the River Crows, to name the two divisions of the nation as it existed when the Sioux first came across it. The Crows wear immense high-crowned black sombreros, which accentuate their height, and they braid their hair in two plaits and tie the ends with small strips of red flannel. Nowadays they occupy a smiling reservation in Montana just north of the Big Horns along the upper reaches of the Yellowstone and around the Pryor Gap country, and their superintendent is a Crow.

Nor were the Crows unrelated to the Sioux. This was to be something of a family quarrel. The Crows are also of the Siouan family. They are members of the Hidatsa substock, but at some time in unrecorded history the Crows had broken away from the main branch and drifted farther west.

Almost with the first coming of the white man the Crows recognized an ally, not because they liked the whites, but because they hated the Sioux. They were a small nation, only about ten thousand of them; the Sioux were as numerous as cottonwood leaves in spring. But, even with their recognition of white usefulness, it was a long while before the Crows could altogether give up the occasional stealing of white horses. It was in their blood.

The Crows were the keenest traders and the best horse thieves in the West. Unlike the Persians, who were taught to ride well, shoot straight and tell the truth, the Crows were taught to ride well, shoot straight and steal horses. The last was the principal instruction given the young. The instruction began somewhere around the age of four. To be able to steal a horse in such a fashion that nobody knew you were around was the wittiest and most honorable feat a young Crow brave could perform.

Later on, when a white man saw a couple of young Crows making their way across country on foot, rawhide ropes in their hands, he knew just what they were doing. That night, on general principles, he corralled his own horse carefully. To go out on foot and return on horseback was, to the Crows, a supreme joy.

They were even better horse thieves, in the more subtle forms of the art, than their hereditary enemies the Blackfeet. For generations before the Sioux came the Blackfeet had been in the habit each spring of raiding down from their country in northwestern Montana and stealing Crow horses and, as an extra bounty, an occasional Crow woman. The Crows retaliated in kind. The juices of the year stirring in their veins, bands of young Crows would ride north, or bands of young Blackfeet would ride south, and surprising each other's camps at night would start for home with as many ponies as they could run off. Then the Blackfeet would pursue, or the Crows, as the case might be.

But the Sioux were different. These distant kinsmen of the Crows meant business. They were after territory. They were following the buffalo. They were seeking grass for their recently found ponies. They were founding a kingdom.

It took the Sioux about thirty-five years to find the Powder, and when they had found it it took them about twenty more to make it actually their own.

About 1760 a Sioux hunting and exploring party came upon the Arikaras, by now settled in strongly fortified villages along the Missouri. The Arikaras had horses, they also had Spanish saber blades to tip their buffalo lances, mysterious weapons that had drifted north. The Sioux had guns and ammunition as a result of their contact with the French in Minnesota.

Here was a wonderful trade in potential deadliness, and the trade was made.

The Sioux seem to have been natural horsemen from the beginning. They began to mount those circling, whirling, charging squadrons that were to make them famous. That red cavalry of red dawns and red sunsets. Panoplied they started their century-long ride to death. But before those hundred years were out they were to take hundreds of white men and some white women with them.

They drove back the Crows, they completely dominated their allies, the Cheyennes, and the other tribes of the Dakotas, eastern Montana, and Nebraska, and they brooked no interference on the Powder. Even the mighty Blackfeet steered clear of them after the first two decades of the new century. When the white soldiers came in the sixties, the Sioux beat them again and again.

A vast and sudden rise to power, this, on the part of a foot-nation that had been fairly consistently defeated by the Chippewa a century earlier!

Until the sixties and the Sioux Wars, up to the very edge of those wars, spilling over a little into them, the Sioux and the Crows raided each other with much mutual content. There was a great honor to be gained and not too much death or risk. For forty years, from the time of their solid conquest of the Powder until the Civil War, during the twenties, the thirties, the forties and the fifties, the Sioux, those that kept to the Powder and away from the lures of the Oregon Trail and Fort Laramie to the south, led a pleasant life. This was the Golden Age of the Sioux.

In the winter a well-made tepee of skins is a comfortable place with its little fire of crossed sticks resembling a tiny tepee. . . . You keep pushing the ends in. If snow piles deep, a tepee is even more comfortable, well insulated, almost airproof, filled with nice warm thick drowsy smells. With spring there are berries and roots, and all summer long there are berries and roots. Everywhere along the Powder in that golden period the buffalo were black. Half the time you didn't even have to bother with the rest of the meat, you merely ate the humps. Humps made a man strong and rounded him out. During the spring and summer and fall there were dances, and stated festivals to make things go well, and powwows, and visits from other Sioux and from friendly tribes.

In the summer nights the old men sat long in circles and talked, and the young men chose their brides. And then to keep your riding straight and your bowstrings taut and your lances well pointed and your few guns from rusting, there were always the Crows. The

Crows raided you before the hunting and, the hunting over, you raided back, or the other way round.

A wonderful life!

The Spanish had brought horses to a country and people which had never seen them. By trading for horses with the Spaniards of Texas and New Mexico, stealing them and breeding them, the Indian tribes soon became cavalry instead of infantry. And this change altered the relative power of that great warrior nation, the Sioux, and their enemies.

A great deal might be said about these Spanish horses and their influence on America's development. They conquered the West; and they are there today; Barb and Arab, descendants of kings, though they have lost something of their old look of caste. Gentlemen, however, equine or otherwise, grow small and lean, and some of them misshapen if they have to shift too much for themselves. Also their coloring is likely to become variegated. In addition, if for generations you've had to fight off bears and mountain lions and wolves, you grow wary and swift and suspicious, and so fall into the habit of curving your back, and "swallowing your neck," and "breaking in half" should something land on you. But if you're an Arab you retain the Arab brains, the Arab stamina, and the Arab susceptibility to gentling in good hands. And if you're an Arab living in the Far West of the United States you have in your small body the big lungs that come with high altitudes. Also the wit. Also—it can't be anything else —the sardonic humor. Watch a well-trained cow pony go to sleep between the legs of an eastern fox hunter!

White men like their horses to be bay, or gray, or buckskin; at any rate, all of a piece; but Indians like their ponies gay. And so imagine what a spectacle a

battle between Indians must have been—between the
Sioux and the Crows, for instance—with its multitude
of pintos—"paints," black spotted, brown spotted, red
spotted, especially beloved because of their gaudy coloring, and palominos, those lovely horses, taffy colored
with cream or golden manes and tails, and palmettos—
grays with small black Arab spots on their flanks. And
mouse blues. And buckskins with the black stripe down
their backs. And pure whites with red-rimmed eyes.
And all these daubed with color like their naked riders.
Shields, too! And pinioned lances! And the occasional
war bonnet of a chief!

Indians treat their horses roughly. Also, as a final
indignity—that is, in white men's eyes—Indians mount
their ponies from the wrong side, from the right; from
the off side, that is, instead of the near.

White men's horses buck if you do that, and very
justly.

Someday—in heaven—those who don't know the
cow pony will understand him, and appreciate him, and
stop talking about him to those who do.

The Sioux are quite different from the Crows.
They, too, are a big fine-looking people, but lighter red
on the whole than the Crows and squarer. More Manchu looking, perhaps, less nomad Mongolian. And
graver, and more fierce. Inclined to be grim. A proud
people, well aware of their departed greatness. A chiv-
alric people in their own way, who made war and made
treaties formally, as has been said, and kept the latter
with a strictness the white man intended perhaps, but
never was quite able to accomplish.

A young uncle of mine—subsequently he became
an Arizona and California cattleman—in his undergraduate days was a member of a college geological ex-

pedition that had come to eastern Wyoming in search
of fossils. The expedition, happily encamped among
lonely coulees and foothills, was ignorant of the fact
that there was unrest among the Sioux and that many
of them were off their reservations in the Dakotas. One
day my uncle, riding alone, came up over a rise straight
into the arms of a young Sioux, naked and in war paint,
his pinto pony painted and beribboned.

The young Sioux held up his arm and asked my
uncle his business.

My uncle told him.

"Go back," said the young Sioux, "and stay quiet
and do not go too far away from your camp. This time
we are fighting the white soldiers, not the white man."

And the oddest thing about it was that this young
Lakota warrior not only spoke perfect English, but
English with a university accent.

White men should stick together and not deprecate
their own color, ugly as it often is, but had the situation been reversed—that is, with the average white
man, not my uncle—it is doubtful if the young Sioux
would have been let off as easily as he let off my uncle.

During Indian troubles white men seldom stopped
to ask the particular trade of any Indian they came
upon unexpectedly. Frequently they didn't even ask
the sex.

CHAPTER FIVE

John Colter Discovers Wyoming

THE Sioux held the grass country of the Powder; the Crows held the Big Horns; and the Blackfeet and the Crows hunted over the grasslands of Montana. But it was inevitable that the day of the wild herds and the primitive hunter should pass in America as it has passed in other now civilized parts of the world. Into the wild hunter's land came presently the explorer and the soldier and the trader; these in their turn were the forerunners of the settler, the man seeking a homesite, land to plant, and grass for his stock.

During the latter half of the eighteenth century French trappers from St. Louis and the settlements south of it had been pushing farther and farther up the Missouri into the western wilderness. And traders of the Hudson's Bay Company and the Northwest Company of Montreal had begun to trade with the Blackfeet, who lived in what are now Alberta, Saskatchewan and Montana, and with the Mandans on the Missouri near the present Bismarck, North Dakota. Here was a huge territory rich in furs and perhaps in other forms

36

of wealth too; the Missouri evidently rose very far west, in the mountains, and beyond the mountains was the Columbia River, which led to the Pacific Ocean. A long route, no one knew how hazardous, but worth exploring if there were men who dared to do it.

Two men made the American Northwest, and a third . . . practically singlehanded . . . discovered Wyoming. The first of these three men was that far-visioned violin player, Thomas Jefferson, who, almost alone in his vision, perceived what a great country the United States could become. The second was that extraordinarily astute, venturesome and mean immigrant, John Jacob Astor, whose object was to wrest the fur trade from the great Canadian companies. The third— the man who discovered Wyoming practically single-handed—was John Colter, one of the greatest of American explorers, although only seven years of his life, 1803-1810, were spent in the Far West and he died practically unknown and is still entirely lacking the renown that should be his.

Jefferson dispatched Lewis and Clark with a large and well-equipped expedition to find the path to the Pacific, to make scientific as well as geographical discoveries, and to open trade with the tribes of the territory through which they would travel. Among the enlisted men with Lewis and Clark was John Colter.

From now on it is no longer a matter of legendary men in armor and wandering explorers in buckskin with French weapons, who may have seen Wyoming. With the advent of John Colter history takes the place of myth.

Colter had accompanied Lewis and Clark to the Columbia and was with them, on the return journey, at the Mandan towns in the middle of August, 1806. At the mouth of the Yellowstone the expedition fell in with two trappers named Forest Hancock and Joseph Dickson, the only Americans, outside the men of the expedition, to penetrate so far into the wilderness. These men and Colter struck up a friendship and Colter asked for his discharge so that he could join his new friends in a trapping venture.

In the journals of Lewis and Clark under the dates of August 14 and 15, 1806, there is this entry:

In the evening we were applied to by one of our men, Colter, who was desirous of joining the two trappers who had accompanied us, and who now proposed an expedition up the river, in which they were to find traps and give him a share of the profits. The offer was a very advantageous one, and, as he had always performed his duty, and his services might be dispensed with, we agreed that he might go, provided none of the rest would ask or expect a similar indulgence. To this they cheerfully answered that they wished Colter every success and would not apply for liberty to separate before we reached St. Louis. We, therefore, supplied him, as did his comrades also, with powder, lead, and a variety of articles which might be useful to him, and he left us the next day.

Thus parted three of the greatest explorers in American history without the slightest notion on the part of two of them that they were saying good-bye to a remarkable third.

Within a year Colter—trapping, not exploring . . . he seems to have been a completely pragmatic explorer; although much excited and interested—had discovered western Wyoming and Yellowstone Park, earning for himself, because of the latter discovery, the reputation of being the biggest liar in the United States. "Colter's Hell," Yellowstone was called by the skeptical, and Colter died before those who laughed at him found the laugh turned on themselves.

Nowadays thousands of people go through "Colter's Hell" every summer, and of these thousands there are still a goodly number who believe nothing . . . until bears bite them.

Not believing anything until a bear bites you is a glandular deficiency, not a question of information.

Colter, almost immediately, joined forces with Manuel Lisa, the leading trader of St. Louis, who lost no time about plunging inland for furs after Lewis and Clark had returned in 1806 with their marvelous story. On November 21, 1807, Colter and Lisa began the building of their trading post, which they named Fort Raymond—but to everyone else it was "Manuel's Fort." The fort was at the mouth of the Big Horn, in the present Montana. The season was winter, the ground snow-covered, the air sharp with winter cold; yet John Colter on snowshoes, or "webs," a supply pack of thirty pounds on his back, and a rifle, set out at once to find the Crows and any other tribes to the south who might like to trade with white men. He covered five hundred miles on that journey; and he traveled alone. John Colter in the depth of winter on foot and alone in the Absaroka Mountains, beside the Three Tetons, along Jackson Lake: traveling north through Yellowstone Park and home to Fort Manuel at the mouth of the Big Horn River, John Colter alone where no white man had trod before! He was back in the spring, safe and sound. The Crows and whatever other Indians he met had liked him. He started out again almost immediately, in fact, he made several journeys into Yellowstone Park—he saw and named the Stinking Water, now the Shoshone River—and came down along the Big Horn, and he drew some extraordinarily accurate maps.

Colter was the hero of an almost unbelievable adventure, and yet it has been well attested.

He was caught by the Blackfeet in the vicinity of Three Forks, Montana, the headwaters of the Missouri, while trapping with his partner, John Potts. Potts was killed. The Blackfeet, having a sense of humor, stripped Colter naked, gave him a start of one hundred yards, and told him to run. The ground they had carefully selected was covered with the short, sharp cactus of the Northwest. Colter was a swift runner. Even though his feet were filled with cactus needles, he kept the lead for five miles, outdistancing the Blackfeet, all but one man. This man was an even faster runner than Colter and he carried a spear. Desperate, Colter suddenly turned, and the Indian, taken by surprise, stumbled and his lance struck the ground and broke.

Colter seized it and killed the Blackfoot, and ran on. He reached the Madison River, and seeing a beaver house, dived in, coming up in the air space. All day he stood in the icy water while the Blackfeet looked for him. That night he swam the river in the darkness, and then walked, naked, without food except roots, the cactus needles still in his feet, for he had no way of taking them out, seven days across Montana, some two hundred and twenty miles, to the fort on the Big Horn.

Colter became a very quiet man. It seems as if he deliberately sought oblivion. Perhaps the reception which had met his discovery and description of Yellowstone Park sobered him. That is often the case with idealists; with highhearted men and women; explorers; men with an inner fire. Mankind is never very "bright" at the moment; it is only "bright" in retrospect. The accepted truths of the present are largely the prophecies, visions and discredited discoveries for which our ancestors were hanged, shot, silenced, or ruined. Coronado was ruined, Columbus was ruined. The Vérendryes were ruined. So was Meriwether Lewis, and calumniated as well—like the others. Colter, apparently, was silenced. At all events, he went back to Missouri, settled on a farm and from then on very little is known about him.

Colter should not be news to Americans, but nonetheless he is. I can do no better than to quote from the notes on Colter's life by W. J. Ghent, of Washington, D. C., the leading authority on the subject, which appear in the *Wyoming Annals* of July, 1938. These notes form a panorama of American frontier history; the gaps; the sudden bright heroisms.

John Colter [writes Mr. Ghent] was the son of Joseph and Ellen (Shields) Colter and was born in or near Staunton, Va. His birth-date is unknown, but was probably some time in 1775. The surname was variously spelled, both his great-grandfather Micajah and his grandfather Michael seeming to prefer the form Coalter. Of his early youth nothing is known. It is apparent that several Colters, about the 1780's, moved from Virginia to the region of Maysville, Ky., on the Ohio River, some sixty miles east of Cincinnati; and it is further apparent that on one of these migrations the boy was taken along. . . .

The younger Colter is first mentioned as a volunteer who at Maysville was provisionally accepted by Capt. Meriwether Lewis on his voyage down the Ohio. Some days later, October 15, 1803, at Louisville, where Lewis and Capt. William Clark united their little squads, Colter formally enlisted for the journey to the Pacific. Doubtless he was already experienced in woodcraft and the use of firearms; and as he was strong, active and intelligent, his fitness for the journey was quickly recognized. At the winter encampment, on Wood River, opposite the mouth of the Missouri, he was at first somewhat unruly, as one might expect a young frontiersman to be, and at one time was deprived of permission to leave camp for a period of ten days. Very soon, however, he settled down to a strict observance of discipline, and he became one of the most dependable members of the company.

I will skip now to the last paragraphs of Mr. Ghent's article, which have to do with Colter's final years. Colter was in his early thirties when he entered Wyoming; he was somewhere around thirty-nine when he went back to Missouri.

He now took up a tract of bounty land on the south bank of the Missouri, near the present village of Dundee, in Franklin County, and turned to farming. Also he married a young woman whose first name appears to have been Sally. He must often, however, have been in St. Louis, called there by business troubles. He had never received the money due him for his service in the famous expedition, and so he brought suit against the estate of Lewis, ultimately scoring a partial victory in the case. . . .

Back on the farm, on March 18, 1811, he saw a part of the expedition of Wilson Price Hunt passing up the river on the way to Oregon. Bradbury, who was to voyage with the party as far as the Arikara village, came ashore and talked with him. "He seemed to have a great inclination to accompany the expedition," wrote the Englishman, "but having been lately married he reluctantly took leave of us." He must also, a little later, have seen Lisa's party beating its way up the river in a frantic effort to overtake Hunt, and again he must have fought an inner battle as to whether he should return to the wilds or remain on the farm. We know nothing further of the hero's life. In November, 1813, he died, as James says, of "jaundice." On December 10 following, his personal property was sold, bringing $124.44½.

In recent years Dr. E. B. Trail, a dentist of Berger, Mo., has interested himself deeply in the Colter legend and has sought to ascertain what can be learned of Colter the farmer. He fixes the home of the explorer on Boeuf Creek, near its entrance into the Missouri; he accepts the neighborhood statement that Colter left an only child, Hiram, and he finds that Hiram had eight children, a fact that would seem to explain the considerable number of Colters who now live in that section. He also accepts the local tradition that Colter was buried on what is known as Tunnel Hill, a nearby bluff overlooking the Missouri. In June, 1926, the Missouri Pacific Railroad opened a large cut in the hill. During the excavation a number of human bones were found, the remains of probably a half-dozen or more bodies that had been buried many years ago. To Dr. Trail it seems certain that among the remains dug up from this little burial plot and dumped on an embankment were those of John Colter.

Nowhere, insofar as the present writer is aware, is there so much as a marker to the memory of this indomitable hero. Even his bones are but scattered dust, and the place of his sepulchre has been obliterated. Is it not time that in some place—at the Three Forks, or in Yellowstone Park, or on the Missouri, near his last home—his life should be commemorated by a monument?

In conclusion one should call attention to the fact that what Colter told of his routes of travel was confirmed a year later by Andrew Henry who, with a small party, had passed the winter of 1810-11 near the present St. Anthony, Idaho, and one should quote two remarks made by Thomas James, Colter's old associate in the Far West.

"Dangers," wrote James, referring to Colter, "seemed to have for him a kind of fascination." Again he wrote, "His veracity was never questioned among us." By which he means men like himself who had known John Colter in the wilderness.

It is dangerous to call a man a liar simply because he knows more than you do.

CHAPTER SIX

Tracks in the Snow

AFTER Colter, other trappers and traders of Manuel Lisa's band—among them Edward Rose, whom we shall meet presently—went southwest from Fort Manuel into the western mountains of Wyoming, and perhaps southeast too. It is possible they even reached the Powder country as well as the Platte, although most of the trapping and trading along the North Platte was done by men from Lisa's other post, Fort Mandan, on the Missouri. It was later, about the beginning of the thirties, that the American trappers were to discover the virtues of the country about the lower reaches of Powder River. Not as a fur territory—the alkalied Powder never was good for beaver—but as a mild, and balmy comparatively speaking, wintering place. There the trappers could camp all through the cold season in stout tents, like the Sioux, sheltered from the fiercest winds, with plenty of meat on hand because the buffalo, too, liked to winter on the Powder.

The furs were in the western mountains; and the traders went where the furs were. So we have this curious fact: it was the western mountains of Wyoming that were first explored, developed and settled, the western part of Wyoming—if you can call trapping and the erection of fur posts, development and settlement—not eastern Wyoming. After four decades or so the peak of the fur trade was passed and the mountains of northwestern Wyoming became again terra incognita, went back to their old loneliness, except for the Indians and such game as the trappers had left. For forty years, until well into the eighties, they were little known.

Nowadays most people, including those who live in Wyoming, quite mistakenly regard the south and the east as the oldest parts of the state.

It is difficult to leave John Colter. Difficult to leave a man so quiet, so courageous, so cool, and so strangely and unintelligently forgotten. And it is particularly difficult for me to leave him because I live in the mountains he discovered and know their snows and their canyons, and their bright and beautiful and terrible rivers, swift as sunlight, and their never-ending forests.

John Colter's snowshoe tracks left a deep webbed pattern on American history during that incredible winter journey of 1807.

Think of it! Five hundred miles through a country where the snow often lies six to eight feet on the level and twenty to forty feet in drifts! Through a country where sometimes a snowstorm lasts for two weeks and at any moment may become a blizzard! Through a country the average altitude of which is six thousand feet! Through a country where the mercury falls to thirty and forty below zero with the sinking of the sun, no matter how blue and warm the winter day has been! Alone through a country where no white man had ever been before!

Crossing streams where the slightest misstep or a wrong ford would have swept him away. Finding his way through forests longer than a man can think. Coming out of them to see crystal peaks eleven thousand, twelve thousand, thirteen thousand feet high. Finding wonders in which other men would not believe and which had kept the Indians away because they thought them devils. A thirty-pound pack on his back, an old long rifle, a knife, a tinderbox, that was John Colter.

Even today men do not go through that country, trappers, the snowshoe patrols of the Forest Service and the National Parks, unless they know exactly what they are doing and are well supplied.

It has been suggested that the winter of 1807 must

have been an extremely mild winter or else Colter would have perished. I don't know about that! Brave men do extraordinary things.

At all events, Colter went five hundred miles alone through a Wyoming winter. His only recorded remark when he came back was that "loaded wagons could cross the mountains where he had been." The one time, I think, when he exaggerated: unless, contrary to the opinion of western historians, he had hunted with his Crow friends as far south as the entrance to South Pass, which seems at least a vague possibility, for the Crows knew the pass. He said "where" he had been, not "anywhere." Another valuable trait of Colter's was his ability to get on with Indians, and that was why he had been dispatched upon his remarkable journey. The Crows really trusted him, so much so that he is given a good deal of credit for their subsequent amiability toward the white man. But the Blackfeet—those "Scourges of the Upper Missouri"—didn't like Colter, probably because he was the friend of their enemies, the Crows, although they didn't kill him immediately, as they killed Potts, when they captured him. On one occasion when Colter was leading some Flatheads, who had been attacked by Blackfeet, a party of Crows, seeing him in trouble, charged to his aid and he and these Indians, 800 in all, badly defeated 1,500 Blackfeet.

But how incredibly lovely those forests and valleys and mountains must have been as Colter went through them! How clear and clean and quiet that part of the United States must have been with no white men in it! In winter great combers of snow overhang the waters of the streams, black with cold, and through the reaches of the forest where the snow glistens on pine and fir and balsam the camp robbers—the Canada jays—dart like little puffs of gray smoke through the shining whiteness. As you snowshoe, your shadow slides blue before you. It is so quiet that the dropping of snow from a fir branch sounds like the brushing of a giant broom; a falling icicle, like the rattling of a sword. All day you snowshoe, your mind wrapped in the clear dry cold and the rhythm and the swishing of your webs. And then you come out into the dusk, and a river, warmer now than the air, coils in a long line of mist below you in a valley, and every mountain is rose pink, and a planet opposite you hangs down at the level of your eyes.

Five hundred miles of that . . . that was something for John Colter to think about back in Missouri!

CHAPTER SEVEN

Bad Fellows Full of Daring

IN those first, quiet decades of the nineteenth century—quiet, that is, for the white man and for the Sioux, save for the latter's enmity with the Crows—a handful of white men, not many, knew the Powder.

There was Edward Rose, for instance, who became a subchief of the Crows, and Jim Beckwourth, the mulatto, who followed him, and later on there was Jim Bridger, of course. Jim Bridger got everywhere in Wyoming and knew every foot of it. And there was the inevitable English explorer and big game hunter in the fifties. And there was also Father De Smet in the forties and fifties, who in his energetic and delighted peregrinations covered almost as much ground as Jim Bridger. And there was especially, where the Powder was concerned, the mysterious Portuguese trader, Antonio Mateo, Powder River's first white resident. But before Antonio Mateo, there was Wilson Price Hunt, who followed close upon the heels of Rose.

These, and a few fur traders in the twenties and thirties, and a few prospectors in the forties and fifties who have remained almost completely anonymous.

Hunt was one of those young partners of John Jacob Astor who made American history, although in Hunt's case he made it more by good luck and bull-headedness than good management.

Lewis and Clark had blazed the trail to the Pacific. Manuel Lisa had followed on as far as Montana and built two forts for trade. Americans as well as the ubiquitous and intrepid French trappers were going into the new fur country. So John Jacob Astor, who had been busy recently in trying to gain control of the fur trade of the upper Mississippi region and the Great Lakes, conceived the idea of adding all the new-found West to his fur empire.

In 1810 he sent a ship, the *Tonquin,* to the mouth of the Columbia; and the next year his overland party under the leadership of Wilson Price Hunt, having wintered a few miles north of the present St. Joseph, Missouri, set out up the Missouri River to travel Lewis and Clark's trail. At an Arikara village Hunt encountered three trappers just come downstream, who warned him of the perils of the Blackfeet country. Hunt, an Easterner, born in Asbury Park, New Jersey, and for the last eight years an estimable merchant of St. Louis, possessing no wilderness experience and no acquaintance with Indians, did not know that while raiding parties of Indians would pursue three or four trappers in bloodthirsty sport, they were most unlikely to attack such a large party as his—sixty-five men well armed. So Hunt sold his boats to the ever-present, ever-watchful Lisa, bought horses and turned away from the Missouri, under the guidance of Edward Rose. Rose had gone to Lisa's Fort Manuel in 1808 and had lived for several years among those Crows of the Big Horns who had been brought into trade and friendship with the white man by John Colter on that first lone winter journey of his. Rose guided Hunt and Astor's overlanders into Wyoming.

Hunt was undoubtedly the first perfect tenderfoot ever to come west, the first simon-pure "dude" ever to enter Wyoming. Interesting that he should have entered it through the very country where ninety years later the dude business of Wyoming was to begin.

As has been said, other white men, Colter's friends of Fort Manuel or free trappers, may have seen Powder River. But Wilson Price Hunt is the first white man we actually know to have been in the Powder River country with the exception of Rose, and Rose was one-third white, one-third Negro, and one-third Cherokee.

Hunt, under Rose's direction, struck south and crossed into Wyoming east of the main Powder, and came to Clear Creek a little north of where the town of Buffalo now stands. Following up Clear Creek he crossed the Big Horns at an elevation of 8,337 feet and came down what is now called Canyon Creek to the headwaters of No Wood. From there he followed the Big Horn River around the corner of the Wind River Range, to where it becomes the Wind River, and ascended the Wind River valley and crossed the Gros Ventres into Jackson Hole. From Jackson Hole he entered Idaho and eventually found Astoria and the mouth of the Columbia.

But Rose proved no trustworthy guide for Hunt. No sooner had he reached the Big Horns than his loyalty failed him, and he lay awake at night concocting a plot whereby some of his adopted brothers, the Crows, who were hanging about Hunt's camp, were to steal Hunt's horses and seduce away as many of Hunt's men as they could. Hunt, getting wind of this, and displaying uncharacteristic good sense and forbearance, bought Rose off with half a year's wages, a horse, and three beaver traps, and suggested that Rose stay where he was. Secretly he wanted to kill him.

In his diary Hunt wrote: "We had in our party a hunter by the name of Rose. He was a very bad fellow, full of daring." And Washington Irving, taking this diary and contemporary reports, describes Rose as "withal, a dogged, sullen, silent fellow of sinister aspect: More of the savage than the civilized man in his appearance. . . . A wandering individual. . . . One of those anomalous beings found on the frontier, who seem to have neither kin nor country."

Well—I don't know! September and October in the high Far West are warm dreams, the color of pomegranates. And along the green mountainsides the aspens have turned gold, and down the valleys where the aspens are gold and apricot and the cottonwoods yellow, the autumn haze gathers like crystal spiderwebs between you and the sun. In addition, there is considerable difference between being a mulatto in the East and a subchief among the Crows. Nor could Edward Rose have been altogether, and withal, "a sullen fellow." Indians among themselves are not dogged and sullen, and especially perhaps the witty Crows. They become dogged and sullen in the presence of white men because of fear and an inferiority complex. Among themselves they are a noisy people, with a high if somewhat gamy sense of humor, which takes itself out in a great deal of practical joking. They chatter and laugh a lot.

In the middle twenties, shortly after Rose had finally left his friends the Crows, another trapper, the son of a Revolutionary officer from Virginia and a slave woman, Jim Beckwourth, also joined the Crows and was made a subchief by them and given wives.

Beckwourth was a more obviously attractive man than Rose, pathetically proud of the fact that his father had been a Revolutionary officer. One of the most charming and engaging and curious figures the Powder and the Big Horns and the Big Horn Basin have ever

known, a kindlier man than Rose, often ready to help
the whites, and a great and epic liar. A monumental
liar. A liar who set a high standard even in the annals
of the American frontier.

Born in Virginia in 1798, he had come west with
General William Ashley's fur brigade in 1822, the first
organized fur brigade to operate in Wyoming, when
he was twenty-four, and he was with Ashley on the
Green River and in the western mountains of Wyoming
until he joined the Crows in 1826. For six years he lived
with the Crows, and then, after wandering all over
Wyoming, the hero of innumerable adventures, some
true, some fictitious, he joined the drift setting in toward the Pacific and made a home for himself on the
Feather River in California, where he ran a roadhouse
and lived in constant debt due to the fact that he was
unable to refuse anyone a meal. He was content, however, because the recipients of his charity had to listen
to his stories. On the Feather River T. D. Bonner, an
early "ghost writer," came upon him and took down
from dictation, which Bonner altered to grandiloquent
sentences—a remarkable book published in 1856: *The
Life and Adventures of James P. Beckwourth, Moun-
taineer, Scout, and Pioneer, and Chief* [Bonner pro-
moted him!] *of the Crow Nation of Indians.*

CHAPTER EIGHT

Portuguese Houses

EVER since the time of Henry the Navigator
and the century that followed, when the Portuguese
made a great stir from India and Africa to Brazil and
boasted a little, bringing down upon their heads the
wrath and envy of their dour but grandiose neighbors,
the Spaniards, they have kept their mouths shut and
gone about their brown-eyed business quietly.

So it is entirely in keeping with the national character that Antonio Mateo of the Powder, and his "Portuguese houses," are still mysterious.

You can find the faint remains of the Portuguese
houses today on the ranch of John Esponda, a Basque.
They are directly on the banks of the Powder between
South Fork and Salt Creek, fifteen miles east of Kaycee;
the Big Horns off to the west, the badlands off to the
east. Somewhere around 1828 Antonio Mateo built this
trading post and he remained there, or some of his men
did, until 1850. Sublette and Campbell didn't build
Fort Laramie far to the south until 1834. So, discount-
ing even the little post of Astor's American Fur Company that was on the North Platte before Laramie was
founded, the Portuguese houses were probably, after the

two temporary log cabins built by Robert Stuart of Astoria in 1812, the first houses in eastern Wyoming.

Antonio Mateo was just as different as could be from Manuel Lisa, the lordly and well advertised, up on the Missouri. He was one of the quietest fur traders and storekeepers who ever lived. Also, he must have been a very brave man. Either that, or a very imperturbable one. It was sufficiently brave even to contemplate settling in such a treeless loneliness as the part of the Powder he chose, and although the Indians at that time were by no means as dangerous as they were to become later on, they were, with the exception of the Crows, not particularly friendly, and even the Crows liked a quiet afternoon or night off every now and then for horse stealing. When Antonio Mateo built, the nearest trading post was four hundred miles to the north. But it is to be imagined that Antonio Mateo liked all that or he wouldn't have been there. And he had everything to himself.

Beaver, of course, was the principal trade. "Plew" or "pluie" from the French meaning pelt. Everything else, however fine, was "coarse fur." But around 1850 beaver in the Big Horns grew scarce, as it did everywhere else. Meanwhile, Antonio Mateo must have become a moderately wealthy man. The Big Horns were a fur country, but the main fur country was in the mountains to the west, so Antonio Mateo couldn't have had many people to trade with but the Indians, although a few white trappers and gold seekers went through from time to time, and following Hunt there were the beginnings of a used trail from Fort Pierre in the Dakotas past the Pumpkin Buttes, and so on to Wind River. And when the snows came, he had visits no doubt from those trappers who wintered on the Powder, their Riviera. But that was about all.

In those days the prices were such on the frontier,

and for a long while beaver was so valuable, that a man like Antonio Mateo could make considerably more than a living. Sugar, for example, was two dollars a pint. Coffee two-fifty a pint. Flour one-fifty a pint, beaver hides around eight dollars each. Also whisky was extremely profitable, although the American traders were forbidden to sell it and only did so secretly. A necessity for silence, however, which did not bother a man very much four hundred miles away from any neighbors, and which has never bothered Americans very much under any circumstances. Whisky sold for twenty-five dollars a gallon.

In 1829, the year following the establishment of his post, Antonio Mateo was attacked by Indians, some say the Sioux, others the Blackfeet, but he had built well—a stockade of hewn logs two hundred feet square, ten feet high, and inside, many buildings of hewn and mortised logs—and for forty days he stood his besiegers off. From then on they seem to have left him alone. And in view of what was to happen fifteen years after the post was abandoned, it is nice, it seems to me, to contemplate Antonio Mateo, the first storekeeper of Wyoming, the first solid citizen and householder of Powder River; so successful, so quiet, except for this one siege in 1829.

You can see Antonio at night, after the last trading was over, in the quiet of his office, casting up the day's accounts and smoking, probably, a long cheroot or "seegar." Outside everything would be as quiet as a planet, except for the crying of the coyotes. And in the keen, cool air of the night that would come in a little even if the door and windows were closed, the beaver hides and groceries and spices and blankets would smell pungently along with the strong, sweet smell of illicit corn whisky. In the candlelight the beads for trade would shine like marbles.

Just the illumination of Antonio Mateo's trading post in all that vast, unlighted country!

There was one extremely important figure of a different kind in the West in the middle of the nineteenth century. He was Jean Pierre De Smet, member of the Society of Jesus, born in Belgium, known to the Indians as Black Robe.

Storekeeper and frontier parson or priest! You find these two figures, completely dissimilar but equally intrepid, all through the history of the frontier.

Father De Smet knew the Big Horns thoroughly, but he did not like the Powder, and said so, and avoided it as much as possible. The Sioux respected him, but they were not "his children." Strangely enough, however, no man had more to do with the future history of the Powder or the tragedy of the Sioux. Father De Smet had the tiniest of Achilles' heels, and, being a Belgian, this Achilles' heel was an interest in gold. A theoretical, unselfish interest, to be sure, but still an interest. It was a casual, unfounded remark of his, let fall upon one occasion at Fort Laramie, that turned the white man's eyes definitely toward the inviolate country to the north. Father De Smet had just come out of the Big Horns, he remarked that he knew where gold was "in such abundance that it would astonish the world. Gold even greater than California."

Pretty soon, also, the American fur companies began to fight among themselves, and this was bad for the Sioux and had a direct bearing on the troubles of the sixties and seventies. The rival fur companies competed for the favor and furs of the Sioux, not without the constant bribe of whisky, and this drew the Sioux down on the Oregon Trail which was exactly where they shouldn't have been.

CHAPTER NINE

The Great Medicine Road

FOR a few years a scattering of free trappers, individual trappers and their partners, held the western mountains, and then the first of the great fur captains arrived and their fur brigades dominated the valleys and the hills. It is not the fashion of Americans to allow their much-prized, in theory, individual initiative to remain unorganized. The flamboyant era of the American fur trade was beginning; the decades of the twenties, thirties and forties.

In 1834 Captain William Sublette, the second great fur captain working from the western mountains, and one of his partners, Robert Campbell, founded Fort Laramie; first called Fort William in honor of Sublette, then Fort John, finally Laramie after a well-known trapper, Jacques Lorimier—pronounced "Laramie" by the Indians and Americans—who had been killed in the Powder country in the twenties.

It seemed an excellent idea to Sublette and Campbell to persuade as many Sioux as possible to come south and trade at Laramie. About a hundred Oglala lodges came to begin with, and some Brulés. Then more Brulés and Oglalas. After a while some Miniconjous and Sans Arcs followed. These Indians fell into the habit of camping more or less permanently, except when they were hunting, around Laramie. After the government took over the Oregon Trail, the lazier bands became ration Indians, incurring the contempt of their fellows.

The apex of the year in the heyday of fur was the "rendezvous," those annual encampments on the Green and Wind rivers in Wyoming, at Ogden's Hole in Utah; and Pierre's Hole, Idaho, now called Teton Basin and today a very sober place of Mormon farmers and sheepmen. Down from all the far-flung lonely creeks and headwaters came the trappers, two by two, or sometimes alone, or, as the great fur companies began to operate, more and more in brigades of partisans, and

to meet them, the fur traders came out from St. Louis and the East. While the Indians—Snakes and Bannocks, and Flatheads and Crows, and Nez Percés and Utes, and for a while even the Sioux—came from north and south and east and west, from all the surrounding endless horizons. And after the serious business of barter and buying was over, everybody got gloriously drunk for a couple of weeks or longer, and sang, and danced, and fought, and made love.

I have a particular interest in those rendezvous; almost a race memory. At some of the earlier ones was a small, gray-eyed, thin-faced young fur trader; an Irish rebel who had recently fled from Ireland.

He was my great-grandfather.

And then suddenly the flamboyant decades were over almost as abruptly as they had begun. Not only were the beavers disappearing under constant assault, but a queer thing had happened. One of those imponderables that are constantly confusing and remaking history. The world suddenly took to wearing silk hats. The silk hat, of course, had been invented in Florence somewhere around 1760, but for many years the world would have none of it and clung to its accustomed beaver. And now, with its usual lack of warning, the world changed its mind.

The trappers were forced to modify their way of life and their point of view. Trappers don't like crowds or strangers—"pilgrims"—any better than miners or cattlemen do, but the majority of the trappers were now faced with the alternative of either guiding the emigrants and soldiers who were beginning to appear in increasing numbers to the south, or else of starving to death.

The mountains—the long Absarokas, the mighty Wind Rivers, not even today altogether discovered, the incredible Tetons, the broad Gros Ventres—were again almost as lonely as they had been when John Colter first saw them thirty years before. A few trappers— lost men—lingered on, but the majority, like "Peg Leg" Smith and Jim Bridger, the wisest of the trappers, went down onto the Oregon Trail, already something of a thoroughfare. In the spring of 1843—the first year when wagons went all the way to the north Pacific coast—Jim Bridger in the southwest corner of Wyoming opened his fort and trading post, the famous Fort Bridger, the ancestor of the "rest rooms" and tourist stations of the present.

The Sioux on the Powder would have been undisturbed for a long while had it been only for the north and the west; it was the White Medicine to the south that made for battle. From the highest point of the divide between the Powder and the North Platte you could see on a clear day the faint far dust, like smoke, of the "Great Medicine Road"—the Oregon Trail—or at least you could imagine that you could.

It was the fur trade, of course, that had opened up the Oregon Trail. Unintentionally! No fur trader ever purposely lured settlers with axes into a fur-bearing forest!

In 1812 Robert Stuart, bearing letters to Astor from the Pacific Fur Company's fort at the mouth of the Columbia, discovered South Pass and journeyed over a large part of the route that was to become the historic Oregon Trail on his way to St. Louis from Astoria. But it was not until after South Pass had been rediscovered in 1824 by a party of trappers, who learned of it from the Crows, that it became the gateway to Oregon. Stuart never returned to the West. He was unaware of the immense value of his discovery, and he would surely have been amazed had anyone prophesied then the fame that has brightened his name in our day with the recent unearthing and publication of his journal. Stuart's route did not touch the Powder, but he wintered in the state and built the first white men's cabins in Wyoming.

It did not take long for the Great Medicine Road to become crowded, only a dozen years or so after the mountain trappers had rediscovered South Pass. Half the youth of half a continent was waiting, and the upland grass began to turn from green to gray where the wagon tracks ran. By the middle forties the wagon tracks had made a definite trail. By the middle fifties the wagon tracks were eight and ten and fifteen abreast, cutting small valleys below the level of the ground. A nation was on the move. It was neap tide. Two major impulses pushed the waters on.

First, religion. The religious unrest that in the

twenties and thirties so stirred the simple American.
The simple European equally. Tired of bloodletting, at
the beginning of the last century men and women saw
visions and heard voices, and felt a hard, dour desire
for peace and righteousness. The American sought peace
by penetrating into the most dangerous section of his
country.

After religion came the news of gold. Godliness
didn't last very long. Hardly had the religious impulse
died down than gold was discovered. After that, of
course, came the unrest following a great war. And
underlying the three, and finally growing into the most
passionate quest of all, was the quest for land.

Back of religion, back of gold, the most enduring
quest is the search for grass.

As early as 1845 three thousand people in one year
passed "old" Fort Laramie, still a fur-trading post, on
their way west; in the fifties, fifty thousand a year were
passing Laramie, now a government fort. Up the North
Platte through Nebraska, up the North Platte through
Wyoming, west along the Sweetwater, pausing to write
their names on Independence Rock, that strange solitary
hump that Father De Smet called the "Great Register
of the Desert," they came. The movement of troops
and emigrants and supplies to Oregon, California and
Utah was almost constant. The Great Medicine Road
had become typically American. It was littered on either
side with castoff impedimenta . . . abandoned beds,
broken axles, cooking utensils. The American had found
a virgin field in which to exercise his disregard of
scenery.

The grass, like the game and the loneliness, had
withdrawn into the distance. The wagon trains were
obliged to bring their feed with them or buy it where
they could. Firewood was equally scarce. The Great

Medicine Road had become a ribbon-cemetery; a linear graveyard. In 1849 cholera attacked it. In 1852 Granville Stuart—no relation to Robert, but as important to the history of Montana as Robert was to the history of Wyoming—on his way to California from Iowa saw not a single head of game between Fort Laramie, far in the east of Wyoming, and Utah, although at that time there was no settlement between Fort Laramie and Fort Bridger, and not a ranch until Granville Stuart reached California.

Sublette had taken the first wheels over the Oregon Trail, to the mountains. In 1830 he arrived at the Wind River rendezvous with ten wagons. Two years later Captain Bonneville took wagons through South Pass. And in 1838 Marcus Whitman got a cart, well damaged, as far as Fort Boise, Idaho. In 1843 wheels rolled along the banks of the Columbia.

By 1858 Russell, Majors and Waddell, the leading freighters, had three thousand five hundred wagons, forty thousand oxen, and four thousand employees working for them on the Oregon and Santa Fe trails. A year later the same firm started the Overland Stages. A new trail, a subsidiary of the Oregon, the Overland, had been found to be safer and shorter. It was farther away from the Sioux and the Pawnees. The Overland cut across the south of Wyoming, across the Laramie Plains to Bridger Pass. Today, on the Laramie Plains, you can still see the Overland's faint tracks.

The Overland Stages swaying and rocking, and galloping when they could, were the innovations that startled the earliest sixties. On their heels came the most original and exciting experiment of all—the short-lived Pony Express. Russell with two other men, Bee and Ficklin, started the Pony Express in 1860, and it was in operation seventy-nine weeks, with four weeks off during the Paiute war. Ten days from St. Joseph, Missouri, to Sacramento, California. One hundred and ninety stations. Two hundred stationkeepers. Eighty riders, often riding for their lives from the Indians. Letters five dollars a half ounce and written on tissue paper. Some prodigious rides were made. The Pony Express rode straight into the transcontinental telegraph, which was completed in 1861. First conceived —the idea of a transcontinental telegraph line—by Edward Creighton of Omaha in 1860, within a year the line was completed.

Think of that! A telegraph line only fifty-seven years after Lewis and Clark; only fifty-five years after John Colter had first discovered Wyoming; only forty-nine years after Robert Stuart had traveled on foot a part of the Great Medicine Road.

Time was moving faster and faster. It was beginning to take on the beat of a voodoo drum. Up over the eastern horizon was coming the black breath of the "Iron Horse."

Event followed event stirring anxiety in the minds of the Sioux, lords of the Powder grasslands and the buffalo herds. In 1842 and '43-'44, Frémont, then a lieutenant, was on the Great Medicine Road, or near by, with his two government topographical expeditions. In 1847 the Mormons trudged past on their incredible hegira. Thousands, many of them old men and women pushing handcarts. Travel the same road today and wonder! In the center of the state of Wyoming, a little west of Devil's Gate, where the Sweetwater pours through a lovely canyon to emerge at Independence Rock, is a monument to a Mormon train, two hundred members of which perished in a November blizzard in the early fifties.

In 1848 gold was discovered in California. A year

later the forty-niners were on the Medicine Road. California was now the principal goal, no longer Oregon. Five years before gold, such as it was, had been discovered on the Medicine Road itself around the South Pass in Wyoming. Mining settlements had sprung up there.

In 1857 Albert Sidney Johnston and his army went through to harry the Mormons.

CHAPTER TEN

Sheet Lightning

THE mountainmen, the early trappers and traders, had got along with the Indians fairly well, all but
the Blackfeet. The mountainmen went through, or
stayed in, a country quietly. They were almost invisible.
They had protective coloring. They wore moccasins.
They left no scarring tracks. Nor did they want land.
Nor had they herds of horses or oxen. The game they
sought was small game, not the game on which men
lived. Also, they spoke Indian and many at least temporarily took Indian wives. There were only a few of them
at the most. The Indian still felt himself a big, safe man.
The mountainmen flattered the Indian's amour propre
—the most sensitive Indian characteristic.

Now there were white men—more and more of
them—who either feared the Indian, and so were given
to sudden, fierce outbreaks of brutality, or else despised
him openly. Moreover, these white men made a wilderness, so far as the Indian was concerned, wherever they
went, and the government sent soldiers to hold this
wilderness with guns.

Vaguely the western Indians began to perceive
that back of these white men were millions of others,
and that, being white men, the intruders would never
rest until everything was theirs.

With all due respect to the small and gallant professional army before the Civil War, its privates were
hard-boiled and its officers—those on the frontier—

65

were for the most part young and arrogant West Pointers.

As to the emigrants, they knew nothing of the Indians. They merely cherished the fear and hatred that had been handed down generation after generation in the East and Middle West. Fear begets fear. It is the secret of most trouble and ninety per cent of all cruelty. Hindsight, however, is easier than foresight.

The government didn't begin to take the Northwest seriously, except for Oregon, until the emigrants began to pour through. And then it took Wyoming seriously only as a highway. If you protected the highway—and that wasn't done very successfully—what more was necessary? The country was huge. Who would want such an isolated, self-contained tract as the Powder? It was off by itself. It had no connection with any thoroughfare. A splendid place to keep the Sioux contented. A nice thing to do for them.

The government didn't even realize what the Sioux were.

In the end it would have been the same anyway. The Sioux were too powerful to handle by peaceable means. They would have come down around Fort Laramie and the Oregon Trail even had they not owned the Powder. The North Platte valley, in Nebraska, the Laramie Plains, in southern Wyoming, were part of their hunting grounds.

Sublette had sold out his fur interests to a company of fur trappers which included Jim Bridger; and this company next year sold out to the American Fur Company, from which Astor had retired, foreseeing the end of western beaver. In 1849 the government bought Laramie from the American Fur Company and turned it into a military post. Frémont in his journals has left us a charming picture of Fort Laramie in the comparatively quiet forties, while it was still a fur fort.

But even the forties were not altogether quiet; not down around the Medicine Road. Already the Sioux were beginning to be restless and dangerous. The old chiefs of the bands encamped around Fort Laramie, Otter Hat, Breaker of Arrows, Black Night, Bull Tail —Brulés mostly—warned Frémont not to go farther. At the moment their young men were out to the west hunting. The "hearts" of these young men were "bad." The emigrants had killed some of their relatives. Then the old men ended in typical Indian fashion. The Indian capacity for begging at inopportune moments has again and again brought the Indian into contempt at just the wrong moment.

Why hadn't Frémont brought valuable presents? Horses, and guns, and blankets, and things like that? The Great White Father was rich; the Sioux were poor and naked and starving.

Frémont was always a friend of the Indian, but this added irritation to resentment. He rebuked the old men sharply in his famous defiance.

"We are the soldiers of the great chief, your father," he said. "He has told us to come here and see this country, and all the Indians, his children. Why should we not go? Before we came we heard that you had killed his people, and ceased to be his children; but we came among you peaceably, holding out our hands. Now we find that the stories we heard are not lies, and that you are no longer his friends and children. We have thrown away our bodies, and will not turn back. When you told us that your young men would kill us, you did not know that our hearts were strong, and you did not see the rifles which my young men carry in their hands. We are few, and you are many, and may kill us; but there will be much crying in your villages, for many of your young men will stay behind, and forget to return with your warriors from the mountains.

"Do you think that our great chief will let his soldiers die and forget to cover their graves? Before the snows melt again, his warriors will sweep away your villages as the fire does the prairie in the autumn. See! I have pulled down my white houses, and my people are ready; when the sun is ten paces higher, we shall be on the march. If you have anything to tell us, you will say it soon."

That was in 1842. Brave words! Frémont was unmolested. He went on to the first scientific exploration of Wyoming. And a few years later, to the taking of California for the United States. Then he went into politics and, like so many other Americans, lost most of the gallant and deserved reputation he had won.

It was thirty years and more before the Great White Father thought seriously of covering the graves of his soldiers, and of other white men, who meanwhile were to lose their lives along the Medicine Road and the Powder.

It was thirty years and more before the Great White Father began to sweep the Indian villages as fire does the prairie in autumn.

In the forties, when Frémont spoke at Laramie, and the wagon trains were growing longer yearly on the trail, the Powder still slept but for the mutually agreeable forays of Sioux and Crow. In the winter the Powder was silver and gray. Springs came, light green. July and August, yellow and ocher, with their mirages. Autumn, many colored. The grass was still high, bending before the breeze like wheat, and everywhere you looked was the distant darkness of buffalo and antelope, the shaken grass between like shifting patches of sunlight. But now the old men, talking in circles, spoke more and more of the news from the south, and there were constant visitors from the Oglala and Brulé bands down around Fort Laramie and the Oregon Trail, and every now and then runners came, grim with news.

Around the Powder there was tightening a loop, a giant coil flung by the white man.

CHAPTER ELEVEN

Red Thunder

I SUPPOSE, if you can set a definite date anywhere in a long and cumulative period of increasing anger and fear on both sides, you can set it with the not-undeserved killing of Lieutenant Grattan and his men in the August of 1854.

In 1849 the army had moved into Wyoming. Both the whites, the few there were, and the Sioux were happy. Both thought the army had been sent to protect them. And, as a matter of fact, this was the entirely amicable, impossible and mutually contradictory aim of the government and the growing party known as the "Indians' Friends" back in the East. That the intention was unrealistic was speedily shown.

The Medicine Road was the trouble. Once that was really open, the handwriting was on the wall and there was no evading it. No turning back. More and more clearly the Sioux began to perceive this, but in the usual vague, disconnected Indian fashion. Only great and exceptional Indians have the gift of continuing perception. For a while the Oglalas and the Brulés and the Miniconjous around Fort Laramie tried to keep the peace, especially the old men. And for a while the government did not take the guarding of the Oregon Trail very seriously. Washington apparently had forgotten the lessons of earlier days and, like General Braddock, thought a hundred Indians no match for one regular. Not only did the War Department undergarrison absurdly its new posts, but it persisted in the quaint habit of forming the tiny garrisons entirely of infantrymen. It cost a lot of money to transport hay for cavalry horses. The government seemed unaware that during the summer these horses could have been grazed on the finest natural grass in the world and that during the winter it was possible to stack wild hay.

In 1854 Laramie was garrisoned by exactly fifty soldiers of the 6th United States Infantry under a first lieutenant. There were thousands of Sioux, six or seven thousand of them, in the immediate vicinity near the fort or strung out along the valley of the North Platte. The result was the so-called "Grattan massacre."

Second Lieutenant Grattan was a gay young man, just out of West Point. The life at these miniature posts in Wyoming was idle and boring. Lieutenant Grattan longed to whet his virgin sword and often said so. In August of 1854 word was brought to Laramie that some Miniconjous had stolen and butchered a beef belonging to a Mormon wagon train that had camped a little east of the fort. No very serious matter, with proper handling. And the Sioux did not as yet envision serious trouble. An occasional brawl! Brawls were part of any hardy man's life, but active war, no!

Brave Bear of the Brulés, the leading chief in the neighborhood and an extremely friendly one, came in at once to Laramie to straighten out the difficulty. He said it had been a mistake and that the Miniconjous were willing to pay for the beef; but the garrison wanted action. Here was an opportunity to show the might of the army, and Lieutenant Grattan begged to be allowed to lead the punitive expedition.

The next morning, against the advice of every experienced frontiersman he set out with twenty-nine soldiers and two howitzers to make an arrest. You shouldn't arrest an Indian except for a deadly offense, he doesn't understand it—or rather, the Indian of those days didn't—and besides, the military authorities were not supposed to make arrests for civil crimes.

Grattan marched into a village a little way down the North Platte composed of about five thousand Oglalas, Brulés and Miniconjous. He demanded the culprits. There was some hesitation, some shaking of lances, some movement to escape, and Grattan lost his nerve and fired. He was killed with all his men save one. The survivor, desperately wounded, died afterwards. Brave Bear also was killed, a fate which frequently befell Indian peacemakers.

The Grattan fight was merely the most formal of numerous incidents that occurred in the years before war came, real war. And by now, in increasing numbers, there were bands of Indian troublemakers: Sioux, Cheyennes, Arapahos, and occasionally Utes up from Colorado, hanging about the Medicine Road, stealing and every now and then raiding and scalping.

The emigrant trains were bad enough. The Overland Stages added to the growing apprehension of the Indians. The Pony Express increased this fear. The telegraph in 1861 was the most alarming magic of all. Here was word that went between the whites with no sound except the singing of the wind in a wire, faster than a pony could gallop; even faster than signal fires could flash from peak to peak.

The Indians hated the telegraph and cut the poles and wires whenever they could.

There were wolves furthermore—human ones—adding their quota, a considerable one, to the growing unrest. Wolves, human or otherwise, hang about the outskirts of frontier settlement.

There was John Richards, for instance, and Joseph Bissonette—"Old Joe"—and the strangest of all, Major Twiss; Thomas Twiss. These three caused about as much trouble as everything else put together, and the Powder can almost claim them as residents because when the wiser of the Sioux, wishing to get away from the dangers and temptations of the Oregon Trail, began to withdraw permanently into the Powder River country around 1856, Richards and Bissonette and, after a while, Twiss followed them and settled on the Oregon Trail as far north as was possible and as near to the Powder as was safe.

Richards had the distinction of being the first white man along the Oregon Trail to smuggle whisky up from the Mexican border to the Indians; a French Canadian, he had been a factor for Pratte, Cabanne & Company, one of the small independent companies that had maintained a post near Fort Laramie while that still belonged to the American Fur Company. This was around 1840. Subsequently, Richards became all too well known to the military authorities. When the wiser of the Sioux moved, he moved with them and opened a store at Deer Creek where the North Platte makes its big loop about fifty miles south of the Powder. This was at the end of the trail leading from the Powder to the North Platte. A most convenient and profitable location. The emigrants went through from east to west; the Indians came down from the north and went back.

Old Joe Bissonette had also been a Pratte and Cabanne man until that firm went out of business. He, too, followed the Indians up as far as Deer Creek in their final tragic attempt to escape the whites and there he raised a large family of half-breeds, the famous

"Reshaw Boys." Old Joe made much money, for in addition to a trading post, a post office, an emigrant store and a stage station he also built a ferry across the Platte. His steadiest income, however, like that of Richards, came from selling whisky to the Indians on the Powder.

One of the most curious characters ever to appear on the frontier, which is saying a lot, was Major Twiss. Born in Switzerland of an excellent family, he had been brought to this country at an early age and had graduated with honors from West Point. Afterwards, for a while, he had served with distinction in the army. Resigning, he had gone into the Indian Bureau and had been appointed agent at Fort Laramie because of his knowledge, his splendid service and enlightened attitude.

At first he had many plans for the improvement of his charges—too many—including experimental farms, but he failed to stand up under increasing temptations, and became the epitome of a corrupt Indian agent. President Lincoln relieved him in the first years of the Civil War. Some time before that the old man in the most highhanded fashion and by nobody's leave had moved the agency up to Deer Creek in pursuit of his friends, Richards and Bissonette. After his dismissal, it was returned to where it belonged. By now Twiss had had a young Oglala wife and a pet bear, and had fallen completely in love with the Sioux and wanted to be near them. Moreover, the Deer Creek country was a much pleasanter place to live than Laramie. There were more trees.

When the fighting broke out in the middle sixties, Twiss, white-bearded and vaguely wild, disappeared into the Powder River country. He had gone over to the enemy, a strange fate for a West Point honor man.

Wandering along the Oregon Trail at this time

was no less a person than Sir Richard Burton of *Arabian Nights* fame. Sir Richard Burton was very much interested in Thomas Twiss's curious character.

The Civil War could not have come at a more unfortunate time for the Sioux and the northwestern frontier. As has just been pointed out, a great many of the Oglalas and Brulés and Miniconjous had withdrawn permanently to the Powder. Only the more friendly bands were left down around Laramie, those and the "ration Indians." But up on the Powder, as everywhere else, it began slowly to dawn upon the Indians that the Great White Father had his hands full with a new enemy far to the east. Fifty-eight years later hundreds of grandsons of these same Sioux were to serve with the American army in France, but now they perceived a different opportunity where that army was concerned.

And the army on the frontier had abruptly changed, and for the worse. The casual, blundering, but on the whole fairly tolerant, regulars had been withdrawn and in their places had been substituted far western and middle western volunteer cavalry; men with the fierce and implacable, ingrained mistrust and hatred of the Indians characteristic of the later frontiersman.

As time went on, serving with these men were a number of what might be called "reverse-English" volunteers; Confederate prisoners granted their liberty on condition that they volunteer for frontier duty. These men were known as "Galvanized Yankees."

And now, out of a clear sky, the Sioux in Minnesota struck; the Santees who, as you remember, had stayed behind when their kinsmen, the Tetons, had drifted toward the Rockies. Unexpectedly, terribly the

Santees struck. In 1862 under their chief Little Crow, the Santees rose in rebellion; the Minnesota massacre. Solemnly Little Crow, supposed to be a Christian Indian, attended the services at a missionary church, and that afternoon fire and slaughter spread across Minnesota and lasted for months. Finally, General Sibley, for some reason more famous for the army tent he invented than for his successful campaign, killed Little Crow and crushed the rebellion, and drove most of the Santees west.

The Indian has always had a genius for doing the wrong thing at the wrong time. The Santee massacre revived all the terror and cruelty of the early frontier days. By now eastern Minnesota was a land of farms and quiet people. The Santees were looked upon as quiet Indians. Through this quiet country, in these delicate times, troubled by distant war, when so many of the young men were away, the Santees struck.

On the distant and still unsettled frontiers men swore vengeance and tightened their belts, and to the dread name of Sioux new dread was added.

The Santees, nevertheless, had had some cause. They had an agent who, taking a leaf from Marie Antoinette's notebook, had told them when they were hungry to eat grass. And on top of the Santee uprising came the hanging of two Sioux chiefs at Fort Laramie. You shouldn't arrest an Indian, and even if you fear and dread Indians you shouldn't hang one. An Indian's dearest possession is his "face"; his dignity. His tribe will not take his hanging with a good grace.

Now, in 1865, two years after the Santee Sioux uprising, these two friendly Oglala chiefs—at least they had always been friendly up to the moment—Blackfoot and Two Face, were hanged in artillery trace chains at

Fort Laramie. No wonder Jim Bridger and all the other scouts present shook their heads.

Nobody knows the truth of the Eubanks incident. A few months before, a wagon train east of Laramie had been attacked and everyone killed except a certain Mrs. Eubanks. She had disappeared. Eventually Mrs. Eubanks was found in the camp of Blackfoot and Two Face by some Sioux police . . . already some of the Sioux were beginning to serve as policemen. Blackfoot and Two Face were arrested and brought into Laramie. An unfortunate volunteer soldier, Colonel Thomas Moonlight, of the 11th Kansas Cavalry, was in command. Colonel Moonlight was temporarily absent in pursuit of some hostiles, or supposed hostiles. During those years of the Civil War the two were often confused. In Colonel Moonlight's absence a brutal subordinate was in charge.

Mrs. Eubanks was hysterical and, undoubtedly, had been maltreated, but Two Face and Blackfoot claimed that they had discovered her with a hostile band and had bought her, and were bringing her back as a friendly act and for possible ransom. Maltreated women are notoriously dangerous witnesses. Two Face and Blackfoot's records were in their favor, but this did not save them.

All night in the guardhouse fronting on the parade ground they sang their death chant, and the next day they were hanged.

Colonel Bullock, the post trader, who knew Indians, had done his best to save the lives of the two chiefs. He was met by this sententious statement:

"So you think, sir, there will be a massacre? Let me tell you, Colonel Bullock, there are two Indians who will not take part in it. Good day, sir!"

The hanging at Laramie turned even the friendly

Indians—even the "ration Indians"—overtly or secretly against the government.

Poor Moonlight—Moonlight of the 11th Kansas Cavalry, with his charming but unmilitary name—he was as moonstruck as his name. Not long afterwards he set out again in pursuit of actual or supposed hostiles; refusing, despite advice, to guard his horses properly at night, they were all stolen and he and his troopers had to walk back eighty miles. This was too much for everyone, including General Dodge then in command of the Department. Moonlight was court-martialed.

Storm along the Powder, storm anywhere in the Far West, especially summer storm, reaches its climax at noon or dusk; its height of aerial drama. The valleys are so wide, the mountains so high, the horizons so far that you can see the storm coming for miles before it reaches you. See it marching across country, cutting the sunshine off mile by mile, turning the gold and green and tawny yellow into gray and black. Making the light, clear heat of July or August suddenly cold, for in high altitudes the temperature—the seasons—are entirely a matter of the sun. And, if the wind does not change, the storm will surely reach you.

In those great spaces thunder is long and loud and interminably rumbling, and the lightning stands high like forked trees reflected in a lake.

All about the Powder to the east and the south the storm was gathering. The tall-headed nimbi were piling up, scarred by occasional streaks of light. The dusty noon was taking on a crimson tinge.

PART TWO

Red Noon

You mount your horses from the right; Indians mount from the right

CHAPTER TWELVE

Crimson Parson

THE Reverend J. M. Chivington, colonel of the 2nd Colorado Volunteer Cavalry, was as unpleasant a man as you'll come across in frontier history. A loose-lipped, boasting, fanatical fellow. A minister of the Methodist Church in civil life, and a presiding elder in Denver before he entered the army with the Civil War. In his speech to his troops before starting the campaign which was to make him memorable, he exhorted his men to "kill and scalp all Indians, big or little," since "nits make lice." His second in command, Major Downing, admitted afterwards "the toasting of Indian shins before little fires" in order to obtain information.

Chivington's men followed his instructions to the letter; there was precision in their scalping and mutilation. Fantasies, incidentally, often indulged in by the white man. The first, scalping, was impressed upon the colonial Indian by bounties and made extremely profitable for him by the British, French and Americans in Revolutionary and pre-Revolutionary days. At all events, it is no Indian invention. Herodotus mentions it as a custom of the Scythians.

Some bands of hostile Cheyennes and Arapahos had been making trouble in northern Colorado and along the Medicine Road, and Chivington was dispatched with his regiment to bring them in. He did not find the troublemakers, in that bitterly cold November of 1864, but he did find the village of White Antelope and War

Bonnet composed of friendly Indians. They were Cheyennes and Arapahos, however, which was enough for Chivington.

The Indians were encamped in the valley of Sand Creek, asleep in their tepees, and Chivington fell upon them without warning and killed every man, woman and child he could lay hands on, three hundred Indians in all; seventy-five warriors, the rest old people, women and children. Chivington lost fourteen men killed and forty wounded. Stumbling from their tents, the Indians either begged for mercy or tried to flee. A number escaped. Among the Indians killed was a three-year-old boy who, left in the deserted village after the massacre, walked out of a tepee and started uncertainly in the direction he thought his mother and father had gone. It took three shots from three different troopers to kill him; and much profanity and laughter.

Not satisfied, Chivington even shot the unfortunate half-breed whom he had forced at the point of a pistol to guide him to White Antelope and War Bonnet's sleeping village.

Sardonically enough, the Cheyennes at the moment, and as they always did whenever possible, were speaking for peace, a wise intention that sometimes got them into trouble with their blood brothers and allies, the Sioux.

General Miles called the Sand Creek massacre "perhaps the foulest and most unjustifiable crime in the annals of America."

A government commission appointed in 1868 and headed by Generals Sherman, Terry and C. C. Augur, had this to say:

It scarcely has its parallel in the records of Indian brutality. Fleeing women, holding up their hands and praying for mercy, were shot down; infants were killed and scalped in derision; men were tortured and mutilated in a way which would put to shame the savages of interior Africa. No one will be astonished that a war ensued which cost the government $30,000,000 and carried conflagration and death to the border settlements. During the spring and summer of 1865 no less than 8,000 troops were withdrawn from the effective forces engaged against the Rebellion to meet this Indian war.

The generals were conservative. The war was by no means over when they and the civilians with them made their report.

The war lasted from 1864 to 1877, and the worst was yet to come. In 1868 there was a deceiving truce.

As for Chivington, it is pleasant to report that he died in disgrace after going back to Ohio and starting a newspaper, and attempting to run for the legislature. "Sand Creek" followed him. Sand Creek had been too strong even for the piquant taste of the frontier.

The Cheyennes had been talking and smoking peace, but they weren't talking peace now. Not after Sand Creek.

Chivington had loosed the winds if ever a man had.

Somehow from now on, for a while at least, you cannot get red out of your mind. Wherever you look the color in all its variations dances like a mirage before your eyes.

Straight north to their allies, the Sioux, and the sanctuary of the Powder, the broken and outraged Cheyennes and Arapahos of Sand Creek marched, picking up recruits on the way. North from Colorado through Nebraska to the Black Hills of South Dakota, and then, circling these to the north, south into the valley of the Powder where, in the gray noons, the lodges of the Powder River Sioux sent smoke up into the frosty air. Eight hundred or more lodges marching. Cheyennes,

Arapahos, 150 lodges of Oglalas, 250 lodges of Brulés—
most of the friendly Indians, friendly until Sand Creek,
of northern Colorado, southwestern Nebraska and southeastern Wyoming, met along the Oregon Trail.

Only the confirmedly friendly or fearful bands and
the "ration Indians" were left down around Fort Laramie. Pretty soon a number even of these were to join the
others on the Powder.

For four hundred miles the Indians from Sand
Creek had marched through the December and January
of a particularly bad winter, bringing with them all
their women and old people, and children and dogs, and
their immense herds of horses, cattle and mules. Both
those they had started with and those they had captured
on the way.

The marching lodges had taken a terrible revenge
for Sand Creek: they had killed more whites than Chivington had killed Indians.

For four hundred miles fire and slaughter lay behind them. Burned stage stations and lonely ranches.
Burned wagon trains. Dead white men and women and
children, their frozen eyes staring up at the sky and
where their hair had been that strange, dark, horrid
amorphousness that means scalping. For a hundred miles
the Medicine Road and the Overland Stage route had
been cut as if a blizzard had roared across them. Telegraph poles were down, stations out of commission or
else turned into miniature forts, mail and passengers unable to move. For a while the mail had to be sent east
again and across Nicaragua—the old route—to California. Julesburg in the extreme northwestern corner of
Colorado, just below the Nebraska line, just east and
south of the Wyoming line, was a smoldering ruin. The
soldiers, taken utterly by surprise, were bewildered and
kept pretty closely to their posts.

The march of the war pipes was only the beginning.

To the Sioux of the Powder—the Oglalas, the Brulés, the Miniconjous and the Sans Arcs who, a few years earlier, in 1856, had withdrawn from the Oregon Trail and had since then lived a fairly quiet life, broken only by pleasant forays with the Crows—the war pipes came. To the Sioux in Nebraska, mostly Sans Arcs, the war pipes came. To the Northern Arapahos and the Northern Cheyennes. Finally, to the fierce Hunkpapas up along the Missouri in Montana, the most withdrawn of all the Sioux, the least in contact with the white man, never amenable, never friendly, and now less than ever, for it was to the Hunkpapas that the Santees, reeling from the blows of Sibley, had fled with their tales of the Minnesota wars of '62 and '63.

Most of the Sioux and the Arapahos smoked. Some of the old chiefs were doubtful. A number of the Brulé chiefs down at Fort Laramie would not smoke at all. Even during the twelve years that followed numerous Sioux remained peaceful. Curiously enough, the Northern Cheyennes continued to work for peace.

As quickly as Antonio Mateo, in the comparatively quiet days of his trading post, had put out his cigar and locked his doors and gone to bed, war had come to the Powder, up to that time inviolate and apparently secure and fairly peaceful. War, and the premonitions of war, had been circling all about the Powder. Now war was on the Powder itself and the Powder was to be the seat of war. And the word "Wyoming," a second time, was to sound in American tales of horror.

Wyoming, not as yet officially named, still a part of the Dakotas, had for a long while been known unofficially as Wyoming. When it became a territory in 1868, four years after Sand Creek, it formally borrowed

the Delaware Indian name of a Pennsylvania valley
where, ninety years before, in July of 1778, Esther
Montour—"Queen Esther," half-breed and supposed
granddaughter of Frontenac—with her Senecas and
British soldiers had scalped, burned, tortured, and killed
upwards of four hundred Americans.

But Wyoming by itself—Maughwauwama—without these memories, is a lovely name. It means "wide
plains" or "alternate plains and valleys."

CHAPTER THIRTEEN

The Bloody Bozeman

JIM BRIDGER had told them not to lay it out where they did, this new short cut to Montana, this side trail that soon was to become too famous.

Bridger had told them not to put it to the east of the Big Horns through the country of the Sioux. He said that, if they did, it would never be safe for use and that it would only add to the growing resentment of the Oglalas and the Brulés, and almost at the same time he laid out his own safe trail to the Montana gold mines, the Bridger, to the west of the Big Horns, up the Big Horn Basin through the friendly country of the Crows.

"Never safe for use?" Well, today the old Bozeman is to all intents and purposes the Casper-Sheridan Highway—No. 87. But at the time, Bridger was right as he always was.

The world, however, is not much in the habit of paying attention to experts, and even John Bozeman himself, and he was an old-time trapper and mountain-man and knew the Indians, did not listen to Bridger. In 1863, in company with John Jacobs, another trapper, he prospected and laid out the trail named after him.

North from the Great Medicine Road, crossing the Middle Fork of the Powder west of where the South Fork enters, and from there hugging the Big Horns until it bent around their northern tip and made for Virginia City and the new gold towns of the Madisons, the Gallatins, and the Bitter Roots.

In confirmation of Bridger's prophecy, Bozeman, cooking supper in camp, was killed four years later far north on his trail, whether by Sioux or by a band of raiding Blackfeet is not surely known.

It is clear, of course, why a short cut to Montana was needed and was in the minds of men. At the beginning of the sixties gold had been discovered in Montana's western mountains, and pretty soon the backwash from California and eager men from the East were building towns there and organizing local governments. Not long afterwards the discovery that western Montana was a fine grazing country was also made and, so, small mountain ranches began to appear. But eastern Montana remained as wild as the Powder—Indian and buffalo country—up until the eighties. It is still a lonely country of wide, unbroken plains.

Up to the time of the Bozeman and Bridger trails there were only two ways to reach western Montana and both were long and expensive. Either you came up the Missouri to Fort Benton and there transferred to wagon or pack outfit, a further journey of several days, or else you used the Oregon Trail and when you came to Utah turned north through Idaho.

A trail heading diagonally across Wyoming would cut off two sides of a wide trangle and shorten a journey of several weeks into one of seven or eight days.

Besides, the Big Horns were beginning to have their own attractions. There was Father De Smet's remark about fabulous gold; there were a couple of stories credited to Jim Bridger; and there were the tales of lonely prospectors and trappers who from time to time disappeared into the Powder River country to reappear months later. There was old La Pondre, for example.

Old La Pondre was a familiar sight around Fort Laramie and up at the trading posts along the Missouri, although no one knew much about him. He was merely an old French-Canadian trapper who frequented the Big Horns. And then word was spread along the Oregon Trail and along the Missouri that La Pondre had "struck it rich." Looking for furs, La Pondre had stumbled across gold.

La Pondre, it seems, on his way back to St. Louis to sell his year's catch of furs had stopped at Fort La Pierre in South Dakota and "had shown Paul Packet and Bruère and Lamireaux," and some other trappers a tobacco pouch filled with nuggets. These stories are always bolstered heavily with names and dates. Everything about them is factual except the main point. Old La Pondre hadn't bothered much about these nuggets. He was a trapper, not a prospector, and had merely picked them up out of curiosity. But since his friends, Paul Packet and Bruère and Lamireaux, were interested, he promised, upon his return from St. Louis, to take them to where the gold was.

"The gold was just lying about on the bed of a creek. Loose. Plenty of it!" But La Pondre never guided his friends to the creek, for he died on that trip to St. Louis.

As for Bridger, he was reported to have told the following story after his return from the expedition of 1859 led by Captain W. F. Raynolds for which he had been head guide. His language, as you will notice, is the language of the reporter, not Bridger's own. In those days, as we have already seen in the autobiography of

Jim Beckwourth, reporters and ghost writers fell into the exact opposite of the error of today. All characters, however rough, spoke beautifully and with feeling, instead of all characters, however gentle or supposedly refined, speaking roughly.

"I," said Bridger, or at least this is what is written, "feeling thirsty, got off my mule and stooped down at a small brook containing clear and inviting water from the snow-capped mountains to drink, and while so doing my attention was attracted by the curious appearance of the bottom of the stream. It appeared to me like yellow pebbles of various sizes, from that of a head of a common pin to a bean and larger. Though well acquainted with the appearance of gold, I was somewhat in doubt of its being the precious metal, since it had never occurred to me that gold could be found in that locality; but my curiosity being excited, I scooped up a handful of the stuff, and rode up to Dr. Hayden and Captain Raynolds. Both at once pronounced it pure gold, and asked me where I had procured it. After I had told them where I had found it, Captain Raynolds got very excited, and insisted that I should cast it away, and not tell anyone of the party of the matter under any circumstances, he fearing that a knowledge of gold in such abundance and of such easy access would certainly break up the expedition, since every man would desert to hunt for gold."

Jim Bridger may have told such a story. When it came to anything serious, he told the truth and told it clearly, but like most mountainmen, in his idle moments he liked to exercise his fancy. His stories of the "wonders of the Yellowstone" are classics, and the sale of his Fort Bridger to the Mormons was a Gargantuan joke and a profitable one.

But even without Father De Smet, or old La Pondre, or Bridger, prospectors would by now have been seeking the Big Horns. Gold was in the minds of men, and gold was being discovered to the west and to the north of the Big Horn River. You can't keep men out of a virgin country where there is any chance of gold. For many years the United States government tried with a definite and distinguished lack of success.

So there was every reason to put a trail north through Wyoming, but just why Bozeman put it through the Sioux country is not so clear. To be sure, in 1863 the Sioux were still fairly peaceful; Sand Creek had not yet happened. But the trail was in direct violation of the treaties the government had made with the Sioux. The Powder was their country and they were to be left alone in it. White men entered only at their own risk, and they were supposed to keep out.

I suppose John Bozeman, paradoxically enough, put his trail where he did because he was a mountainman and an old-time Indian fighter. He felt that men like himself would be safe. As for the emigrants, they would go through in numbers and on the alert. Pretty soon the Sioux would get used to this invasion, anyhow, as the Indian had got used to such invasions everywhere. Furthermore, in some ways Bozeman's trail was simpler than the trail Bridger blazed through the Big Horn Basin. It was shorter and there were no obstacles in the way, just rolling, gentle country throughout. The Big Horn Basin Trail had to go through rough country for a while on the Wyoming-Montana line where the Big Horn River plunges through its mysterious canyon, not even yet well known.

The mountainman was not afraid of Indians. Give him plenty of ammunition, a companion or two, and some shelter, and he was quietly sure he could take care of himself. He had done so again and again. He was master of the most deadly, morale-shattering weapon ever invented, the rifle. He never wasted a shot. In the history of the West there is nothing more striking than the way in which a handful of trappers, scouts, mountainmen, would stand off hundreds of Indians; the same Indians who had very little trouble massacring soldiers, emigrants and ranchers.

In his reports, General Dodge, at the time commander of the Department of the Plains, speaks of having interviewed an old trapper after the Wagon Box Fight of 1867.

"How many Indians were there in the fight?" asked the general.

"Wal, gineral, I can't say for sartain, but I think nigh on to three thousand." (The old trapper multiplied the number of Indians to about double. A common habit.)

"How many did you kill or wound?"

"Wal, gineral, I can't say for sartain, but give me a dead rest and I kin hit a dollar at fifty yards every time, and I fired at a dead rest more than fifty times at them varmints."

"How many times did you fire altogether?"

"Wal, gineral, I can't say, but I kept eight guns pretty well het up for more'n an hour."

This self-confidence of the mountainman was not like the ignorant self-confidence of the soldier, professional or volunteer, until he learned better. The mountainman was as wary as he was self-confident, and he knew every move, and trick, and sign of the Indian. He was an Indian himself so far as his knowledge went; his knowledge of tracking, of countries, of how to be unobserved, of what was going to happen; but he was an Indian with the added intelligence, doggedness, second wind, and deadliness of the white man.

John Bozeman, however, did not know the full

capacity of the Sioux. It is doubtful if anyone did except Bridger, and Bridger, where the Indian was concerned, had extraordinary intuition. What the Sioux thought of the Bozeman Trail was soon evident.

At first they paid little apparent attention to it. The older chiefs still hoped by means of treaties and conferences to make things right, and the Powder was a huge country. Men, except in large numbers, were swallowed up on its horizons. A few wagon trains got through safely to Montana; a number of prospecting parties. But the Sioux, nonetheless, realized fully that here, unless it was cut, was another Medicine Road, even more destructive than the original. This new Medicine Road passed right through their buffalo and antelope country.

Also they began to perceive clearly, as it affected them, the significance of the ancient, continuing, universal search for grass. If enough white men went up the Bozeman Trail, pretty soon some of them, seeing the lovely valleys at the foot of the Big Horns, would want to settle, and the buffalo herds, the lifeblood of the Sioux, would go. The Sioux knew what their great Powder River chief, Red Cloud, expressed some years later in conference with the whites:

"The Buffalo North and the Buffalo South," he said; "that is the game that has brought our Nation where it now stands."

On top of the growing apprehension came Sand Creek and the pipe bearers from the south.

On a still day sound travels far in a country like the Powder. On a still night it travels even farther. After Sand Creek the tom-toms sounded often. And there was much dancing, and the rising crescendo of the rattles was like the furious challenge of a myriad disturbed snakes.

CHAPTER FOURTEEN

The Powder River Expedition

SUDDENLY and as confusingly as it undertook all Indian affairs during this period, the government decided that the Indians who had marched north from Sand Creek—and their Sioux protectors—must be taught a lesson and that the Powder River country must be brought under control; not taken away from the Sioux, but brought under control.

The government at long last had arrived at a conclusion held by all those who knew Wyoming, a conclusion eagerly desired by the wiser officers of the army. The Powder River country was the Sioux base of supplies and their general headquarters; the Sioux Service in the Rear. It was a pool, a citadel, a donjon of Indian power. And a very convenient one. If you were an energetic Sioux with a grudge, down over the Teapot Dome Divide you came, down to the loop of the North Platte, and there was the Oregon Trail for you to cut, guarded at that point only by a miniature military post. Eastward there was nothing to stop you. You could ride east, and through Nebraska south, and once more there was the Oregon Trail to cut. Just a few days' work for hard-riding young braves.

Afterwards you could go back to the Powder, and lick your wounds, and fatten your ponies on grass, and fatten yourself on buffalo meat, and lay plans, and by means of dancing and drumming and singing restore your fighting edge.

By now the government was in a position to turn its attention a trifle more formally toward its new provinces in the west. The Civil War was almost over.

Outraged by the cutting of the Oregon Trail after the Sand Creek massacre in the autumn of '64 and the

slaughter along it—as much outraged, indeed, as the Indians had been by the massacre itself—the government decided to send an army into the Powder the following spring. The intention was to build a strong post there and make a demonstration in force. Volunteer troops were still garrisoning the West, and a volunteer general was chosen to lead the expedition, but a good one. A short, fiery, red-haired Irishman named Connor, General P. E. Connor, originally from New York. Connor was the man who, a few years before, had put the fear

of the United States government into the hearts of the
recalcitrant Mormons at Salt Lake.

The expedition was carefully planned all that winter. In the spring, Connor was to march north, build a
post on the Powder, garrison it strongly, and from there
proceed up along the Big Horns. Two other columns
were to effect a junction with him: Colonel Walker
with 600 men, a Kansas regiment; Colonel Cole, with
1,400 men. Connor was supposed to have at least 3,000
men.

Walker was to march north through Nebraska,
paralleling far to the east Connor's march until he came
to the Black Hills. There he was to join Colonel Cole,
who was to march northwest from the Lower Platte.
Turning southwest, the combined column was to find
Connor. In this way, the Sioux on the Powder would be
taken from the front and the rear, and the Sioux in
Nebraska and South Dakota would see what the government could do when aroused.

Connor's expedition, the first hostile expedition to
enter the Powder River country, was known officially as
the "Powder River Expedition."

Until recently the government had been extremely
vague about the Powder River country. As late as 1851,
in the treaty of that year made with as many of the
Plains and Mountain Indians as could be persuaded to
attend the conference at Horse Creek, just east of Fort
Laramie, the Powder River country had been spoken of
as Crow country, the commissioners apparently unaware that the Crows had lost control of it fifty years
before.

Over in the friendly Crow country, or down
around Fort Laramie, Bridger shook his head. He could
scent Indian trouble as stock scents water. But it was

the experience of the old-time guide and scout—it is still the experience of the guide and scout—that people listen to him only when, having tried everything but his advice, they find themselves in serious difficulties.

Bridger, a man of useful apothegms, one of the most useful being that when you saw no Indians "thar was the time to look for 'em," was accustomed to not being listened to. They tell a story about him that on one occasion guiding a detachment of troops under command of a second lieutenant across the Big Horn River in flood, when he made suggestions as to safe swimming, he was told by the embryo officer to mind his own business since he was merely a "civilian scout." The result was that a trooper was drowned. When eventually Bridger got the troops across without further loss, the young officer, a very religious man, knelt down on the bank and loudly and publicly thanked God. Bridger watched him in silence till he had finished, then raised his eyes devoutly to the skies.

"And, pardner," he said confidentially, "he never once mentioned Jim Bridger!"

CHAPTER FIFTEEN

1865

ONNOR never had a chance; he was a good deal like the French king who marched up a hill and then marched down again. At the time the government had a gracious habit, a habit not unknown to governments past and present, of discrediting numerous excellent officers whose only faults were the government's lack of support and its own division of opinion.

Connor never received proper support, and he no sooner got started than he was accused of undue severity. He had been told to impress the Indians and, being an old Indian fighter, he knew what impressed an Indian, but the Indians' Friends, excellent ladies and gentlemen in the East, most of whom had never been west, were still powerful and, despite the intention to give the Indian a lesson, the government still couldn't quite make up its mind about the Sioux. An uncertainty that lasted for eleven years; indeed, up to the Custer massacre.

Connor never got away from Fort Laramie until July 30th, and, when he did, it was with only about one third of the troops he was supposed to have, and not half the supplies and horses he needed. Meanwhile, the Sioux had taken things into their own hands. They had struck at Platte Bridge, raiding down from the Powder across the Teapot Dome Divide. In a small skirmish, Lieutenant Caspar Collins of the 11th Ohio Cavalry and some of his troopers had been killed. The present town of Casper, misspelled, is named after Lieutenant Collins.

Up on the Powder the drums and the rattles, the dancing and the councils, had reached a climax, and for a while the young chiefs, and the warrior societies, and the fire-eaters were in control.

There had been a great council that spring lasting for two months and bringing together over 1,000 lodges; upwards of 3,000 warriors; Oglalas and other bands of Tetons with Arapahos and Cheyennes. Well aware of what was happening down around Fort Laramie a couple of hundred miles south, and of the preparations for Connor's expedition, the Indians had finally decided to get in the first blow.

Formally they marched south—this was intended as formal war—the warrior societies of the Oglalas and Cheyennes in the lead: the Oglala Crazy Dogs, the Cheyenne Dog Soldiers. A formidable army that accomplished even less than Connor's. The leaders of this army could not even prevent the younger warriors from attacking a wagon train that was pulling into the post at Platte Bridge and so giving the whole show away before a surprise attack could be made on the tiny post itself.

Lieutenant Collins, with the cool, gallant and fantastic lack of realism which characterized the United States frontier army, volunteer and regular, up until the desperate seventies, rode out with a handful of men to rescue the wagon train . . . rode straight into the Sioux army. He was killed with most of his men. A few managed to get back to the post.

The Indians circled the post for a couple of days, shook their guns and lances, shouted at the defenders, and then rode happily back to the Powder.

In their minds they had won a major victory and

had shown the Great White Father where that mythical gentleman got off.

It has been said often, and with much truth, that the white man taught the Indian how to fight. Taught him deadliness. Certainly death, accurate and intentional, followed the white man through the East and then westward like the knife of a mowing machine. Even those grim and serious-minded people, the Sioux, never learned how to conduct a real campaign. Even less than their eastern brethren did the Plains Indians seem to have any idea of actually besieging a fortified position; beleaguering it; starving it out; forcing it to surrender. Later on Fort Phil Kearny, that disastrous post, was in the hollow of the Sioux's hands, yet at no time was it actually beleaguered. Always the garrison could come and go about as it pleased, although often at the risk of its lives.

The white man can outdo the Indian in everything the Indian does. He can outshoot him, outride him, outmarch him, and even outtrack him, that is, if he is willing to learn the last: but the principal advantage that the white man has is his second wind. The Indian's second wind is confused by his primitive psychology and traditions. Clearly he has immense bravery and endurance, and has shown both again and again heroically and almost unbelievably. But the Indian's second wind depends too much upon his sense of loss of face. At all events, given any chance at all, the white man invariably defeated the Indian, and began to fight about the time the Indian stopped. And the Indian never became a good shot, once he gave up the bow and arrow and took to a gun.

Indian fighting, until the white man came, was largely a matter of ceremony and boasting, of tradition, of dressing up, of drum music, of dancing, of horse raiding and woman stealing. The taking of coups, that is, the touching of an enemy's body with a coupstick, the stealing of his horses or women, was a much more important business than killing him. There was a great deal of forming of battle lines, of individual champions, of shouting back and forth, of the shaking of lances. Nor would the Indian fight consistently.

Why should any sensible man want to fight consistently? You fought a battle, and won it or lost it, and then you went home and celebrated your victory, or mourned your defeat, and the next spring, or fall, when you were all ready again, you hunted up your enemies, unless they had hunted you up in the meantime, and fought another battle, and won it or lost it. The white man took all the fun out of fighting. Besides, consistent fighting interfered with the real business of life, which was hunting.

I have a suspicion that the Indian, like most primitive men, disapproves the civilized theory that war is one of man's most fundamental impulses: that, and women. Food was much more important to the Indian, and as a rule all his serious fighting was done because of food. His traditional enmities arose over disputed hunting grounds. As for women, they are not exactly the same thing as the urge for reproduction. Usually there are enough women around locally without going to war over them. Stealing women was merely a beau geste, added to the beau geste of a raid.

The alimentary canal was what counted, and I am sure that careful history would show this to have been the case around Troy as well. That, and not Helen's beauty.

But the white man, of course, as is his custom, did everything in his power to make his enemy dangerous.

The white man seldom hesitated to supply the Indians with ammunition and firearms, even if he knew that the next day they would be used against him and his family and neighbors, and he kept the Indian in a sporadic mood for provocative incidents by furnishing him, despite the efforts of the government, with firewater.

During all these parlous times, Richards and Bissonette and Major Twiss, and others like them, were busy up around the Platte River Bridge.

The Sioux and their allies could have taken the Platte River Bridge, and cut the Oregon Trail, and destroyed the little post at the Platte, and thrown things out of kelter for a long while, but they didn't.

Six days after the fight at Platte Bridge, Connor moved north.

The Powder River Expedition was the last appearance in force of the volunteer troops on the frontier. Pretty soon the regulars were back. Connor's roster reads like a roll call of the states. The 7th Iowa Cavalry. The 11th Ohio Cavalry. The 2nd California Cavalry. The 2nd Missouri Artillery. The 6th Michigan Cavalry. The last were to be left to garrison the post on the Powder which Connor was to build. Not full regiments, you understand, but companies and detachments. And with Connor also were 75 Pawnee scouts, under no less a person than Captain Frank North. In addition to the Pawnees were 70 Winnebagos and Omahas; 195 teamsters and wagon masters; and 185 wagons.

The Omahas and Winnebagos and Pawnees had a wonderful time lifting Sioux and Cheyenne and Arapaho scalps. They were the only people who really enjoyed the expedition, the Pawnees especially, those tried and true friends of the United States and bitter enemies

of the Sioux. The Sioux for years had harried the Pawnees in their Nebraska villages along the North Platte,
invading and occupying the Pawnees' hunting grounds.
From now on the Pawnees, with their famous Pawnee
Battalion of Scouts, Captain North in command, began
to take a full and terrible revenge.

We forget the part the Indian played in presenting
us with our country, which was once his. Among his
numerous defeatist characteristics, the most fatal was
the Indian's inability at any time to see himself as a
member of a race. He would not fight as such.

To the white frontiersman of the West—except in
the case of a few notorious renegades, more terrible with
their white man's eyes staring at you than any Indian—
the white man in danger was always a white man, no
matter how much, in times of peace, white men might
quarrel among themselves. To the Indian an Indian was
not another Indian, but a member of another tribe, or
even of another band of the same tribe: and, if hostile,
that Indian's scalp was as pretty a souvenir as any white
man's scalp. Indian tribes on all frontiers—and in particular the Pawnees and Crows, where the Northwest
was concerned—helped the white man mightily in the
final humiliation of their own people. From the time
the fighting began in the middle sixties until the end of
the seventies, the Crows, Pawnees and Shoshones were
among the best scouts and fighters the army had.

Connor marched to the Powder and built his post
and called it Fort Connor. A year later, with the arrival
of Colonel Carrington and the second Powder River
Expedition, the post was moved a little down the river
and its name changed to Reno. Connor was not even
allowed to retain this mild honor. After leaving the
Michigan regiment in garrison, Connor marched north
to meet Colonels Cole and Walker. From there on, with

the exception of Connor's own column, the campaign
became a comedy of errors.

Walker and Cole never found Connor. From the
moment they marched into the Powder River country
from the north they were in trouble. Their troops were
sullen, unwilling, frightened and tired out; the Indians
hung on their flanks, appearing and vanishing, stealing
horses and cutting off men whenever they got the
chance, and finally the combined column managed to
lose itself in the endless badlands east of the Powder.

It was lucky that Connor had built his post and
that Cole and Walker could hardly help finding it if
they marched south long enough; and luckier still that
they stumbled across a scout who guided them.

Meanwhile Connor, close to the Big Horns, had
been as successful as Cole and Walker had been unsuc-
cessful. He had marched steadily north as far as Tongue
River at the northern end of the Big Horns, defeating
the Indians in small skirmishes wherever he met them.
They would not meet him in full battle. The nearest
approach to a real battle was Connor's defeat of Old
David and Black Bear on the Tongue. Nonetheless, at
the end of September, Connor was recalled to Fort
Laramie in partial disgrace.

Connor had issued an unfortunate general order.
"You will not receive overtures of peace and submission
from the Indians," it read, "but will attack and kill
every male Indian over twelve years of age."

As soon as the Indians' Friends heard of this, Connor's fate was sealed.

Just to add to the confusion and the growing Sioux
belief that they were invincible, also to their anger
and their dread of what the white man intended to do,
another bewildered expedition had penetrated the Powder that summer far to the north near the Montana line.

Aware now that the Powder was a short cut to western Montana, the government had decided, largely because of local pressure, to build a wagon road from Niobrara, in northwestern Nebraska, to Virginia City, in Montana. This was intended more or less to take the place of the Bozeman and so quiet the Sioux. It had, of course, the opposite effect. Despite what was going on at the moment, the government had called another conference with the Sioux chiefs—all those who would come—in the spring of '65 down at Fort Laramie, and at this conference had signed what was known as the Harney-Sanborn Treaty. No really hostile chiefs were present, especially those on the Powder, but Spotted Tail, persistently friendly, and Man-Afraid-of-His-Horse, still friendly, had signed as well as the chiefs in the neighborhood of the fort. On condition that the white man would go through the Powder River country quickly and not linger there, the chiefs who signed had promised safe travel on the Bozeman.

The attempt to establish the Niobrara-Virginia City wagon road did not add to the authority of these friendly chiefs or increase the goodwill of the hostile chiefs on the Powder. Colonel James Sawyer, lately retired from the Civil War, was appointed to lay out the Niobrara-Virginia City road. For these purposes he was granted an appropriation of $50,000, two companies of infantrymen and a few cavalry.

No one has ever been quite sure whether Colonel Sawyer hadn't obtained both the soldiers and the appropriation to further a private plan to convey a large emigrant train from Niobrara to the Montana gold fields. At all events, he set out with this emigrant train and his soldiers, and it did not enhance the already weakened prestige of the United States that when Dull Knife, later to become so famous, met him with his

Cheyennes and some Sioux and barred his progress, Sawyer bribed the Cheyennes and Sioux with a wagon load
of provisions not to attack him.

This, Dull Knife and the chiefs with him agreed to
if Sawyer would get out of the country and stay out.

By this time Sawyer was about as badly lost in the
badlands of the Powder as Cole and Walker had been.

The upshot of the summer of 1865 was that the
government decided to call another big conference at
Fort Laramie the following spring.

If talking could convince the Sioux and edge them
peaceably out of their country, the government was determined that every tongue should wag.

But perhaps this isn't fair. What the government
really had in mind was the thoroughly incompatible
program of keeping the Powder still inviolate and yet,
at the same time, opening it up freely to the coming and
going of the white man.

Nor is it invidious to remark that the government
probably also had in its mind that conditions on the
frontier would soon be different. Before long the government would be in a position to replace volunteer
troops and volunteer generals with hard-riding profes-
sionals.

Connor, Cole and Walker had had bad troops.
Never especially good, they had been made especially
bad by the fact that they knew the Civil War was over
and were tired and wanted to go home. Walker's Kansas
regiment had mutinied at Fort Laramie on the eve of its
march north and had only been forced to proceed, lag-
ging and ill-tempered, by loyal troops and the threat of
executions.

Up until the summer of 1865, as far as the records
show, no white man had been killed along the Powder.
Sioux and Crow deaths, of course, had continued to
happen in sporadic and galloping fashion. As late as

1861 the Sioux and the Crows were still raiding each other. In 1859 something like a real battle had occurred when the Sioux had killed a Crow head chief and thirty Crow braves, and again, in 1861, the Sioux had killed a Crow chief while they were raiding into the Crow country under command of no less a person than Red Cloud. But now the color of death along the Powder was to change. Red death and white death were to be intermixed. And the Powder, so slow and coiling and sleepy in summer, was to raise its head and strike.

Suddenly the Powder, known hithertofore only by the name of a few creeks and mountains and buttes, by the old faint line of the Pumpkin Buttes Trail and the new line of the Bozeman, was, with dates and death, to become as pockmarked as the moon.

Here are a few from the bloody sixties and seventies. The Bozeman became as red as a vein.

Fort Connor: 1865. Far to the north, the Battle of Tongue River where General Connor defeated Black Bear and Old David. That was also in 1865. Fort Reno: 1866. Twenty miles north, Crazy Woman Battlefield: Lieutenant Daniels and Sergeant Farrel, killed July 20, 1866. Fort Phil Kearny. Up in Montana, Fort C. F. Smith. The Fetterman massacre. The Wagon Box Fight —August 2, 1867. November 26, 1876, Dull Knife against Colonel Ranald Mackenzie—a tragic fight.

And, the most tragic of all but antedating the last, the Little Big Horn, June 25, 1876.

These are only a few of the dates that mark the Powder. A country almost without history became abruptly crowded with what has long been recognized as that not very happy series of events.

We will come later to the dates which mark the actual arrival of the white man as an inhabitant.

CHAPTER SIXTEEN

Red Cloud

I T is generally believed that great events make great men, that, the times calling, great men appear. History is not so simple as that; it is a matter of action and reaction. You could say with equal truth that great events are made by great men. Now, in any case, there appeared a great Sioux. Great because he had the un-Indian power of wide vision. Great because he had the un-Indian gift of organization. Great because, unlike most Indians, he could be patient and plan far-reaching plans.

Perhaps he did not see so clearly as old Spotted Tail who from the very beginning realized the power of the white man and so throughout remained peaceful. Nor was he ever the spectacular warrior, the great battle leader, that some of his younger braves were, especially his son-in-law, Tashunka Witko, Crazy Horse; the young paladin, the greatest warrior the Sioux ever had. But Red Cloud came near to being a statesman in a way few other Indians have been. Just a few equaled him: Pontiac, Tecumseh, King Philip, a handful of others.

Nor was Red Cloud a young man when he came into his greatness; he was somewhere around forty-two years old.

A hawk-faced Indian, Red Cloud, an Oglala, with the quiet eyes of a dreamer and immense dignity in his face, and a self-made man. Early in life he had made a

reputation for himself as a more than ordinary horseman, a keen hunter, a good warrior, and a mind wise in
council, but he was not born an hereditary chief, although just what that meant among the Plains Indians,
and how much power was attached to the position, no
one exactly knows. All we do know about Red Cloud's
childhood is that he was born somewhere around 1822
and that his father, Lone Man, amounted to little. There
is a tradition that Lone Man was a drunkard. His
mother's name was Walks-as-She-Thinks.

No one knows how Red Cloud got his name. Some
of the present-day Oglalas have an easy and poetic, although probably untrue, explanation. They say it was
because Red Cloud's followers with their crimson blankets made a red sky along the horizon. Also that, as a
signal to charge, Red Cloud often waved a blanket of
the same color. But according to contemporary reports
Red Cloud's men did not wear red blankets.

George Hyde, author of *Red Cloud's Folk,* writes
me:

Spelling of Sioux names seems to be largely a matter of
taste. In spelling Red Cloud's name some use "q" and others
"k." I make it Makhpiya (cloud) luta (scarlet). The whites
always made it Red Cloud, and in later life he was commonly called by his own tribesmen Makhpiya sha (sha—
red). As for "makhpiya," it is usually translated "cloud,"
but it often meant sky, as you can see when the Sioux speak
of "makhpiya to" (blue cloud).

Red Cloud was born about 1822, at about the time the
meteorite passed over the Sioux country from west to east
(it exploded over the post of Fort Snelling at the mouth of
the Minnesota River on the night of September 20, 1822,
as recorded in Keating's book, published in 1825). I have
always believed Red Cloud was named for this event, which
greatly impressed the Indians. Inkpaduta, the great Sioux

chief, had twin sons born about 1822 and evidently named
for this event. One was called Roaring Cloud, the other Fire
Cloud. This meteor passed over in a blaze of light and with
a great roaring sound.

Very early in his life Red Cloud conceived a cool
consistent dislike of the whites. He never trusted them
and the fact that his father was a drunkard, on white
traders' alcohol, undoubtedly helped to harden this attitude. Red Cloud as a boy went down to the posts with
his family along with those Oglalas and Brulés who suc-
cumbed to the lures of Fort Laramie and the Oregon
Trail. Red Cloud resented the way the fur companies in
fierce competition bribed and debauched the Indians,
especially with whisky. The different bands had begun
to fight among themselves and there was occasional
brawling and occasional private murder, the last something rare with Indians except when they are drunk.

Red Cloud first came into prominence in 1841
when he was still a young man, only nineteen. There was
at this time near Fort Laramie an old Oglala chief, Bull
Bear, who although an excellent chief in some ways was
a bully and a tyrant. He was a friend of the traders and
respected by them but could not get along with a number of his own people. His principal rival and enemy
was another Oglala, Smoke, now chief of the band to
which Red Cloud's father, by this time dead, had belonged. The enmity between Bull Bear and Smoke
reached its climax in the autumn of 1841 during a
drunken fight among their respective braves, and Red
Cloud is credited with having shot Bull Bear. The quarrel separated the Oglalas into two distinct factions; and
the break influenced that tribe's entire history.

The Bear people, Bull Bear's followers, eventually
drifted toward Nebraska and Kansas and the southeast.

Into the Platte valley near the Oregon Trail. They were the Oglalas who made trouble in the first place but eventually they settled down and became quiet. The Smoke people, Red Cloud with them, when they found conditions unbearable along the Oregon Trail and near

Fort Laramie in the middle fifties, drifted permanently north. They were the Oglalas who, with part of the Miniconjous and some Brulés and Sans Arcs, settled on the headwaters of the Powder. Peaceful for a decade or so, removed for a while from the white man, pleasantly preoccupied with hunting and the Crows, and deluded by the notion that the government was strongly determined to keep the Powder River country sacred for them, these Smoke people were the Oglalas who in the sixties became the spear point of the Indian attack.

It is doubtful if Red Cloud, however, ever believed much in the promises of the government. Where the Indian was concerned, the government was never its own master. On the one side it had the emigrants, the few settlers, the stage companies, the miners and the soldiers and their generals; the constant complaints and pressure of these, their determination to open up the Powder River country. On the other side were the Indian Bureau and the Indians' Friends.

Red Cloud foresaw war from the moment Sand Creek occurred. Perhaps he foresaw it from the time the Santees fled west to the Hunkpapas after the Minnesota massacre. In any case, he began to lay his plans early. During the summer of 1865 he skirmished with the columns of General Connor and Colonels Walker and Cole, and he was one of the Sioux chiefs, the most prominent, with Dull Knife and his Cheyennes when Dull Knife humiliated Colonel Sawyer and put a stop to the proposed Niobrara-Virginia City wagon road. Red Cloud was not present at the Harney-Sanborn conference of 1865. It is doubtful if he would have been present had he been able to go, and it is still more doubtful if he would have signed. At the time he was lying in his tepee up on the Powder with a convenient excuse, a wound made by a Crow arrow in a spring raid. He recovered just in time to take part in the attacks on the Powder River Expedition, and he was sufficiently strong to be a major factor in the great council of the Sioux which ended in the march down to the Platte River Bridge. A year later Red Cloud found his great opportunity.

The government stepped blindly into Red Cloud's trap. All that winter after Connor's expedition Red Cloud had been sending messengers among the Sioux and Cheyennes and Arapahos telling them they could not trust the government and that they must prepare themselves to make war. The words of the white man, he said, were written in water.

The great and much-heralded conference at Fort Laramie in the early summer of 1866, the conference that was to make the Sioux at last completely secure in their possession of the Powder and at the same time make the white man safe in his travels, followed the prescribed pattern perfectly. This conference was intended to wipe out all memory of Sand Creek and the Connor expedition and smoothly square a circle. But, just as before the Harney-Sanborn conference of the previous spring, when the government had been preparing to send an expedition north to make a demonstration in force and partially fortify the Powder, so now the government was preparing to send an expedition north and completely fortify the Powder. Before the conference met, Colonel Henry B. Carrington, late general in the Civil War, had been ordered to march with his regiment up the North Platte valley from Nebraska, and then up into the Powder River country.

Carrington had seven hundred men, the 2nd Battalion of the 18th United States Infantry—regulars this time. He was to relieve the volunteers Connor had left at Fort Connor and after that build two forts along the Bozeman Trail, one in Wyoming, one in Montana. Nothing could have been in more open violation of the proposed treaty or of the treaty of the year before. And the government didn't even bother to tell Carrington about the conference at Fort Laramie. The unfortunate colonel marched straight into the conference, camped on its edge one night, and the next morning appeared blithely in the concourse of commissioners and Indians, got off his horse, and strode up to the commissioners and shook hands with them smilingly.

Red Cloud, sitting in the circle of chiefs, sullen and watchful, must have smiled suddenly and delightedly.

He arose, stalked forward, and pointed at Carrington's shoulder straps . . . his silver eagles . . . then he turned dramatically to his people.

"Look!" he said. "Here is the white eagle who has come to steal a road through the Indian's land!"

For a moment he was silent, before steadily, quietly, passionately he spoke for war.

He said the peace commissioners were treating the chiefs like children, pretending to negotiate for a country they intended to take by conquest. He said the government had broken faith in every transaction with his people. He said the white man year by year had crowded the Indian back until there was left only this little country to the north; the Indian's last home and last hunting ground. If this were taken, the Indian would die of starvation. As for himself, he preferred to die fighting. If all the Sioux and the Cheyennes and Arapahos would combine, they could keep the white man out of their country. It might be a long war—yes, but in the end, since they were defending their hunting grounds, the Indian would win.

Red Cloud broke up the conference. Big Mouth, Spotted Tail, Swift Bear, Two Strikes, with about two thousand Sioux, mostly Brulés who had no interest in the Powder River country, or who belonged to the kept and rationed bands that wandered about in the vicinity of Fort Laramie, abided by the treaty. Red Cloud and Man-Afraid-of-His-Horse—the latter had for a long while tried to keep the peace and because of this had lost some face with his immediate people—and the other hostile chiefs went back to the Powder taking some six hundred lodges with them. The Miniconjous, and half of the Oglalas, and a number of Brulés, and a few Sans Arcs, and the Northern Cheyennes and the Northern Arapahos.

They told the white man to keep out. They told him he could build no fort nearer than Fort Connor on the banks of the Powder. They told him he could not use the Bozeman. That way, they said, lay death.

CHAPTER SEVENTEEN

Fort Disastrous

L ITTLE BEAR, a Cheyenne chief who died not long ago, as a boy of eleven hid with his father behind a rock somewhere up near the Clear Creek fork of Powder River, somewhere, that is, near the site of the present town of Buffalo, and watched Carrington and his men go by.

This was in July, 1866, an especially hot, dry year and month, so word comes down to us.

"My son," said Little Bear's father, "you have seen the white soldiers. The Indian cannot hope to defeat these white soldiers. There you see marching the end of your people. But do not give in. Do not surrender. And never make a friend of a white man." And for many years Little Bear tried to follow the last injunction, although when he came to die his final message, oddly enough, was to a white friend.

Carrington's men were as hard as their alkali-stained faces; they were as limber as the long strides they took. In the blazing heat of a high country drought which sucks every drop of moisture out of a man's body, they were marching sixteen, eighteen, twenty miles a day. Some of them were mounted on horses, but not many, and those that were weren't good on horses. The government had intended to mount them all before they left Nebraska, but as always the government's plans went astray. So they were marching, these foot soldiers, up into a country of clouds of disappearing horsemen.

Little Bear's father must have had a vision, which was like a Cheyenne. The Cheyennes were a sensible people, and visions as a rule—sensible visions—are no more than common sense projected into the future. The Cheyennes had known the white man longer than the Sioux; they had fought the white man down along the Oregon Trail before the Sioux took to the same pastime.

There was nothing in the surface appearance of Carrington's tiny army, unless it was its hardness and its discipline, to cause Little Bear's father to say what he did. Even Red Cloud, the wise, was for a long while optimistic. Little Bear's father must have realized that here was no question of temporary success, nor of present numbers, nor of equal gallantry or endurance. This thin blue trickle in the vast shining country, this thread of blue, gray with dust, was the first warning of the flood behind; the first break in the dam.

And there must have been something about Carrington's men that convinced Little Bear's father that the government was at last in earnest.

These were no careless and badly disciplined volunteer cavalrymen. These were victorious veterans of the bloodiest war the world had as yet seen, and they were flushed with victory, and back of them were mysterious forces, released, of which even they were totally unaware.

Along with Carrington marched Invisibles, Powers and Principalities. Demiurges, that were presently to roar along the ground, and dig deep into it, and to speak over wires and belch forth smoke, and make gray ghosts walk on screens, and bring death in a score of terrible and unheard-of ways.

In a certain fashion, Connor's cavalrymen had been

closer to the Sioux than to these marching veterans of Carrington. Carrington's marching infantrymen marked the end of the Civil War: the world had changed. Connor's cavalrymen had garrisoned a far and temporarily forgotten frontier where the horse was still the swiftest means of transportation. They had lived on a frontier still close to its beginnings; to the fur trade, to the mountainman. A frontier that was looked upon as Indian country where the white man was either an intruder or a temporary guest, and men still wrote and spoke of the country farther east as "the States" and as "home."

A year after Carrington marched, the railroad reached Cheyenne, and all along it from the Nebraska line to Utah little towns sprang up. Two years after Carrington marched, in 1868, Wyoming became a territory with all the pride, expenses and officeholders that implies. People could now ride through Wyoming in the slow safety of jolting trains where only three years before emigrants, guns on their shoulders, had trudged beside their oxen, or the swaying Overland Stages had galloped. From the car windows this new form of traveler could see every now and then Indians on the horizon, as unsubstantial as sun-brightened earth-clouds before rain.

Even the buffalo didn't like the railroad. Sometimes they held it up for hours with their not-to-be-hurried crossing. The buffalo had apparently not liked the telegraph line either when it had gone through in 1861. Every now and then they uprooted the poles by rubbing against them to get rid of their winter hair.

Carrington's marching infantry marked the definite end of the Stone Age man. The southern planter, the southern farmer had gone down before Carrington's veterans and men like them; now the Indian hunter was to go down as well.

But for a little while the old order was still to hold its own on the Powder as, for a little while, it had held its own thousands of miles to the east and south below Mason and Dixon's line. And if Carrington's infantrymen represented something new, something extremely old was with them, for as they marched, Death, the familiar, the accustomed, a war bonnet on his head, marched on their flanks.

Everywhere behind concealing buttes and hills, rippling pools of bright color and sober hues, mirages in the deep swales, were the scouts of the Sioux and the Arapahos.

Carrington's steel-wire veterans might have lost some of their jauntiness, their hardness, had they known that within six months so many of them would die, their stained faces lonely in the winter dusk.

Carrington arrived at Fort Connor, where he relieved 250 discontented Michiganders, finding them irritable and in very low spirits, as they well might be. He changed the name of the fort to Reno and moved its site a little down the Powder, and then he marched north in the shadow of the Big Horns. Across Crazy Woman, across Clear Creek. On the 13th of July he came to Piney Fork, forty miles above Reno, and chose that as the location for the first fort he was to build on the Bozeman, Fort Phil Kearny. Later on, he built another fort, Fort C. F. Smith, ninety miles north, across the Montana line where the Big Horns make their final bend to the west. Fort Smith had its share in the fighting as well, but never anything like Kearny. Kearny was the especial hatred of the Sioux.

On the 15th of July, after a reconnaissance as far north as Tongue River, Carrington returned to Piney

Fork and began to build. From the very first his garrison was in daily danger. His timber was five miles away in the Big Horns. Whenever he sent out a logging crew he had to send other soldiers to guard it. He cut wild hay, but his men went out in force and heavily armed to do the cutting. Carrington had chosen, at least so it would seem to later observers, about as poor a site as possible; a triangle between two creeks in a small bowl-shaped valley where the Bozeman Trail, coming out of open country, ran between high close-pressing hills. Carrington could see nothing; his enemies could look down on him and see everything. Anyone but Indians would have had that fort in no time. Carrington put a lone mounted man on a butte about a mile away and this lone mounted man signaled the approach of hostile bands, and then galloped for his life. Nor did Carrington even build a wing of his fort to enclose a strip of one of the near-by streams. Later on, when Kearny was more closely watched, the water detail was in constant danger.

But it was a fine fort; large, solidly constructed, 800 feet long by 600 feet wide, and equipped in every detail. It was completed, except for a few buildings such as the hospital, by the 31st of October: a muster-for-pay was held, the fort was dedicated, and the flag was run up. Carrington made a speech.

It was a bright, cool day; quiet as October days in mountain countries are. The aspens had turned gold and apricot, and five miles to the west the Big Horns were splotched with color. It was a very quiet, bright October day. Still, and touched with winter, like a fallen leaf.

Carrington said:

"Three and one-half months ago stakes were driven to define the now perfected outlines of Fort Phil

Kearny. Aggressive Indians threatened to exterminate this command. Our advent cost us blood." (Carrington named nine enlisted men and a lieutenant who had been killed during the building of the fort.) "These men have given their lives to vindicate our pledge never to yield one foot of our advance, but to guarantee a safe passage for all who seek a home in the lands beyond.

"Fifteen weeks have passed, varied by many skirmishes and both day and night alarms, but that pledge holds good. In every work done your arms have been at hand. In the pine tracts or hay fields, on picket or general guard duty, no one has failed to find a constant exposure to some hostile shaft and to feel that a cunning adversary was watching every chance to harass and kill.

"And yet that pledge holds good.

"Surrounded by temptation to hunt the choicest game, lured by tales of golden treasure just beyond you, you have spared your powder for your foes and have given the labor of your hands for your proper work. Passing from guard-watching to fatigue-work, and after one night in bed, often disturbed, returning to your post as sentry; attempting with success all trades and callings; and handling the broadaxe and hammer, the saw and the chisel, with the same success as that with which you sped the bullet; your work has proven how well deserved was the confidence I reposed in you.

"And the pledge holds good!"

Carrington concluded:

"And now this day, laying aside the worn and tattered garments which have done their part during weeks of toil and struggle, the veteran battalion of the 18th Infantry, from which perhaps I shall soon be parted in the changes of army life and organization, puts on its fresh full-dress attire of muster and review."

Chaplain White offered a prayer. The flag rose to the top of the flagpole. The guns spoke. Their echoes were as long as thunder in the Big Horns.

A very quiet, cool October day!

Carrington was a good man, honest, earnest and religious. More of an engineer than a soldier. A strict and detailed disciplinarian. All during that summer of peril one of his main preoccupations had been to keep his soldiers off the grass of the parade ground. He had issued upward of a hundred minute special orders. Moreover, he was curiously optimistic. To be sure, during July he had asked for reinforcements of which only a handful—a few cavalrymen—had arrived, but when General Hazen passed up the Bozeman Trail in the autumn on a tour of inspection, both officers had agreed that everything was in splendid shape and Carrington had no sooner started his march up the Powder than he had sent word back to Reno that the country was safe for freighters and emigrants, and that they would need no escort so long as the members of each expedition kept close together.

The freighters and emigrants would be perfectly safe, he had sent back word, he and his soldiers would protect them.

During the first six months of Fort Phil Kearny the Indians made fifty-one hostile demonstrations, killed 154 white men at the fort or along the Bozeman Trail, and ran off over 650 head of stock, some of it belonging to the government.

During the building of the fort, every hour of every day, as Carrington had said in his flag-raising speech, the garrison had been in peril; not a detail had dared leave the fort without arms and an armed guard, and not a detail but had been raided from time to time. In addition to the soldiers cut off in this way and killed, several had disappeared mysteriously to be taken to the small, slow-burning torture fires of the Sioux. Even as Carrington and General Hazen talked, almost within earshot were 65 enlisted men, three officers and two civilian scouts who were soon to complete the list of 154 white men killed along the Bozeman in the first six months of Kearny.

Carrington and Hazen were not the only optimists. All that summer the Indians' Friends in the East, and the Indian Bureau, had been claiming that the Powder River troubles were nothing but the work of a few malcontents, and along the Oregon Trail government agents had been encouraging emigrant trains to go up the Bozeman.

The very night that Carrington had come back from Tongue River, the night before he started to build Kearny, as if the conference at Laramie, and Red Cloud, had not been enough, Carrington had been warned again.

At the risk of their lives, certainly at the risk of their reputations with their Sioux allies, four great Cheyenne chiefs—Dull Knife, Two Moons, Red Arm and Black Horse—had ridden into Carrington's camp and asked for a conference. Carrington had welcomed them. He was a well-intentioned, friendly man. The Cheyenne chiefs told Carrington what he had heard before. Told him that the Sioux were willing to allow the troops to come as far as Fort Reno, but no farther. That the Sioux were determined that there should be no travel through their hunting country; no emigrant trains along the Bozeman; and no forts such as this one Carrington intended to build. Carrington's hands were tied, but he seems to have had hardly any perception of what all this meant.

Jim Bridger was at that strange, sudden conference,

and so was Jim Beckwourth, but they said nothing. There was nothing to be said, anyway; Carrington had his orders.

The Cheyennes suffered bitterly for their display of generous common sense. They suffered the most terrible fate that could befall great chiefs. For a while they lost face utterly.

Sorrowfully they departed from Carrington's camp. They did not want war, no, not even despite the memory of Sand Creek. They told Carrington that unless the Sioux forced them into war they would not fight. The following night they spent at the camp of a trader, Pierre Gasseau, or Louis Gazzous—"French Pete" he was called—and while there a war party of Sioux overtook them and, rushing into the tents of the Cheyennes, struck the chiefs across the faces with their bows, counting coup on them and shouting that they were traitors.

The next day French Pete and the five other white men with him were found killed and scalped; their stock run off, their wagons plundered. French Pete had thought himself safe. He had traded with the Sioux for years. He had a Sioux wife. Two soldiers were killed and three wounded when, riding to French Pete's aid, they attacked the Indians who were still hovering around the six dead white men and the burned wagons.

On the 24th, seven hundred Sioux surrounded Hugh Kirkendall's freight train coming up from Fort Reno and would have captured it had not a company of infantry from Kearny arrived in the nick of time. Four days earlier a party of five officers with an escort of ten men on their way to Kearny, Lieutenant Wands having with him his wife and children, were attacked on the Crazy Woman, and Lieutenant Daniels and a sergeant were killed. Between July 15th and 29th, eight wagon trains were attacked between Fort Reno and Fort Kearny.

And so July and August and September and October passed, and Carrington remained unperturbed and confident, issuing his minute special orders.

"The pledge holds good!"

By December the Sioux were in the mood really to fight—their annual hunt was over. Meanwhile, they had forced the Cheyennes to go on the warpath and had even attempted, but without success, to enlist the Crows.

There is a ghost story on the Powder. The tradition of an army of ghosts, ragged and grim, who had marched up the Bozeman a little while before Carrington, unharmed and hardly noticed, and had disappeared into the mountains of western Montana. The ghosts wore uniforms, whatever remnants were left, of a different color from Carrington's men.

You remember, perhaps, Price, the Confederate general who fought in Texas and who was the one Confederate general whose army never surrendered, and who himself fled to Mexico? The story goes that part of Price's army marched up from Texas, marched all those long, arid miles, and then up the Bozeman to the edge of the Bitter Roots, where it scattered and settled.

There seems to be little basis for this story, but it is true that numerous Confederate veterans took up land in western Montana as they did all over the West.

Anyway, it's a nice ghost story.

CHAPTER EIGHTEEN

Scarlet Snow

I T is still a lonely country, the country to the east of Kearny; lonely as a hawk. It has changed hardly at all except for a hidden distant ranch, a wire fence and a narrow winding road, since that December day over seventy years ago. Over the buttes to the west, only a mile or so away, down in its narrow valley stood Fort Phil Kearny, the flag above it.

Between the present towns of Sheridan and Buffalo, just to the north of the site of Fort Phil Kearny, between some low buttes the narrow road takes off to the east from the highway. If you go along it you come to a higher butte in a country of tangled buttes, and on top of this high butte is a monument. The inscription on the monument reads as follows:

ON THIS FIELD ON THE 21ST DAY OF
DECEMBER 1866
THREE COMMISSIONED OFFICERS AND
SEVENTY-SIX PRIVATES
OF THE 18TH U. S. INFANTRY AND OF THE
2ND U. S. CAVALRY, AND TWO CIVILIANS
UNDER THE COMMAND OF CAPTAIN BREVET-
LIEUTENANT COLONEL WILLIAM FETTERMAN
WERE KILLED BY AN OVERWHELMING
FORCE OF SIOUX UNDER THE COMMAND OF
RED CLOUD
THERE WERE NO SURVIVORS

Captain Fetterman was the exact antithesis of his commander. He was a fighter pure and simple. His family for generations had been army people and he himself had had a distinguished record in the Civil War. He chafed under the routine and caution of Carrington. Like Lieutenant Grattan twelve years before, down on the Oregon Trail, Fetterman got his chance.

On Friday, December 21st, a bright clear day, but bitterly cold, a wood train of fifty-five men had started for the Big Horns. Around eleven o'clock the lone cavalryman stationed on Pilot Butte signaled that the wood train had been attacked. Forty-nine men of the 18th Infantry and twenty-seven men of the 2nd Cavalry were assigned to the relief under the command of Captain James Powell, later to distinguish himself in the Wagon Box Fight, but Fetterman pleaded so hard to be allowed to go in place of Powell that Carrington consented. Fetterman, also like Lieutenant Grattan, wanted to "whet his sword." Carrington gave strict orders, however, not to pursue the Indians for any distance, orders which Fetterman disobeyed.

Powell was a very cautious man, steady and cool; Fetterman was dashing and reckless. With Fetterman went Lieutenant Grummond and Captain Brown. Grummond had been married a little while before, and his bride watched him go. Brown was to be transferred within a few days to Fort Laramie, but he was eager, as he said, "to get a scalp" before he retired to that comparative safety and dullness. Fetterman, who had arrived at Fort Kearny only a month before, had remarked on several occasions that if given eighty men he would ride through the entire Sioux nation.

That day he had his eighty men, but he rode only a short distance, and never again. He rode into an ambush.

When he crossed the first hill he saw a few Indians galloping desperately away as if to escape him, and he followed them laughing and in high spirits. Over the next hill, the jaws of the bloody trap closed upon him.

East, west, north and south, in every draw and behind every butte were the Cheyennes and Sioux.

Fetterman must at once have realized the seriousness of the situation.

The infantry halted halfway up a ridge, the cavalry reached the top of the ridge. The infantry, Brown and Fetterman among them, went down before a mass of Indians. Only a few of the Indians had guns. Hatchets, clubs and spears were enough. Before long the cavalry was wiped out, too. Back at the fort they heard the firing and young Mrs. Grummond listened. A sergeant and a trooper were sent to find out what was happening to Fetterman. They came back close to their horses' necks. They said everywhere they had looked were Indians. The country was filled with Indians. Carrington ordered Captain Ten Eyck with fifty-four soldiers, all that could be spared from the fort, to join Fetterman. Just before Ten Eyck reached the top of the ridge behind which Fetterman was fighting, the firing ceased.

From the summit, Ten Eyck saw more than two thousand warriors galloping up and down the valley below. He sent a message back to the fort for reinforcements. Carrington dispatched forty more men; released the prisoners from the guardhouse; armed the band and the cooks.

Ten Eyck rode down the farther side of the butte looking for Fetterman, and as he rode the galloping Indians below him disappeared. In a little space of not more than forty feet square Ten Eyck found Fetterman and Brown and their forty-seven infantrymen. Brown and Fetterman had saved their last bullets for themselves. The "little torture fires" of the Sioux were even more expertly planned than most torture fires; they began at the feet and bit by bit worked up. All the bodies were scalped and mutilated. It was now night, and Ten Eyck came back to the fort with the dead infantrymen.

That night young Mrs. Grummond waited, not knowing whether her husband was alive or not. If he was alive he was probably a captive and that was worse than death. The next morning Carrington set out himself to find Grummond and the cavalryman. Before he left the fort he placed all the women and children in the magazine under the supervision of an officer who had instructions to blow up the magazine should the Indians take the fort.

Carrington found the cavalry scattered along the ridge a considerable distance from where the infantry had fallen. There was evidence that for a few moments a dreadful panic had set in. A quarter of a mile beyond most of the bodies, a dozen men had fought fiercely. The two mountainmen—the civilians—Wheatly and Fisher were there, ringed around with empty cartridges. Ten dead Indian ponies were near this group of dead white men and on the ground were fifty or more pools of Indian blood.

Pools of blood usually meant dead Indians or Indians badly wounded. Indians always tried to take their dead off a battlefield.

The Sioux claimed that only ten Indians had been killed and fifty or so wounded in the entire fight, but the Cheyennes years later said the killed were between fifty-five and sixty.

Red Cloud had directed the battle, but Crazy Horse, as usual, had been the outstanding warrior.

Carrington knew at last what sort of position he was in.

The Plains Indians, as has been said, had practically no conception of taking fortified places by direct assault, but from what was learned later, evidently their plan in this case was to storm Kearny. A blizzard saved Carrington's decimated command.

Now, a blizzard is no friend of man, red or white. It is a hateful thing, but that night a blizzard was a friend to Kearny.

No one unless he has been in a blizzard knows what it is. The blackness, the fury of the wind, the bewildering agony that follows the loss of all sense of direction. It is like a roaring deafness and blindness coming suddenly upon a well man. A million tiny icy fingers pluck at you. You cry because of the insult and the bafflement.

That night the thermometer dropped to thirty below zero and the snow whipped suddenly along the Bozeman, piling so high against Kearny's stockade that the garrison shoveled without intermission lest the Indians walk over into the fort. It was so cold that the men had their hands and feet frozen and could work for only half an hour or so at a time.

Carrington called for a volunteer to ride to Laramie for help. A man named John Phillips—"Portugee" Phillips—offered to go. Phillips was a civilian scout. No one else would go, no one else thought it possible to go, not even the other mountainmen. Fort Laramie was 236 miles to the south. The nearest telegraph station, Horse Shoe Creek, was 190 miles south, 40 miles north of Laramie.

In all the annals of America there has been no such ride as that of Portugee Phillips, nor any more extraordinary feat. The run from Marathon was a holiday compared with it. If Portugee Phillips had been a European, his name would be a household word. Indians themselves are enough without a blizzard; a ride of 236 miles under the best of conditions is an undertaking. But Indians like blizzards no better than white men do. The Sioux and Cheyennes and Arapahos were warm in their tepees although Phillips did not know it; it never occurred to them that anyone would be abroad on such a night.

Carrington gave Phillips his own saddle horse, a Kentucky thoroughbred. Phillips took with him a sack of oats and a few hardtack biscuits.

At first he walked in the careening darkness, painfully on the alert, then, well away from the fort, he mounted and began his endless gallop through the darkness and the whirling snow. How Phillips found his way has ever since been a marvel to the Far West. Horses and men circle in a blizzard, but neither Phillips nor the Kentucky thoroughbred circled.

The third night Phillips came to Horse Shoe Creek, telegraphed to Laramie, and rode on. His hands, knees and feet were by this time frostbitten. The message from Horse Shoe was never delivered.

The fighting had left the Medicine Road and was concentrated on the Powder. Laramie had become fairly civilized; comfortable and safe; no longer the tiny, dangerous post of the ill-fated Grattan. There were plenty of women there now; wives of the officers and men. Phillips reached Laramie on Christmas Eve. The officers' club was called "Bedlam," and the younger officers were giving a ball.

Into the midst of the dancing, the warmth, the uniforms and the women Phillips staggered, told his story, and fainted. A ghostly figure with his frozen beard and snow-covered buffalo coat.

Outside, Carrington's thoroughbred was dying. There was a horse for you!

Two hundred and thirty-six miles north the sentries at Kearny still manned the stockade, frozen apparitions, and the rest of the garrison shoveled, but Kearny, the snow whipping across its stockade, was saved.

Phillips lay between life and death for weeks.

Portugee Phillips had a black pointed beard and narrow, amused, slightly dangerous eyes. His reputation was not altogether good. A few years before Malcolm Campbell, down on the Oregon Trail, had found him quarrelsome and not to be trusted. Which merely shows that not many men are all of a piece when it comes to virtue or heroism. Beauty peeps out of the eyes of a toad when the light is right, and bravery shows itself suddenly like winter lightning.

To square their shoulders Americans can think of Portugee, not a very nice man. And they can think of a myriad other Americans too, many of them not very nice, but nonetheless men and women of incredible endurances and gallantries.

It is pleasant to record that a grateful government presented Portugee Phillips with $300 for his scouting services including his ride, and, after his death at Cheyenne in 1883, voted $5,000 to Mrs. Phillips. The latter, however, was not a reward but a compensation. The Sioux never forgave Phillips and at the first opportunity, six years later, killed all his cattle and ruined him.

Mrs. Grummond met with a happier fate; she became Colonel Carrington's second wife.

Carrington was another man broken for something

that was not altogether his fault. He was relieved and sent to Fort Casper. Colonel H. W. Wessells took his place. The winter was too cold for further fighting. The next summer, on August 2nd, Captain James Powell, the officer Fetterman had replaced in command of the wood-train relief, took a stalwart revenge for the Fetterman massacre.

CHAPTER NINETEEN

Hay Field and Wagon Box

THE Wagon Box Fight has recently been re-assessed by historians, and since historians, like every-one else, have to present new theses in order to be arresting, it is now the opinion of some of them that the Wagon Box Fight amounted to much less than the participants and the frontiersmen then living imagined. The participants and the frontiersmen then living, be-ing simple folk, were convinced that the Wagon Box Fight and the Hay Field Fight, which had taken place ninety miles up the Bozeman, near Fort C. F. Smith, the day before the Wagon Box Fight, went a long way toward destroying Red Cloud's morale, and face. Man-Afraid-of-His-Horse was jealous, naturally, of Red Cloud's rise to power. Man-Afraid-of-His-Horse was the titular chief of the Oglalas, and for some time he had been trying to undermine Red Cloud's prestige. In addition, a number of the young braves were becoming restless. Red Cloud was having trouble keeping them together. They wanted to go hunting. The Wagon Box Fight and the Hay Field Fight came at just the wrong time for Red Cloud.

In any case, after the Wagon Box Fight and the Hay Field Fight, Red Cloud, although he gained for a while from a bewildered government all he had been fighting for, never again made war. For over a year he had been in complete command of the situation, now on an August day he lost that command.

It wasn't much of a fight, the Wagon Box, so far as the white casualty list was concerned, and it didn't last long. The white loss was seven dead and three wounded, and these soldiers from Fort Kearny fought only from the early morning until the late afternoon, but the point was that a mere handful of white men stopped, mowed down, and dismayed the flower of the Sioux nation, 1,500 warriors at the least. Three times the flower charged; three times it was terribly broken.

Captain Powell was as wise as Fetterman had been foolish. His soldiers fought like mountainmen.

But that wasn't by any means all.

The white soldiers were fighting for the first time with Springfield-Allin breech-loading rifles, and the Indian couldn't understand the deadly continuous fire. This was steady death, and the Indian by nature dislikes steadiness of any kind.

That spring, the spring after Portugee Phillips's ride and the relief of Kearny, Red Cloud made war again. All during June and July he harassed Kearny, but a much better garrisoned Kearny now. At the beginning of August a wood detail under Captain Powell was chopping wood in the Big Horns five miles or so from Kearny. Powell had twelve men under a sergeant in the timber, and thirteen other men under a sergeant had been told off to escort the wood train to and from the fort. Near the wood camp Powell, always a careful man, had made full preparations for a possible attack. Out in the open, away from the timber, he had dismounted fourteen wagons and had formed a corral of the wagon boxes piling, on top of these, sacks of grain and anything else that would stop arrows. Across the openings between the dismounted wagon boxes, he had dragged wagons on wheels. Inside this improvised corral were plenty of provisions and ammunition.

Suddenly, on August 2nd, Red Cloud struck.

Here was something easier than Fetterman . . . at least, so Red Cloud thought.

At dawn the Sioux stampeded Powell's horses and not long after the woodchoppers came running out of

the timber, the Sioux behind them. Four of the wood-choppers were killed, the rest reached the corral. That made thirty-two white men inside, including a couple of civilian scouts.

The corral must have looked small and not very formidable. And it was disarmingly quiet. Powell had told his men to hold their fire. He was a very cool man, Powell. He had given his marksmen two rifles apiece, the poorer shots were to load the rifles. On a rise of

ground a Sioux chief—they thought it was Red Cloud
—signaled for the charge by whirling his blanket above
his head.

Crazy Horse was there in the thick of the fighting,
as always; so were High Back-Bone, Big Crow, American Horse. The best warriors the Sioux had were there.
Confident, the Sioux charged, roaring down on their
ponies onto the corral. Suddenly the corral spoke. The
charge faltered and fell back before the dreadful steady
firing.

The Indians returned to the forest and held council.
A little while later they crept up to the corral through
the grass and, with what rifles they had, poured lead
into it. But the Indian, with a few exceptions, has
always been as bad with a rifle as he has been adroit in
concealing himself. The defenders were unharmed and
Powell didn't waste his ammunition, firing only when
an Indian exposed himself.

The Sioux wriggled back into the timber, and
once more they charged, this time on foot, but so serried
and so huge was their charge, so desperate, that it almost penetrated the corral. The white men had their
knives out for hand-to-hand fighting. At the very edge
of the wagon boxes, the charge broke.

Again in the afternoon for the second time the
Sioux charged on horseback. The wagon boxes spat their
withheld, sudden fire. Dazed and stricken, the Sioux
were done. They had never seen anything like this.
There was nothing left for them now but to try to
take their dead and wounded from the field. In the
dusk they withdrew, and in the dusk, far off in the
direction of Kearny, a cannon barked, and presently,
across the hills to the east, came the relief.

The day before the Wagon Box Fight, Fort C. F.
Smith, ninety miles north at the tip of the Big Horns,

had also spoken. The Hay Field Fight was in many respects like the Wagon Box Fight. The same attack upon a small body of troops working in a hay field. The same results.

In their elation over the first clear-cut white victories in years, the white men put the Indian losses of the Wagon Box Fight down at 1,500. In other words, every Indian engaged! Captain Powell estimated that 180 warriors had been killed or wounded.

The Bozeman and the Powder were quiet for a while and fairly safe, and then, a year later, with one of those extraordinary about-faces characteristic of its Indian policy until a few years ago, the government decided abruptly to get out of the Powder River country lock, stock and barrel.

Kearny was to be abandoned. Smith was to be abandoned. All that fine, fussy, meticulous building of Carrington's! Mortises just right! Ridge logs level! The government was determined to pursue a new policy with the Sioux. It was going to be always kind to them, always generous. The government was going to feed the Sioux whenever they needed food, and now—actually—the Powder River country was going to be given back to them. Actually! A dead line was to be established which included the Black Hills as well, also Sioux country, and recently becoming troublesome because of the gold discovered up there. The dead line would take in all the Powder and all the Black Hills. North of this dead line no white man could go, nor west of it. Troops along the dead line would see that this edict was obeyed. The Bozeman was to go back to grass.

Stronger than it had ever been with the Sioux— Kearny and Smith holding the Bozeman firmly and not imaginatively as in the days of Carrington—the government decided to abandon the Powder River country completely.

Once more Red Cloud must have smiled.

No sooner was he defeated than he won. The Wagon Box Fight was as much of a Pyrrhic victory to the white man as, a few years later, the Little Big Horn was to the Sioux.

In August of 1868 the garrison marched out of Kearny. Back of the buttes, on top of the buttes, were Red Cloud and his men; hundreds of them. As the soldiers marched down the Bozeman, Red Cloud and his warriors poured into the fort. The soldiers looked back.

Against the sky was a huge column of black smoke.

It is doubtful if Red Cloud was altogether fooled. More and more he seemed to come to old Spotted Tail's way of thinking, and now he was to see for the first time close at hand the white man's latent power, his numbers, his wealth, his crowded cities.

Those strange years between 1868 and 1874 when the government coddled the Sioux and fawned upon them, and made fools of them through presents and flattery, as previously it had made fools of them through broken promises and brutality, might well be called "the years of the chiefs' visits to the East." Red Cloud went to Washington several times to see the Great White Father, and so did Spotted Tail and other chiefs. Red Cloud was in danger at one time, almost, of becoming a Chautauqua lecturer. His tall figure was familiar in the streets of Washington and New York. On his first visit to the East in 1870 he was taken on a tour, and made speeches, addressing, in particular, an immense meeting at Cooper Institute in New York. New York, as usual, was immensely interested in any cause which was not its business and which did not affect its own pocketbook. It was willing to give away one-quarter of Wyoming. Red Cloud made a deep impression; his dignity, his sincerity, his common sense.

Red Cloud—the Sioux spoke through interpreters —concluded his speech.

"You have children," he said. "So have we. We wish to rear our children well, and ask you to help us. It seems to us that it is not an unreasonable request even though it does come from a savage."

No, not in the least unreasonable, except that to an Indian the raising of a child properly is an altogether different matter than it is to a white man. To raise an Indian child properly, at least in the seventies, meant thousands of square miles of grass and plenty of wandering game. So much of reasonableness is incompatible!

Red Dog, who followed Red Cloud, was less reasonable but even more direct.

"When the Great White Father first sent out men to our people I was poor and thin," he said, "now I am large and fat. That is because I was so stuffed with lies."

New York loved the Sioux. So did Buffalo, the name of which must have puzzled the Sioux. The Sioux were as fascinating as opera singers. The *Times* and *Tribune* threw up their hats. The far western papers were furious. Reasonable or not, the Far Westerner wished to travel and settle as he willed. The East has always deluded itself by the idea that it supports the West; the West knows that the East without the West would be poverty-stricken both in vigor and in money. During the nineties and 1900's most of the big houses in New York were built by far western mines or land.

At the moment in the Far Westerner's recent memory were too many dead friends and scalped relatives for him to read the eastern papers amicably. Red Cloud had spoken beautifully, Red Dog had been humorous, but only four years before both had permitted American soldiers and emigrants to be roasted slowly by little fires.

Poor Red Cloud! After a while he got into trouble in the East. He lost face with his sentimental and moral eastern friends as he had lost face after the Wagon Box Fight with his Sioux followers.

At that time there was in Washington an underworld hotel proprietor of gracious ways whose favorite game was to waylay the chiefs when they arrived, cajole them in every possible manner, and then, when they left, present them with heavy bills for drunken parties which they had not given and for the attentions of Loreleis they had never met. Red Cloud had been warned against this man but insisted upon staying with him. In addition to this, several times he had shown up badly in contrast to Spotted Tail. Spotted Tail was reasonable, courteous, smiling, modest. Red Cloud, his head slightly turned by his notoriety, was jealous of Spotted Tail and indulged in occasional scenes. Red Cloud was a proud, short-tempered man.

Red Cloud's star steadily waned. Years later, almost the last word we hear of him, he was arrested and fined for shooting game without a nonresident license. Arrested in the very country which, twenty-eight years before, had trembled with his name and on the spot where, thirty years before, his Oglala braves had besieged the garrison at the Platte River Bridge. By this time Red Cloud was half blind and living on the Pine Ridge Agency in South Dakota; a crusty, sour, disappointed old gentleman, hating the whites but aware that the only way you could fight them was by stealth and adroitness.

In June of 1894, Red Cloud, his son, Jack Red

Cloud, and Red Cloud's then counselor, Dreaming Bear, an educated Indian who had gone to Carlisle, left the agency without proper credentials to go hunting in the Wind River Mountains. On June 10th, on their way home, they were arrested near Casper and taken before a justice of the peace.

The Indians were "exceedingly sullen and rude." Dreaming Bear refused to speak English. They were fined twenty dollars apiece and costs, and being unable to pay, Red Cloud turned in his wagon and team and was released. For two days, however, Red Cloud and his son and his chief counselor had been confined in the tiny and dirty local jail.

Red Cloud must have smiled for the third time, but wryly and sardonically. The charges, to be sure, were correct. Red Cloud was a nonresident. He was living now in South Dakota, and he was not even an American citizen. But imagine Red Cloud hearing himself described as a nonresident of Wyoming! And imagine him being fined for shooting without a proper license game that had once been his for the asking! Game that had been as thick as the tawny grass of the Powder!

CHAPTER TWENTY

The Dreary Black Hills

IF the government had found it difficult during the sixties to keep white men—the few who wanted to go—out of the Powder River country and the Black Hills, it now found itself confronted by an impossible task. Forces stronger than the government were at work; forces many of which the government itself had released. Another great impulse was sending the nation west. Thousands of young men made restless by war were seeking land, adventure and gold. And to transport these young men there were the railroads; one already built, others in the building.

In 1844 Congress had authorized a preliminary survey for a transcontinental railway, and Frémont during his expeditions of the forties had traced the most direct route. In 1862 Congress passed a further bill subsidizing the building of the Union Pacific and the Western Pacific. In 1865 the building commenced and forty miles of tracks west from Omaha were laid. Two years later the Union Pacific came to the border of Wyoming. By November 13, 1867, it had reached Cheyenne.

From the east to the west, from the coast toward the east, day by day the tracks were being laid. Cheyenne was left behind. All of Wyoming was crossed.

On May 10, 1869, Brigham Young, his beard exceedingly solemn, for he hadn't wanted this intrusion in the beginning, drove a golden spike at Promontory Point, Utah, and the waiting engines of the Western Pacific and the Central Pacific puffed across the remaining ties and touched cowcatchers. This was the beginning of the Union Pacific. The Western Pacific engine was 638 miles east from its home town, Sacramento, and the Central Pacific engine was 1,186 miles west from its home town, Omaha. The cowcatchers touched just sixty-two years after John Colter, more or less by accident, had discovered Wyoming by its back door. Indeed, the first dust of the Medicine Road had hardly died down.

The telegraph line of 1861 had made a faint singing in the wind, leaving loneliness almost untouched. But now there was a roar that came out of the distance, drew nearer, reached a climax, and passed on some urgent business, only to be repeated again and again.

The southern plains of Wyoming heard that strange melancholy cry, distance in its throat, that is so much a part of the American memory and of the American present.

George Francis Train, visiting Omaha the day the first tracks were laid, had predicted in his speech that the road would be done in five years. He had been laughed at. The actual time of building was three years and six months.

A small army had been released, much of which settled in Wyoming. It had taken 25,000 men to build the Central Pacific and these men had been guarded by soldiers especially sent for the purpose. The Indians knew what the railroad meant to them; whenever possible they raided it.

"Buffalo Bill," Colonel William F. Cody, the chief of the hunters employed to supply the construction crews with fresh meat, had in one year, with the help of his rifle, "Lucretia Borgia," and his pony, "Old Brigham," killed 4,280 buffalo. The government was still claiming that the Powder River country belonged to the Sioux, but nonetheless it was permitting the destruction of the buffalo as fast as this could be accomplished. The buffalo were the Sioux commissary. Once that was ended, the Sioux would have to beg their food from the United States.

Overnight Cheyenne had become a town, and all along the new Medicine Road that ran south of the old Medicine Road, and just north of the later Overland, little towns, Laramie, Evanston, Green River, were springing up. Here is a contemporary description of Cheyenne from that most excellent book, *Malcolm Campbell, Sheriff*. Malcolm Campbell was then a young man, just arrived in Wyoming:

There were tents set everywhere without alignment, and the scaffoldings of new buildings were being erected to the tune of many hammers, the lumber having been hauled all the way from Denver. There were tents where men sat on benches before long plank tables wolfing meals; tents with rough shelves of canned goods piled to the eaves, and many others where sat gamblers playing faro, roulette and monte.

Saloons were everywhere with their bourbons, whiskeys, brandies and beers. Hurdy-gurdies could be heard in any block at any time of the day or night. Along the banks of Crow Creek were grouped the canvas-covered wagons of emigrants. Camp fires blazed continuously and shelters had been erected on ropes stretched from wheel to wheel.

The aisles between the tents in the town were swarming

with the roughest of the population. Idlers sauntered from gambling table to dance hall, then on to saloon. Others stood in groups debating the probable boom in real estate values within the next few days. Water wells were being dug at four of the corners of what was to be a business block. Everywhere was expectancy and alertness.

As in the case of all new towns, the gamblers, thieves and so-called sporting elements were running things with a high hand. I heard that it was a nightly occurrence for men to be knocked on the head, dragged off into the dark and robbed of all possessions. Everyone wore guns, minded his own business, and demanded that other men mind theirs.

In December, 1867, the father of George Cheyenne Wise, the first boy born in Cheyenne, stepped down to the Union Pacific office and claimed the town lot offered by that enterprising company for this feat. In September of that same year, two months before the coming of the railroad, Thomas Leland, Cheyenne's first postmaster, had begun to handle mail at the rate of three thousand letters a day for which he received a salary of one dollar a month. In the same September, the Wells-Fargo stages put on a triweekly service to Denver. In October the Cheyenne *Leader* advertised the arrival of the first theatrical troupe, the Julesburg troupe. Julesburg was the Colorado town that only two years before had been burned to the ground by the Indians on their way north from Sand Creek.

Time had become incredibly foreshortened. In my intimate acquaintanceship there is a charming old lady, still alert, who remembers Omaha when that proud, tall city was merely a lonely army post. As a girl—the old lady belongs to an army family famous on the frontier, generation after generation—she often rode out from Fort Omaha with Buffalo Bill, then a young scout.

"He was so charming," she says. "And so hand-some."

Cheyenne with a theatrical troupe! Only two years before it had been nothing but sagebrush and distances. Curious that the Indians up on the Powder thought themselves safe only 280 miles north of a town that was advertising theatrical troupes! Advertising everything else as well. The Cheyenne papers were filled with enthusiastic advertisements. Both advertisements and editorials reflected the gusto of a new town and a new country. "The best of everything" could be obtained "and at remarkably low prices." However, the Cheyenne papers never reached the heights of the Deadwood paper which, in 1875, describing the opening of the Bella Union Variety Theatre, spoke of the occasion as "an evening of refined entertainment and cool toilets."

But before long Cheyenne settled down a little, at least on the surface.

In those small, early far western towns the organization of vigilantes followed closely upon the organization of more formal government. Undesirable citizens began to decorate lampposts. The leading banker of Laramie is a soft-voiced gray-haired gentleman, by no means aged. The morning after he arrived as a youth in what is now that pleasant, tree-shaded, cathedral town —having accepted a job as a teller—he saw on his way to his new position four men hanging from four different lampposts.

Cheyenne is still exciting, but in a mature way. It is one of the smallest of state capitals, and yet it is still the largest town in Wyoming. Cheyenne's population is 17,000. A nice, wide-streeted, green, bright town sticking straight up out of a treeless country, the gilded dome of the statehouse shining against the sky at the end of a long street. On cold days there clings to Cheyenne the lovely smell of soft-coal and wood fires, and there is still something of the cow-town about it.

On Saturday nights the steel-shod boots of cow-punchers continue to strike fire from the pavements of Cheyenne and Laramie.

But no one found gold around Cheyenne. You had to go up to the Black Hills to find that. And if you went from Cheyenne and the south you had to go through the eastern part of the Powder River country, whether or not the government had told you to keep out. As a matter of fact, if you remember, the government had told you to keep out of the Black Hills as well.

In 1868 Wyoming had become a territory. A courteous territory, too. With far western politeness it was the first territory or state to proclaim entirely equal rights for women. Practically nothing a lady could do disbarred her from anything. It must have been a relief to Wyoming to know at last just what its name was and where it belonged; few parts of the United States had belonged to more people or been handed about more. Wyoming's vicissitudes in this respect are fascinating. At one time, and for several years, part of Wyoming was even ruled by Queen Victoria, believe it or not, although that stern disciplinarian was probably unaware of her privilege. Until the Oregon Treaty of 1846 England claimed part of northwestern Wyoming along with northern Idaho, Washington and Oregon.

Meanwhile, at various times various parts of Wyoming had been claimed by Spain, France and Mexico. Wyoming has had twelve Spanish kings, starting with Ferdinand in 1492, and one Spanish queen, Isabella, Ferdinand's consort. Ten French kings, beginning with

François Premier of Valois, 1515-1547. One Spanish-French king, Joseph Bonaparte. And three English rulers, George III, George IV and William IV, in addition to Queen Victoria. Wyoming, moreover—that is, a part of it—also survived the French Revolution, and just missed serving under Napoleon. In 1803, with a gesture possible only to dictators, Napoleon, as First Consul, with the signing of the Louisiana Purchase gave away a section of Wyoming along with a great deal else.

Compared with Wyoming's record, that of the thirteen original states, who had only ten English kings and queens and two lord protectors before they became wearied of them, is mere provincialism.

Nor was this confusion ended when, bit by bit, the United States finally acquired what was to be Wyoming.

At one time or another Wyoming was credited to Louisiana. Then to Missouri. Then to Texas. In 1848, to Oregon. Following this, to Utah. After Utah, to Nebraska. Then to Washington. In 1861, to the Dakotas. Then, to Idaho. And once more, and finally, to the Dakotas. Even after 1868 the infant territory arising to its feet and knuckling the dust from its eyes, was not recognized by the lords spiritual. The Episcopal Church did not recognize the new territory at all. For many years religion, officially, had to travel, first, all the way from the Dakotas and, then, all the way east from Idaho. This meant that the missionary bishop of the Episcopal Church was able to visit his scattered flock only about once every three years. A situation that gave rise to some untoward circumstances.

So far as alien domination was concerned, the Powder River country had been happier than other parts of the principality; it belongs to that part of Wyoming securely held by the United States from the time of the

Louisiana Purchase. Nobody could trade the Powder River country about except to the Sioux.

But Wyoming's new knowledge of what it was, and who it was, did not help to solve the problem of the Powder. This knowledge only complicated the situation. Wyoming was now an entity to be reckoned with.

In the early seventies prospectors were working their way into the Black Hills at the risk of their lives, for the Sioux didn't want them there and the government announced that it would not protect them and would deport them if caught. The last was a threat never very seriously carried out. The route up from Cheyenne was far simpler than the route west across South Dakota. By the middle seventies, the Battle of the Little Big Horn just fought, a gold rush to the Black Hills was at its height. The government was trying to get the Sioux back on their reservations, but nobody cared much so long as the stages ran regularly to the Black Hills and everybody had a gun.

The Cheyenne *Daily Sun* was advertising "The old reliable Cheyenne & Black Hills Stage Line. Shortest. Safest. Best." Six-horse Concord stages left daily for Deadwood, Custer, Battle Creek, Rapid City, Golden, Gayville, and all the other mining camps in the hills. "First-class eating-stations" and "attentive divisions agents" added their share to make the stage line "unequalled for Safety, Comfort and Speed." The IXL Hotel and Restaurant, Deadwood, was "the largest and finest hotel in the Black Hills." Pole Creek Ranch on the stage route, between Cheyenne and Deadwood, Fred Schwartz, proprietor, advertised meals at all hours and "the choicest of wines, liquors and cigars."

Cigarette smoking had just come up from the Southwest with the Mexican-influenced cowboys from Texas. It was looked upon as unmanly. The first cigarette smoked in Montana was rolled by a gentleman I knew in my youth, who, noticing some toilet paper sticking out of the pocket of an Englishman leaning up against a bar, tore off a sheet and filled it with tobacco. My friend had just come north from Cheyenne where he had been working with the Texas cowboys.

But to return to 1868.

The new territory from its inception began to speak with authority. It demanded that the government open up the Powder River country, put the Sioux on reservations, and come to its senses. The Wyoming papers referred contemptuously to the "effete, Indian-loving papers" of Omaha. The Omaha *Bee* was called "Red Cloud's personal organ" because it favored abiding by the treaty of 1868 and feared another Indian war if this was not done. At its first meeting, the territorial legislature of Wyoming had petitioned Congress to give Wyoming "a Custer, a Carr or a Sheridan with a strong cavalry arm of the service. A general who will open up the old Powder River route and deliver the settlements from the constant fear of Indian attack."

Miners' songs, cowboy songs, all folk songs for that matter, describe events and people and times with a conciseness and color neither fiction nor history can attain. From now on I am going to quote several such songs, some of them pretty much in full.

There is a sad song about Cheyenne and the Black Hills of the days when both were young, but you need not worry too much about the singer. He wouldn't have been where he was unless he had wanted to be, and on the whole he probably had a pretty good time. Nobody has a better time than the adventurer and nobody in his leisure moments feels so sorry for himself. All far western ballads have in them the wail of the coyote, but even the coyote doesn't seem to be particularly unhappy except when he is sitting and thinking about himself.

Here is the way this song goes, and it is called "The Dreary Black Hills":

Kind friends, you must pity my horrible tale;
I'm an object of pity, I'm looking quite stale.
I gave up my trade, selling Wright's Patent Pills,
To go hunting for gold in the dreary Black Hills.

The roundhouse in Cheyenne is filled every night
With loafers and bummers in terrible plight,
On their backs are no clothes, in their pockets no bills,
Each day they keep starting for the dreary Black Hills.

I got to Cheyenne, no gold could I find,
I thought of the lunch route I'd left far behind;
Through rain, hail and snow, frozen plumb to the gills,
They call me the orphan of the dreary Black Hills.

Kind friend, to conclude, my advice I'll unfold,
Don't go to the Black Hills a-hunting for gold;
The railway promoters their pockets will fill
By your taking a trip to the dreary Black Hills.

The refrain of this gloomy ditty, to be sung after each verse is:

Don't go away, stay at home if you can;
Stay away from that city, they call it Cheyenne,
For Old Sitting Bull or Comanche Bills
Will take off your scalp in the dreary Black Hills.

Lest anyone who does not know be misled, the Black Hills are lovely mountains.

TO THEE RIVER

PART THREE

Red Sunset

CHAPTER TWENTY-ONE

The Dove of Peace

T HE sixties had been bad enough, but until the treaty of 1868 everyone at least knew what he was doing—he was fighting. For eight years now no one had known what he was doing. An era of unrest, bickering and recrimination ensued.

The government, at the moment entirely under the control of the "Peace party," was trying "kindness" on the Sioux; urging them gently onto reservations, loading them with presents, and bribing them with blankets, clothes and rations. The army, its hands tied, was standing by in a silent rage, every now and then riding to the rescue of some agent in temporary trouble with his charges. The reservation Sioux spoke of their agents as "their white men" in tones of kindly, but not always, patronization and contempt, and at different times adopted every modern tactic from sit-down strikes to picketing. The Sioux thought the agents were where they were for the sole purpose of obeying Sioux orders and handing out rations.

All the agents needed were white beards and reindeer with bells to make the picture complete. One agent, an Episcopal clergyman, even had the name of the Reverend Mr. Wham to make things funnier. Grim fun, however.

Between 1868 and 1875 the government spent over $6,000,000 clothing and feeding the Sioux.

The Sioux didn't understand the government's

change of policy. They thought the white man had admitted defeat and was showing signs of his fear. By now the Sioux were divided into three distinct groups: the really peaceful Sioux, such as Spotted Tail and his Brulés, by this time tucked away fairly safely on reservations, first in Nebraska, then in South Dakota; the restless Sioux, such as Red Cloud and his Oglalas, on reservations also but causing continual subterranean trouble; and the wild nonreservation Sioux, like Crazy Horse and Sitting Bull. Crazy Horse, his band with him, was up on the Powder leading the life he had always led and the life the government had promised the Sioux they could lead in the Powder River country and the Black Hills. Sitting Bull was up in Montana with his Hunkpapas.

As for that new creation, the citizen of Wyoming, he didn't care what happened to the Sioux so long as they were put in their place, which, according to his notion, was clearly not Wyoming, and so long as he was allowed to mine or settle where he wanted. By this time Wyoming was beginning to take on the semblance of a real community, with wives, husbands, mothers, fathers, children, dogs, and even cats on log cabin hearthstones. People were beginning to admit that Wyoming was a place where one actually lived. Along the railroad, and up in the valley of the North Platte, and in the Sweetwater valley, and in the west and southwest of the new territory, men were making homes. Wyoming was becoming self-conscious. Strahorn in his guidebook complains of the way "tenderfeet" arrived in Cheyenne, dressed in what they thought were appropriate costumes, only to experience disappointment at the quiet manners and appearance of the inhabitants.

This is an ancient far western grievance, still unabated.

But what was the use of being a citizen of a full-blown territory, with a governor, and a legislature, and taxes, and counties, every one of the last as big as an average eastern state, if you were halted at a dead line cutting off the entire northeastern corner of your possessions?

The Sioux up on the Powder, largely oblivious of what was going on, were having a fairly nice time. During the summer they lived about as they had always lived, and during the winter, if they needed food, they could go south or east to one of the reservations, and draw rations, and sneer at the tamer Sioux. Every now and then Red Cloud and some of the more restless reservation Sioux managed to slip away and join the Sioux up on the Powder, and there was always the annual hunting which the better-behaved reservation Sioux were allowed to join and the less well-behaved usually managed to join anyhow. By this time the Sioux had found a new and delightful enemy; a foe worthy of their mettle. There was still some Crow and Sioux mutual raiding, but the Crow business was about played out; the Crows were enlisting in the army as fast as they could as scouts and irregular troops, which was a much more effective way of troubling the Sioux, if trouble came, than the old-fashioned method. Besides, it was legal. But now the Sioux locked horns with the Shoshones from the western mountains of Wyoming.

In 1868 the Sioux raided the Shoshones, and in the first raid one of Red Cloud's sons was killed. This made Red Cloud bitter, made his "heart bad," and the following year he led the second raid himself. In 1870 the Sioux, under High-Back-Bone who had taken such a leading part in the Fetterman massacre, raided the Shoshones once more, and in this raid High-Back-Bone was killed.

Bad medicine! The hearts of the Sioux were black! The hearts of the Shoshones were black too, but they were self-confident and contemptuous. They had the white man with them.

Washakie, the great chief of the Shoshones, should also be mentioned as another Indian, along with Pontiac and Tecumseh and Red Cloud, who saw things far and saw them clearly. But Washakie saw even more clearly than these three; he saw as clearly as Spotted Tail and he had more to work with than Spotted Tail. He had his entire nation under his thumb. At his command it acted as one. For sixty years, from 1840 to 1900, Washakie ruled his people, and it was his boast that "no white man's scalp had ever decorated his tepee."

Washakie and his Shoshones were the stanchest friends the white man ever had in Wyoming, much more trustworthy than the Crows. At an early date the Shoshones made safe the western mountains of Wyoming, and the western Wyoming end of the Great Medicine Road.

During the Second Sioux War of the seventies, Washakie and his Shoshones rendered invaluable aid.

The Sioux didn't understand the Treaty of 1868 and there is excellent evidence that it was not explained to them, and that the government was satisfied not to have them understand it too well. One of the principal intentions of the government was to get the Sioux away from the railroad and the settlements in southern Wyoming and in the North Platte valley. In exchange for the return to them of the Powder River country, the Sioux were supposed not to trade any longer at Fort Laramie or to hunt south of the North Platte. In fact, they were forbidden to do so. They were supposed either to go on to reservations or else to go up to the Powder and the Black Hills, and stay there and behave themselves.

Red Cloud elected to go to a reservation, and at first he was on one named after him just north of the North Platte, and subsequently on another, named after him, up in northern Nebraska. But he had no real intention of behaving himself. He had become, by now, as we have seen, a regular visitor to Washington. After his first trip, which had so won the heart of New York, he made three other trips in quick succession. One in 1872. One in 1875. And—his last—one in 1877 after the Battle of the Little Big Horn and the subsequent killing of his son-in-law, Crazy Horse.

Apparently Red Cloud was becoming more and more irritable, and one can hardly blame him. He insisted that he had never understood the Treaty of 1868 and that it had never been explained to him, and that it had never occurred to him that the Sioux were expected to give up their accustomed hunting grounds in southern Nebraska and south central Wyoming. Like most of the Sioux, he objected vigorously when the government, wishing to remove the Sioux even farther from temptation, changed the newly organized reservations from near the Oregon Trail and the Union Pacific to northwestern Nebraska and the country adjacent to the Black Hills.

Red Cloud said, and with reason, this was merely inviting white men into the Powder River country and the Black Hills. By now the government was supplying the Sioux with beef, and along with the cattle came Texas cowboys driving the steers up to the reservations. In addition to this, if the government wouldn't let the Sioux trade any longer at Fort Laramie, then the traders, naturally, would also have to come to the reservations.

The miners filtering into the Black Hills were enough as it was.

They certainly were. It was they who made the Second Sioux War.

Red Cloud's attitude during these years, and later, has puzzled many people, but it is simple enough if analyzed. He was a complete irreconcilable and remained so until his death as a very old man in 1909, but he was an irreconcilable who had seen more than most Indians and had learned several lessons. He was neither a wild, uninformed Indian like Crazy Horse or Sitting Bull, neither of whom realized until the very end the hopelessness of the Sioux position, nor was he a naturally peaceful, informed Indian like Spotted Tail. He hated the white man, but he knew a lot. The Wagon Box Fight had taught him something, his trips east had taught him more. He devoted the rest of his life to fighting the white man, but solely by obstruction, troublemaking, and threats of wars he was never willing to undertake when it came to the point. He sent his son, Jack Red Cloud, to join Sitting Bull in 1876, but he didn't go himself, nor did many of his Oglalas. He was not happy. He would have been happier if he had been killed like Crazy Horse or Sitting Bull.

When the tragic and pathetic Messiah Craze spread from the Southwest to the Northwest in 1890, and the Ghost Dancing began, and for the last time the Sioux breathed deep, Red Cloud's heart—and he was an old man even then—stirred mightily, but nothing came of it.

To the contrary, Spotted Tail protested only once, but when he did the government listened to him. This was when, after the Battle of the Little Big Horn, the government proposed to take all the Sioux down to the

Indian Territory. Spotted Tail said he would rather die
than go.

Of all the sardonic conceptions that occurred to
the mind of the white man in his treatment of the Indian, the cruelest was the idea that cropped up from
time to time of transferring Indians used to mountains,
grassy valleys or plains, cool nights and clear water to
the arid Southwest.

The unrest of the Sioux reached a climax in '75.

Meanwhile two events of the utmost importance to
the future history of Wyoming had happened and few,
caught up as the people of the new territory were in the
search for gold and in the bickering over the Sioux and
the dread of them, realized their significance.

To the southeast the Kansas Pacific had completed
its road, opening a northern market, Chicago, to the
cattle that by now had increased to millions in Texas;
and the same year, the spring after the Fetterman massacre, without any heralding and with no trouble, Nelson Story had gone up the Bozeman Trail with six hundred Texas longhorns for the small new ranches in the
Gallatin valley in Montana.

In 1867 the first drive north from Texas to Abi-
lene, Kansas, took place, and the most famous of all the
cattle trails, the Chisholm, had become a fact.

There was a new smell, a new dust on the Powder,
as prophetic as the dust stirred by the Oglala ponies
ninety-two years before when the Oglalas first rode
down onto the buffalo pastures of the Powder country.

CHAPTER TWENTY-TWO

No Sale

By now the gold rush to the Black Hills was on and it was impossible to keep the miners out of that forbidden territory, except by the use of unremitting force. The government found itself in a quandary it had helped to create.

In 1874 General George Custer with 1,200 men and 110 wagons, and a party of prospectors, had been sent to the Black Hills ostensibly to map that country, actually to discover how much gold was there. There was gold . . . plenty. And so now the government had either to live up to the Treaty of 1868 or else think up something new. The government conceived a brilliant idea; it would buy the Black Hills. Meanwhile, the miners and storekeepers and gamblers placidly, if defiantly, were building towns, laying out lots, and organizing local governments. The Sioux killed a few of these determined settlers, the government told the Sioux not to do so. The soldiers arrested a few more; the local governments released them.

In 1875 a great conference was held on the White River in northern Nebraska halfway between the new Red Cloud and Spotted Tail agencies. The conference was a spectacular one. The commissioners sat under the fly of an open tent, the old chiefs in a sitting circle in front of them, a rigid company of cavalry behind them, and the younger hostile Sioux put on a fantasia. In bands they suddenly appeared over the nearest hill, charged to within a few feet of the commissioners, wheeled and took their stations. This was supposed to frighten the commissioners and impress them. It frightened them, but did not impress them.

The commission offered $6,000,000 for the Black Hills, or else a rental of $400,000 a year. The Sioux demanded $600,000,000 and the promise that the government would feed and clothe them for seven generations. The latter demand had as its basis the fact that the Sioux had already been in the Black Hills for seven generations, and so, naturally, the government should feed and clothe them for seven generations more. What could be simpler?

To the innocent surprise of the Sioux, the government lost its temper and decided to take the Black Hills, issuing a pre-emptory order for all the wild bands to come in and surrender themselves for settlement on the reservations.

The dead line was set for January 31, 1876.

It was a bitterly cold winter, that winter of '75-'76, with all the wild Sioux, including those who had been at the conference, out in their scattered villages. Sitting Bull was far away on the Yellowstone, Crazy Horse was near the South Dakota line, the Cheyennes were on the Powder itself.

None of the wild chiefs paid the slightest attention to the order except that a few of the more polite ones sent back word that it was "too cold to move," and this was probably just what the government wanted, for by now its patience was exhausted and the order had been issued so late in the fall that many of the wild bands would not have had time to come in even had they wanted.

As suddenly as the crack of a whip, the government turned the army loose, and as joyfully as a pack of bloodhounds the army slipped its leashes. It had been taking insult long enough.

All the old Indian fighters knew that the best time to fight the Indian was in the winter. This threw out of gear all Indian ideas of what was proper. Not only in the winter were the various bands widely scattered in their winter camps, but winter is that part of the year in which you stick close to your tepee fires and keep warm. Never before, however, had the army been able to put this knowledge into effect. Now, on March 1, 1876, General Crook with over a thousand men, mostly cavalry, marched out of Fort Fetterman on the Oregon Trail up into the Powder River country.

The hard-riding generals were in command at last, and the government had reluctantly decided that there was just one way to bring peace to the frontier.

But Crook, despite his record against the southwestern Indians, was not so successful against the Sioux. It was a real winter, thirty and forty degrees below zero at night. Crook advanced as far as Tongue River and striking a broad trail to Crazy Horse's camp—Crazy Horse had by now dug in on the Powder—detached Colonel J. J. Reynolds with six companies of cavalry to bring Crazy Horse in. Reynolds failed miserably and his failure resulted in the court-martial of several officers. Reynolds attacked Crazy Horse and burned his village, but Crazy Horse came back, and Reynolds was driven off, and retreated, losing a number of his horses. Crook, furious, his supplies low, his men suffering from frozen hands and feet, marched back to Fort Fetterman. In June he was campaigning again, and was on the Rosebud, in Montana; General Gibbon was marching east from the Yellowstone to join him; General Terry,

Custer with him, was advancing west from Fort Abraham Lincoln in North Dakota.

Everyone was looking for Sitting Bull.

By now Sitting Bull had taken the place of Red Cloud as the great leader and organizer of the Sioux, and the Hunkpapas were the spear points instead of the Oglalas.

Meanwhile, two years before, the enthusiasm of those earnest but never numerous allies of the Sioux, the Northern Arapahos, had been considerably dampened by what is known as Bates' Battle.

The first shot of the Second Sioux War had really been fired in the spring of 1874 by Captain Alfred Bates with Company B of the 2nd United States Cavalry, 50 Indian scouts under Lieutenant Young of the 4th Infantry, and 136 Shoshones under Washakie. This encounter did not take place in the Powder River country but over the Big Horns, in the southern end of the Big Horn Basin, on the divide between Bad Water and No Wood creeks. Just around the corner, that is, from Powder River by way of the southern foothills of the Big Horns.

Bates lost two enlisted men killed and two wounded, and two Shoshones were killed and two wounded. Lieutenant Young was seriously wounded. Nine Arapaho warriors were killed and twelve Arapaho warriors wounded, and a visiting Sioux was killed. The loss among the Arapaho women was almost equally severe—eight killed, eight wounded. The names of some of these women are so curious that they bear repeating. One would judge that they were nicknames, not the names given at birth, and that the physical condition of this particular band of Arapahos was not of the best.

Here are some of the curious names:

Lame Woman, Crazy Woman, Bad Woman, Finger Nails Off, Half Dead Woman (a paralyzed woman), Slow Woman, Funny Face, Poor Flesh.

Bates's so-called battle was the only Indian-white man fight that ever took place in the Big Horn Basin, that valley so safe for the white man, so quiet, in such startling contrast to its nearest neighbor, the Powder, to the east. The Arapahos—a small band of them—inspirited by the attitude of the Sioux had raided to the southwest as far as the main Rockies and the South Pass mining country; burning out some settlers, stealing a number of horses and cattle. They had started back to the Powder when Bates and the Shoshones overtook them. The story is that Washakie halted a massacre; a startlingly un-Indian act, but Washakie was an extremely wise Indian.

"Don't kill them any more!" he is reported to have shouted to his braves. "Don't kill them any more! We have whipped them. Set them a-foot! Don't kill them any more!"

Like so many of these frontier skirmishes, the actual loss on either side in this fight on the No Wood had been absurdly small, but the moral effect upon the Arapahos was large.

A slim, aquiline-faced, proud people, the Arapahos, good fighters, but nothing like the Cheyennes and the Sioux. The Arapahos were among the first Indians to cause trouble to the fur traders trapping along what was, later, to become the Medicine Road. Nowadays the Northern Arapahos are the only Indians—except the Shoshones—left in Wyoming. Wyoming, from the time of the trappers and the Blackfeet down to the time of the soldiers and the Sioux, the fiercest of all Indian countries, as crackling with sudden bursts of fire as the bloody flames of a barbecue, is no longer an Indian country. Just the Shoshones and the Northern Arapahos left over on the Wind River Reservation in the west of the state.

When the government finally herded the Arapahos onto a reservation, Washakie saw his chance. The Arapahos had always been the especial enemies of the Shoshones. As Plains Indians they had had in the beginning a contempt for the Shoshones.

"Brigade them on the same reservation as my people," Washakie told the government, "and I'll keep them quiet and take care of them."

He did.

The Shoshones were brigaded on one side of the Little Wind River, the mountains to the west, and the Arapahos were brigaded on the other. Both tribes dealt at the same store, and had the same agency, old Fort Washakie. Whenever an occasion arose, the Shoshones, whom the Arapahos still thought inferior, pushed the Arapahos out of the way and sometimes even spat on them, and the Shoshones had the government with them. Pretty soon the Arapahos were a broken people. Their face was gone.

They are still pretty much a broken people. Those who deal with them find their morale uncertain. The Shoshones, to the contrary, are doing well. They are fairly successful ranchmen. A broader, squarer, more Mongolian-looking people than the Arapahos.

CHAPTER TWENTY-THREE

Tatanka Yotanka

Yᴇᴀʀs ago when I was a little boy, Buffalo Bill's Wild West Show visited the city where I lived, and my uncle, who knew Colonel Cody, the uncle who was a ranchman in Arizona and who was east on a visit, took me out to see and meet that handsome and courteous gentleman.

I remember the hot July afternoon, the smell of ponies and dust, and the smell of the outskirts of a city in hot weather, and how Colonel Cody in a white buckskin suit and with long hair over his shoulders, shot, from horseback, little glass balls thrown into the air.

Afterwards my uncle and I walked along the row of tents where Colonel Cody's Indians were camped. We were part of a long file of people. In the open fly of one of the tents sat a big, square old Indian in a canvas armchair. He was staring at the sky. As people came up to him, he would stick out his hand and say, "How!" Just that, without looking at them.

When we came up to him, he stuck out his hand and said, "How!"

This was about fourteen years after the Battle of the Little Big Horn, and the Indian was Sitting Bull.

For a year Sitting Bull traveled with the show of his friend—and he was a friend—Buffalo Bill.

Tatanka Yotanka, Sitting Bull, the Hunkpapa, was almost as great an organizer as Red Cloud, almost as fine a fighter as Crazy Horse, although not so glamorous or spectacular as the latter. Like Crazy Horse, he hadn't the slightest fear of the whites; unlike Red Cloud, he knew little about them. To General Terry in the early winter of '76 he sent this contemptuous message. . . . General Terry had ordered him to a reservation and had threatened to come after him if he didn't comply.

"You won't need any guides," Sitting Bull sent word. "You can find me easily. I won't run away."

To General Nelson Miles after the Battle of the Little Big Horn, he sent this note:

> I want to know what you are doing traveling on this road. You scare the buffalo away. I want to hunt in this place. I want you to turn back from here. If you don't I will fight you again. I want you to leave what you have got here and turn back from here.
>
> I am your friend,
>
> > Sitting Bull.
>
> I mean all the rations you have got and some powder. Wish you would write me as soon as you can.

A mental leap is necessary to put oneself in the place of Sitting Bull and the other wild Sioux at this time. They were so ignorant of the United States that they thought the soldiers in Montana and the soldiers in Wyoming belonged to two different nations, and so could not understand why the soldiers in Wyoming would not supply them with arms and ammunition to fight the soldiers in Montana. As to the power of the white man, they had seen, after all, armies of only a thousand or so at a time, and against these they could match armies of two thousand or more. So what then?

Tatanka Yotanka was a square-shouldered, stolid-looking Indian, with a great aquiline nose, high broad cheekbones, and a jutting square jaw. Above these were level, unafraid eyes. He was a medicine man as well as a self-appointed chief, and the most adroit politician among his people. Slowly but steadily he had risen to power, first among the Hunkpapas, then among the Sioux as a whole. When necessary he had visions, convincing and appropriate, and visions have always been useful to dictators. By calling a rump parliament up on the Missouri a couple of years before the crucial days of 1875, Sitting Bull had got himself elected head chief of the entire Sioux nation, although for the most part only the hostile Sioux were present and the vast majority of the agency Sioux were nowhere near.

While the generals were looking for Sitting Bull in the spring of '76, he was calmly waiting for them up near the Rosebud in Montana, not without sardonic amusement. He had sent word to the generals that if they wanted war he would give it to them, and pretty soon, during the annual Sun Dance, his confidence was heightened. He had a wonderful vision. He found himself in a multitude of American soldiers—hundreds of them—and suddenly they all dropped dead about his feet. This encouraged Sitting Bull's followers exceedingly.

With Sitting Bull at the moment were some nine hundred lodges, which meant about two thousand warriors; mostly Hunkpapas, Oglalas and Miniconjous, with a sprinkling of Brulés, Sans Arcs and other Sioux. There were also some Cheyennes. Those of the wild Indians, who had gone down to the agencies for the winter, had drifted back and with them some of the more dissatisfied reservation Indians. A number of great chiefs were present. Crazy Horse was there. Hump, American Horse. That stalwart warrior, Gall. Leading the Cheyennes were Dull Knife, Two Moons, and Little Wolf.

On June 17th Crook found Sitting Bull and fought the Battle of the Rosebud. It was a bad battle for the whites. Crook's cavalry almost rode into a trap up a canyon, and only by the hardest fighting did Crook drive the Sioux off. The next day they were back at him again, and Crook, fighting a rear-guard action, withdrew to his base camp to await reinforcements. Crook had thirteen hundred men with him; the Sioux had put about fifteen hundred warriors into the field. Leading Crook's Shoshone scouts was Washakie, and at the head of the Crow scouts were those two famous Crow chiefs, Alligator-Stands-Up and Plenty Coups.

After the Battle of the Rosebud, Sitting Bull and Crazy Horse went west and camped in the valley of the Little Big Horn. It was a huge camp; between two and three thousand warriors with all their women and children. The valley where the Sioux camped is about five miles long and about half a mile wide; a fine, well-grassed valley, the Little Big Horn running through it. All around are low buttes and hills. The Indians apparently did not expect attack. Why should they? They had shown Crook what they could do and for any sensible opponent that would have been enough. The younger braves wanted to go hunting, wanted to turn their attention to something important, and Sitting Bull, not so confident as they, had trouble keeping them together.

Sitting Bull was having the same trouble with his younger warriors that Red Cloud had had ten years before when the latter chief was trying to besiege Fort Phil Kearny. Even now in their final—although they did not know it was final—campaign, and their most desperate one, the Sioux would not fight consistently and effectively. Even now, when on their flanks like wolves were the hard-riding generals. They exhibited the customary Indian combination of self-esteem, ignorance and inability to change age-old custom.

Every nation and every breed has its peculiar stupidities as well as its peculiar virtues, and victory usually means little more than that the virtues, in the case in question, temporarily have been luckier than the stupidities.

There is an ancient sporting axiom that no one ever wins a game; that is to say, either you or your opponent loses it. From the distance of today, the majority of the Indian campaigns in which the United States government indulged seem a desperate effort on the part of the white men and the Indians to see who would lose first. In this odd pursuit, the Indian was more successful than the white man.

On the whole the record of the United States Army on the frontier was a gallant and irritating tragedy of errors, persistently complicated by political stupidity, but the white man was dogged. That was why he won. Had he taken the trouble to find out something about the Indian he would have saved himself an infinite amount of trouble and bloodshed. General Hugh Scott, one of the few soldiers who ever learned to know the Indians, who studied the way their minds worked, and therefore one of the few soldiers ever trusted by the Indian, a trust that prevented much disorder, in his autobiography states that when he was a young lieutenant in Wyoming in the early eighties only two other officers in the United States Army could talk the sign language; the lingua franca of the Plains Indians, a language that can be picked up in a couple of months. As for the actual languages of the various tribes, hardly anyone bothered about these except General Scott, and the mountainmen, and the Indian traders. Practically all the mountainmen talked some Sioux, or Cheyenne, or Arapaho, or Crow, or Shoshone, or whatever else it was that they needed. That was another method they had of preserving their long hair.

No wonder that the favorite taunt of the trapper or cowboy was to send in word to some near-by post asking if it needed the protection of four or five qualified civilians. All this, of course, over and beyond the amazement of the frontiersman and cowboy that anybody should be willing to lead the ordered-about, badly fed, poorly paid life of the frontier army.

Nor, on the other hand, would the Sioux change their tactics of warfare. They had only one method of attack, the method they had used so successfully with Fetterman, and which they had almost succeeded in using against Crook at the Battle of the Rosebud. They invariably tried to decoy and ambush their enemies, and when this failed they were at a loss. After a while even the United States Army began to recognize what the formula was.

Now, however, there was to happen a battle in which the Sioux needed no tactics at all; the army supplied the Sioux with all they needed, and the Sioux, surprised and cornered, fought as they never had before.

The Battle of the Little Big Horn did not actually take place in the Powder River country, any more than did the Battle of the Rosebud. Both took place in Montana to the north, across the Tongue River divide, but both are part of Powder River history because they marked the end of the Sioux fighting on the Powder, and the end of the Sioux.

The night of June 24th was cold and clear but for a little mist that rose from the coolness. June nights in those high altitudes are always cold, and very quiet, except for the far-off barking of coyotes.

The great Indian village along the Little Big Horn slept. Nothing moved except the dark shadows of the ponies feeding and every now and then, near the tepees, the small shadow of a dog. The tepee fires had died out, so that through the tepees no light shone.

Along the Little Big Horn the mist of the coolness of June nights stood up, like drifting ghosts, for a few feet above the banks of the small river.

CHAPTER TWENTY-FOUR

Little Big Horn

Custer rode into it if ever a man did, and as he rode he slapped his thigh and cried out "Custer's luck!" because he had come upon Sitting Bull's trail and could follow it, and annihilate him.

General Terry had sent Custer and his 7th Cavalry in advance to locate the Indians and the plan was for Custer, if he found the Indians, to wait for Gibbon, who was following with an equal number of men. The combined columns would then attack the village. But Terry, just before Custer's departure, had added an unfortunate verbal command. Because of Custer's reputation as an Indian fighter, Terry had told him, were the circumstances right, to use his own judgment. This was enough for Custer.

Custer was one of the most gallant cavalrymen who ever put foot into a stirrup, but he was also one of the most arrogant and fiery. He was a spoiled child of fortune. Now, as it usually does, fortune was turning against him. Custer, moreover, was in a dangerous mood. Dangerous for himself and dangerous for others.

There have been a number of theories, some of them absurd, advanced for the Massacre of the Little Big Horn. It has been said that Custer was drunk. It has been said he committed suicide. The facts are simple enough. All during the Civil War, all his life, fortune had smiled upon Custer and his golden curls, and his reputation for gallantry and success and luck had stead-

ily mounted. He was the darling of the popular imagination. The beau idéal of all the "hard-riding generals."
The beau sabreur. It takes a steady head to bear coolly
that reputation, and beaux sabreurs are not by nature
cool. Custer was in trouble with President Grant and
the War Department. At the beginning of the Civil
War Custer had been only twenty-two, at the Battle of
the Little Big Horn he was only thirty-seven.

Custer was beginning to lose his popularity with
the army, which had never been so great as with the
public. He was an erratic but overly severe disciplinarian. He gambled with his younger officers. He did not
discipline himself the way he disciplined his men. Smoldering charges were piling up against him at Washington, and it was with these smoldering charges in mind
that Custer rode into battle. Besides, hadn't he the finest
regiment of the finest cavalry then in the world? Five
hundred and fifty of them! He could ride through the
entire Sioux nation! And here at last was the chance to
restore his reputation and once more bring the country
to his feet.

The night before, coming upon the trail of the
Sioux, he had made a forced march. Around ten o'clock
in the morning he rode over the divide into the valley
of the Little Big Horn. The Sioux were in a trap. Custer
had them encircled.

Major Benteen with three troops was to go to the
east to attack from that side. Custer with five troops
rode to the northwest. Major Reno with three troops
was told to ride straight down into the village. Reno was
to strike the head of the village; Custer was to strike
the lower end. Benteen was to cut it in half, and the attacks were to synchronize. It was a three-pronged spear
and Sitting Bull was to be impaled upon it, but Reno
missed the head of the village by about two miles, and

while he was still totally unprepared, the Sioux were upon him . . . hundreds of them. The Sioux had surprised Reno, not the other way about. Reno was fighting against enormous odds and his Arikara scouts at once deserted him. At first Reno dismounted his men and then, mounting them once more, he fought a desperate rear-guard action, back to the river and a strong position.

One of the most horrible stories of the day is that of two of Reno's troopers whose green horses bolted into the ranks of the Sioux. The ranks opened and the troopers disappeared as if into a red and bleeding mouth. But it was a day of horrible stories.

Fighting a hand-to-hand fight, officers and men going down, the Sioux on his flanks, Reno and his men finally gained a bluff across the Little Big Horn, and the Sioux halted in the valley below them. After a while Benteen, who had found no Indians, came over a hill and joined Reno. Neither Reno nor Benteen knew where Custer was, but Benteen had a note from Custer asking for reinforcements and ammunition. This had been brought to him by Trumpeter John Martin, the only man of Custer's immediate command to survive.

In the middle of the afternoon a strange thing happened. The Indians in the valley below Reno and Benteen suddenly stopped their circling and galloping, and for a moment were still. Then, without any apparent reason, they raced, the vast majority, madly over the hills to the north and west. They left just enough warriors to keep Reno occupied. A little while after, Benteen and Reno heard heavy firing.

This was Custer.

It was then that Reno had his chance and failed.

No one knows just why he did not move. His officers urged him to. He seemed bewildered; refused to answer questions, would not issue commands; sat on a rock staring, a sweat-soaked bandanna around his head. One captain set out with his troop against orders but was turned back by the Sioux. Finally, Reno retreated to the top of a neighboring hill from where, with glasses, he could see Custer's battlefield. He saw clouds of dust; a mass of Indians; no soldiers. Presently toward dusk the Indians attacked Reno again.

The next day they attacked once more at dawn and all day kept up a desultory firing. Toward night they did another strange thing—they abruptly struck their tents and marched away.

Reno was as bewildered by this move as he had been when he had heard Custer's firing. But the next morning he knew why the Indians had retreated. Up the valley of the Little Big Horn came a long cloud of dust. This was Terry and Gibbon, a great column of blue behind them. Still no one knew what had become of Custer. And then, far off to the east, naked in the sunlight, strange white blotches sprawled carelessly in the grass and through the brush and on the slopes, Gibbon's scouts came upon Custer and his men.

The Battle of the Little Big Horn was the worst defeat suffered by the white men in the history of Indian fighting. Not a man of Custer's immediate command was left alive except the fortunate trumpeter, John Martin. On that warm and bright June day, Custer and the 208 white men with him had gone down. Five troops of the 7th United States Cavalry, including the famous Gray Horse Troop, had been wiped out. A fatal day for the Custer family too. Among the dead were two of Custer's brothers: Lieutenant Thomas Custer and Boston Custer; his brother-in-law, Lieutenant James Calhoun; and his nephew, Autie Reed.

Thirteen commissioned officers; 191 enlisted men; four civilians and guides . . . that was Custer's loss. Over the hills to the southwest Reno at the same time was losing three commissioned officers, 48 enlisted men, and four scouts and interpreters. Two hundred and sixty-four dead white men in all. Fifty-two of Reno's enlisted men were wounded.

Nor were these troopers volunteer cavalrymen. They were hardened and accustomed veterans of the frontier. They belonged to the most famous regiment in the cavalry branch of the United States Army; an army that a little while before, at the end of the Civil War, had been admittedly the greatest army in the world. An army so huge and well trained that the mere hint that it would be sent into Mexico had caused Napoleon III to abandon Maximilian to his fate.

The humiliation felt by the army and the nation as a whole was almost as great as the shock of the massacre. The unfortunate Reno was made the scapegoat, and he never regained his reputation. Nor was this any more fair than it usually is. Reno had been taken utterly by surprise; he was tremendously outnumbered; he had difficulty saving his own men; and, having a much smaller command until Benteen joined him, undoubtedly he expected aid from Custer rather than the other way about. Reno's indecision on top of the hill when he first heard Custer's firing was what ruined him.

Custer's men were widely scattered. Custer, apparently, had been as much taken by surprise as Reno. After the Sioux charged he had retreated toward the top of the little hill on the slopes of which are the serried monuments of himself and his men, but a band of Sioux had come over the hill and attacked him from the rear. Some of Custer's men had dismounted and fought on foot. Far off to the east, in the direction from which Custer had come, was found the body of Lieutenant Calhoun. Strung out behind him were the bodies of some troopers. They had fought their way at least as far as that.

There is a story that Custer was the last to go down on the slopes of that small hill, and that on his knees, wounded in several places, two revolvers in his hands, his yellow curls flying back of him, he roared with laughter and when his guns were empty flung them in the faces of his enemies. Nobody knows if this is true.

From the score of stories surrounding the massacre an especially grim one survives. Frank Grouard, the famous scout, on a mission for Crook, was on the battle-field the very night of the fight. He did not know there had been a fight, he did not know that Indians were near, until he stumbled in the darkness across the bodies of Custer's dead.

First he smelled blood. Then his horse shied from something on the ground. Grouard dismounted and searched. For a moment he raised his head and listened. Very quietly he got on his horse again and rode for his life.

He need not have worried. There were no Indians around. They knew all about the coming of Terry and Gibbon. They had scouts out too. Indeed, it has always been a question whether the Sioux had not known about the coming of Custer just as accurately as they did about the coming of Terry and Gibbon, and if their apparent lack of preparation had not been a trap.

In any case, the Battle of the Little Big Horn meant business where the government was concerned. From now on the government looked neither to the right nor to the left, but straight ahead.

Trailing north, the great caravan of Indians began to break up and drift apart in separate bands. The Sioux were contented with their victory. Hadn't it been decisive enough? What further lesson did the white man need to teach him to keep away from the Powder and the Montana hunting grounds? The Sioux were temporarily tired of fighting. What sensible people wouldn't be? Moreover, they had used up all their ammunition.

One by one, through the summer and autumn and following winter, the hard-riding generals hunted the chiefs down. General Miles, summoned from the Southwest, overtook Sitting Bull up in Montana, and after a conference in which Sitting Bull was defiant, harried him north over the Canadian line. Colonel Ranald Mackenzie, Crook's chief of cavalry, found Dull Knife and his Cheyennes in winter camp far down in the Powder River country, tucked away in the folds of the Red Fork of the Middle Fork near the Hole-in-the-Wall country, and burned the village and killed about thirty Cheyennes. This was on November 26th, at dawn, and the broken and fleeing Cheyennes performed the first of those feats of tragic endurance that were to make them famous.

There was deep snow on the ground and the Cheyennes, men, women and children, naked and barefoot, driven from their lodges where they had been asleep, walked seventy miles north to Crazy Horse's village on the Powder. Their trail was clear because of the blood.

In January, General Miles came up with Crazy Horse, and after a desperate fight Crazy Horse was defeated and fled, only to surrender a few days later. On April 22nd, Two Moons surrendered with three hundred Cheyennes. Ten days later, Lame Deer, a Miniconjou, the last of the wild chiefs at large except Sitting Bull who was now up in Canada, also surrendered.

Less than a year after their greatest victory the Sioux were done. Their nomad principality had collapsed. Their hegira of a hundred years was ended.

For a year or so there was nothing to crop down the grass of the Powder. It grew undisturbed. The buffalo were gone. The Indian ponies were gone. The white man's cattle and horses had not yet come.

CHAPTER TWENTY-FIVE

Death Rides a Pinto

CRAZY HORSE was killed at the Spotted Tail Agency in the fall of 1877, five months after he had surrendered. Just how he was killed will remain forever a mystery; there are two diametrically opposed stories. One suggests murder, the other places the blame upon Crazy Horse. You can take your choice.

The first story is that Crazy Horse having married, the spring of his surrender, the daughter of a half-breed interpreter at the Red Cloud Agency, found that his wife had tuberculosis and, since the doctor at Red Cloud could do little for her, against the express orders of the agent at Red Cloud, he took her to see his friend Dr. McGillicuddy at the near-by Spotted Tail Agency. When he reached Spotted Tail, the agent there and the army officers, having the deepest suspicions of his purposes, lured him into the guardhouse and attempted to put him under arrest. Crazy Horse exhibited the usual reactions of an Indian to this, especially an Indian who was a great warrior. He drew a knife and attempted to escape, and this version of his death claims that in the subsequent brawl he was bayoneted by a soldier.

The other story is that Crazy Horse from the very moment of his surrender began to make trouble and, throughout the summer of 1877, was constantly trying to reorganize his own band and attract other Indians to it for the purpose of going back to the Powder or, if that was impossible, to the Canadian line in Montana, there to resume the life and habits he loved. This story claims that Crazy Horse, finding that practically all the Sioux were now against him, even the majority of his own band, started to flee north when he heard an order for his arrest had been issued by General Crook; but, being deserted by most of his followers, circled back to the Spotted Tail Agency hoping that his personal influence would induce some of his Miniconjou friends to join him. Arriving at the agency he was arrested by the Indians themselves and turned over to the officers.

From there the two stories are similar except that, in the second version, Crazy Horse is supposed to have stabbed himself accidentally when one of the Indians holding him bore down on his hand that held the knife.

Both stories agree on several important points. They agree that Crazy Horse was held by one at least of his own warriors and by some of Spotted Tail's Brulés. They agree that Spotted Tail's Brulés hated Crazy Horse although he was Spotted Tail's nephew, and although Spotted Tail himself, invariably kind and sensible, did not hate him. They agree that General Crook and the army feared Crazy Horse's influence and reputation and put no trust in his ability to keep the peace. And they agree that the government was contemplating sending Crazy Horse to the Dry Tortugas in Florida, that deadly military Alcatraz. They also agree that the rumor was out that Crazy Horse had sworn to kill General Crook and that Crook believed the story. The more faithful of Crazy Horse's admirers claim that this rumor was untrue and that, when told of it, Crazy Horse indignantly repudiated it. At all events, the army believed that Crazy Horse made the threat and that he intended to keep it.

The important fact is that Crazy Horse was dead, and that with his death the Sioux lost their greatest warrior. Their firebrand. The point of their lance. Their oriflamme. Crazy Horse was only thirty-three years old when he died.

Crazy Horse was gone. Two Moons had surrendered. Dull Knife had been rendered impotent. American Horse was dead. Little Wolf, the great Cheyenne, had enlisted as a scout in the United States Army. Up in Canada, Sitting Bull and his Hunkpapas, kept in unaccustomed order by a handful of imperturbable redcoated Northwest Mounted Police with whom they got along fairly well, stayed until 1881, and then came back to the United States and surrendered.

For a couple of years Sitting Bull was held a prisoner at Fort Randall and then he was allowed to go to his former home near the Standing Rock Agency in Montana. One year, as has been seen, he toured the country with the Wild West Show of his old friend Buffalo Bill. Sitting Bull had many white friends and they liked and respected him. In 1889 the Messiah Craze spread from the Southwest up into the Sioux Nation, spread among all the Indians of the Far West, and for a little while the Sioux were greatly troubled, for a little while a strange vague metaphysical hope stirred in their breasts. This so-called "craze," similar to the hopes of the early Christians, and compounded of mission

Christianity and Indian myths, had been started by a single visionary red man far down in the Southwest. This prophet had seen visions which predicted that because the Indians were broken, and defeated and humbled, a God was coming among them who would raise them, without fighting, without trouble, above their conquerors, the insolent whites.

Blessed are the meek, for they shall inherit the earth!

In the midst of the excitement and the Ghost Dancing, Sitting Bull apparently behaved with a good deal of sense, but the government still feared his influence and told Buffalo Bill to persuade his old friend to come in to the Pine Ridge Agency. At the last moment Buffalo Bill's orders were countermanded, and a squad of Sioux police dispatched in his place.

The government—perhaps it did not care—seemed never to get through its head that you could not arrest an Indian.

The Indian police rode into the Hunkpapa village, attempted to arrest Sitting Bull, and at once a fight was on. Four Sioux policemen were killed and two wounded, and nine Hunkpapas were killed, including Sitting Bull and his seventeen-year-old son, Crowfoot.

As in the case of Crazy Horse, no one will ever know just what happened or why it happened. The eastern papers cried "murder," the western papers and the army bitterly resented the charge. In any case, Sitting Bull's death, coming at the height of the Ghost Dancing, had tremendous reverberations among the Sioux. About four thousand left the agencies, and for a while it looked like serious trouble. The majority of the Sioux, however, remained peaceably where they were. There were enough out, however, to furnish the troops with a few small skirmishes and to furnish Colonel Forsyth, now in command of the 7th Cavalry, the opportunity for which the 7th Cavalry had been looking ever since Little Big Horn. Big Foot, the last recalcitrant chief to surrender, furnished the 7th the opportunity for the Massacre of Wounded Knee.

Big Foot had surrendered, and the day after the surrender his tepees were in a square guarded by the troopers, a Hotchkiss gun at each corner pointing in. A bad way to place Hotchkiss guns, if you think it over, since in case of trouble the bullets are just as likely to hit the guards on the other side of the square as they are to hit the prisoners for whom they are intended. And this, according to most contemporary reports, was exactly what happened.

Orders had been given for the troopers to search the tepees for guns and although the Indians were peaceable they were restless as the soldiers moved in and out of the lodges. In the silence, Yellow Bird, a medicine man, was haranguing the Sioux to resist because the Messiah would protect them, but there was no other sound, or movement of any kind, until someone shot off a gun. No one knows who fired the shot, and the bullet struck neither soldier nor Indian, but the slaughter was on. When it was over twenty-nine whites were dead and thirty-three wounded and over two hundred Sioux had been killed, including at least fifty women and twenty small children.

And now, as a fitting climax, we come to another bloodstained march of the Cheyennes. The Cheyennes seem to have had a genius for memorable drama.

Portugee Phillips and Fort Kearny for the whites! The trek of Dull Knife and his Cheyennes for the Indians! Those were things of which any race, red or white, can be proud.

The government had listened to Spotted Tail when he had protested against the plan to transfer the Sioux to the Indian Territory, but the government was not so kind to Dull Knife. Dull Knife and his Cheyennes were exiled to Oklahoma and kept there for two years under a stupid and brutal agent. Even their ponies could find no feed.

Desperate, starving, seeing no hope of any kind, in September of 1878 the Cheyennes broke for the north and home, the latter almost a thousand miles away from the sand dunes of the new reservation. Leading them, along with Dull Knife, was Little Wolf, who had been an outstanding chief in the Fetterman fight, the Battle of the Rosebud, the Custer massacre, and during Ranald Mackenzie's attack on Dull Knife's village.

North the Cheyennes rode for twenty-two days to the Nebraska line, red Quixotes, on their gaunt ponies; the few they had kept with them, the ones they had managed to steal on the eve of their flight. Loping, trotting, riding sixty and seventy miles a day, the Cheyennes sought their home. Women, babies, old people; only about eighty able-bodied warriors in the whole lot. They shook the pursuing cavalry off after a few small skirmishes. They burned a village in Kansas and killed everyone in it, eighteen white men, women and children. They burned the ranches they passed. As they went they collected guns, ammunition, horses. When they came to the Kansas-Nebraska line, heavily guarded by the troops along the Union Pacific, they divided themselves into small groups and slipped across at night. Presently they had reached their own country in northern Nebraska.

Little Wolf wanted to go on into what he still thought were the impregnable fastnesses of the Powder; Dull Knife, old, tired, with that curious ignorance and innocence that so often afflicted the Indian, wanted to stop. The Cheyennes were in their own country, he said. No one would bother them any longer. They had come home. They had only done what was right. Dull Knife and Little Wolf separated.

On the 23rd of October the cavalry found Dull Knife in the Nebraska sand hills and he surrendered. He was taken at once, with his small gaunt band, to Fort Robinson in Nebraska. Little Wolf reached Montana and wintered there, and surrendered in the spring, making final peace with the government. But Dull Knife's journey was not over.

Once again it was a winter as bitter as the winter of 1875-1876 when Dull Knife and his people, after Ranald Mackenzie's destruction of their village on Red Fork, had walked through the bloodstained snow across the foothills of the Big Horns to Crazy Horse's camp. The Cheyennes were being held in barracks at Fort Robinson. In December, Dull Knife was told that he and his people must go back to the Indian Territory. In January, while a blizzard was raging, word came from Washington that the Cheyennes, under military escort, were to depart at once. For the second time the strange icy agony of the Cheyennes was to be re-enacted. When they had been searched in the sand hills at their surrender they had managed to conceal a few weapons; some revolvers, five rifles broken up into their various parts and hidden by the women in their dresses. These they had put together again. They had also managed to conceal some ammunition. The rest of their weapons consisted of clubs, knives, floor boards and stove handles.

Red Cloud and some other Sioux chiefs had been brought over from the Sioux agencies a month before to advise with Dull Knife, and the Sioux had counseled peace, telling the Cheyennes that even the Sioux knew better now than to fight the government, but Dull Knife and his people would not go back to the Indian Territory.

Suddenly one night, just after guard mount, a shot rang out, a sentry dropped, and the handful of Cheyennes broke from their barracks and fought their way to liberty. For eleven days, the garrison on their heels, 37 of the Indians dead, 52 wounded or captured early in the flight, Dull Knife's son dead, his daughter dead, without supplies of any kind, in weather so severe that even the buffalo-coated troops had their hands and feet frozen, the Cheyennes fought, slipped away, fought again, struggled toward the Powder. Finally, with only three cartridges left, they were surrounded.

Here is the end! Three young Cheyenne braves climbed from the shallow ravine where the remnants of their band were and charged straight at the soldiers; two had knives, one an empty pistol.

A man will fight hard for his home; especially if there are mountains and rivers and grass—

The government, for once in its relations with hostile Indians, did the right thing. It did not send the Cheyennes back to the Indian Territory. Dull Knife had won his point. The blind heroism of the Cheyennes had made even their most bitter enemies generous.

In all American history there is nothing finer than the loping march of the Cheyennes up from the Indian Territory and their subsequent incredible frozen flight. The march of Xenophon and his Ten Thousand was as nothing compared with it.

For a thousand miles the Cheyennes, a mere handful, had ridden their starved ponies without resting through country that had changed greatly in the fourteen years since Sand Creek. Now this country was fairly well filled with towns, ranches and cowboys, and also it was held together by railways and the telegraph. And the entire country was up in arms against the Cheyennes. Between them and their destination, moreover, or within easy call, were 13,000 soldiers and four generals. Crook along the Union Pacific. Bradley up in Nebraska. Gibbon along the Yellowstone. And down on the Santa Fe Trail, Pope. Straight across this country the Cheyennes rode, and then, captured, imprisoned, disarmed, without horses or food or supplies of any kind, clad only in the thin clothes they were wearing, surrounded by a thoroughly equipped garrison, they broke through again and for eleven days fought off their pursuers and their even more implacable enemies, starvation and cold.

An Algonkin people, the Cheyennes, driven west from Minnesota by the Ojibway and, like the Sioux, not coming into their own until they found the plains and horses. An extremely handsome people, with beautiful women. A tall people, brave and honest, but even a smaller tribe than the Crows—only about three thousand of them.

Of all the hostile northwestern Indians, the Cheyennes were the best liked, the most admired, by the men who fought them. And today they are the best liked by the old-timers who knew them when they were by no means easy or safe to know.

Dzi-tsii-tsa they call themselves, "The People," or "Our People"; not an exclusive name, for many tribes also call themselves the "People." Sha-hi-yena the Sioux called them, or "people of different speech," a word corrupted into Cheyenne by the French-Canadian trappers and which sounds much more French, and like the French for dog, than it is. The name has proved confusing to many people, even experts, since, oddly enough, the great fighting society of the Cheyennes was known as the "Dog Soldiers."

Dull Knife had said: "All we ask is to be allowed to live, and live in peace."

Big Mouth had said: "You have set the prairie on fire."

Spotted Tail had said: "The land on which we stand is full of white men; our game is all gone and we have come on great trouble."

Touching-the-Clouds, Crazy Horse's friend, watching him die, said: "It is good! He has looked for death, and it has come!"

Chief Joseph . . . Hin-mah-too-yah-lah-kekht, Thunder-Strikes-out-from-the-Water . . . the great Nez Percé, as a youth had stood by his father's death-bed and heard these words:

"This country will hold your father's body. Do not sell it. Never sell the bones of your father."

Charlot, chief of the Flatheads, that fine tribe of the Bitter Roots up in Montana who never killed a white man and remained throughout the white man's stanch friends, in desperation said:

"You are liars! I do not believe you. My young men have no place to hunt. They get whisky. They are bad. My women and children are hungry."

Whatever else may be said about the Indian he had a gift for apothegm.

CHAPTER TWENTY-SIX

Arapaho Love Song

A FULL moon was up over the mountains to the west and the mountains, sharp as goats' horns, were thin and high as if they had been cut from the night by the knife of some whittling god. The valley was silver, and from the road on which we were, you could see, a more shining silver even than the valley, the silver of the river. The forests, save at their tops, were black.

It was September, a cold night, and the pines smelled, and the sagebrush.

On the front seat beside me were two Arapaho braves, one a chief. On the back seat, huddled in blankets, were their women. We were driving back to an Arapaho camp, twenty miles up the valley. Along with the smell of the pines and the sagebrush, the frosty smell of the night. And the peculiar smell of the Indian, a smell like old wet moccasins held too close to a fire. For half an hour now the braves had been singing the same song over and over. Indian music is like Chinese music; the first ten minutes are fascinating. On the whole, the moment was romantic.

"What's that song?" I asked.

"That . . . ? That famous Arapaho love song."

"What are the words?"

"Those . . . ? Very fine words. They say, 'I love you, darling, and I'll get you whether you're married or not.' "

A huge motion-picture company had come into
the valley and for two months had destroyed its peace,
its temper, and its ability to concentrate. On the edge
of a little lake were the painted tepees (provided by
the motion-picture company) of 400 Crows, Cheyennes, Arapahos and Shoshones. With the pony herds
out on the flats at night, and a sickle moon in the sky,
and the dying campfires, the mountains as a background, the camp was a spectacle. Even by day it was
fine.

The script called for a scene in which four braves,
one a chief dressed in full war paint, out scouting, discovered a wagon train and galloping back to the village
alarmed it for attack. At the entrance to the village sat
four women grinding corn. One spoke English, the other
three didn't. As the four warriors came shouting and
galloping back from the hills, the four women were
supposed to rise and express interest and concern.

Six times the warriors came shouting and galloping
back from the hills, and each time only the woman who
spoke English showed interest. The others knew it was
merely a play.

The director finally decided to put that scene off
for another day.

Meanwhile the village had been awakened six times
to life and six times a couple of hundred warriors had
ridden past within ten feet of me at a full gallop, shouting and shaking their spears. Leading them was a naked
and fierce young Crow. Each time they passed my heart
jumped with the color of it and the thunder of the
ponies' hoofs. A hundred of these ponies were mine,
incidentally, and—white men's ponies—they had a baf-
fled look in their eyes due to days of Indian riders, and
the red and yellow paint that had been smeared upon

them, and the strips of red flannel that had been tied to their manes and tails.

With the order "to cut," the Indians got off their ponies, and the fierce young Crow saw me and strode over to me. "Why, old man," he said, "hello! I haven't seen you for years!" and slapped me on the shoulder with what used to be, but no longer is, a collegiate gesture. "Where have you been?" He still had his guttural voice and it had lost none of the inhuman, ventriloqual effect of the Indian voice speaking English, but the phrases were fashionable. I told him where I had been and asked him where he had been.

"I? Oh, I've been in Paris. With the pictures. You know Paris? Cognac? . . . That French cognac!"

Several years ago, just before he died, I ran across my old friend White Horse—Tom Crispin was his agency name. Tom was a chief, a medicine man, an Episcopalian deacon, a graduate of Carlisle, president of the Arapaho Farmers' Progressive and Benevolent Association, and the best drummer of the Arapaho nation. He was also a quarter-Cheyenne; grandson of famous old Two Moons.

Years ago Tom came over the mountains to visit me. He and his wife made a little wickiup out of willows down near our irrigation ditch and lived there three days very happily. One night I asked Tom to drum. At first he said he wouldn't, although I knew he loved to drum. He said he had a headache. But I told him some people were coming especially to hear him drum, and then I added that he was the greatest drummer the Arapahos ever had, and everyone knew it, and that of course meant that he was a better drummer than the Shoshones or Cheyennes had ever even imagined. At this, Tom weakened a little and his headache got slightly better. Presently, when I told him how many people were coming, and how far they were riding . . . this was before the time of automobiles . . . and how interested they were, his headache got completely well.

Once he started drumming, he drummed from eight o'clock until midnight.

Now, the finest drum music the Arapahos have is their Thunder Music, and I wanted Tom to play that, but at first, and for a long while, he refused. Eventually it occurred to me why. The pass over the mountains in those days—the pass is forty miles long—was just a clay wagon road, all right in dry weather, bad in wet. We had been having a minor drought for three weeks and the road was fine. Naturally Tom didn't want to ruin it by any Thunder Music, but I finally persuaded him, and vanity getting the better of common sense, the tom-tom spoke.

Within two hours it poured rain and rained all the rest of the night.

Tom was very gloomy when he set out with his wife the next morning to recross the pass.

When I ran into old Tom again, ten years later, he was in a group of Indians and white men. Again we had been having a drought, this time a serious one.

"Pretty dry!" said Tom.

"Very. Couldn't be worse."

Tom looked at me with the secret shy look that peers from the ambush of Indian eyes when an Indian, and he seldom does, speaks of what is actually at the back of the Indian mind.

He took me aside; he spoke swiftly and softly.

"You like me make rain for you again?"

"Of course."

Tom turned away and went back to the group he had left.

Half an hour later he hunted me up.

"Look," he said, "I make you a proposition. You know that Harry Smith, eh? Friend of yours? Well, he want to trade me his Buick. You get him to take two hundred dollars off and I make you rain—plenty."

This, if you remember, was a Carlisle graduate, the president of the Arapaho Farmers' Progressive and Benevolent Association, and a deacon in the Episcopal Church. But he was also an Indian and a medicine man. Finally, he was an American citizen, not untouched by business ideals. And in all that lies just the point of the story.

If you can unravel Tom's psychology and tie it up into a neat and logical bundle, then you can understand the Indian, something no white man has ever completely done.

The greatest misfortune that befell the Indian was that he wandered onto a continent that was to attract the white man hundreds of years later; and, at that, the northern white man—not the Latin who also kills the Indian but understands him better. For some reason the white man's progress has been toward the west; toward the setting sun. If the Indian had migrated west himself, instead of east, counterclockwise instead of clockwise, he would have been all right. He would have been with the Russians, who are also Orientals.

The second great misfortune that befell the Indian was that, almost with the first coming of the white man, certain white men and women, innocent souls, most of whom saw little of the Indian, found him romantic.

The Indian is an exceedingly pragmatic man, far more pragmatic than the white man ever thinks of being. When an Indian says a thing he means it exactly. His knowledge is limited but precise. His statements and intentions are equally so. He has none of the white man's misty imagination, none of the white man's long and hazy visions, none of the white man's willingness to compromise or the white man's dogged intention somehow to muddle through.

One of the great tragedies of history is that the Indian and the white man had to meet. No two races could have understood each other less.

For one thing, an expanding race met a static one. A force in motion met an immovable object. A man of the Machine Age met a man of the Stone Age. A settler met a nomad. An Occidental met an Oriental. A growing civilization met one that centuries before had stopped growing. It was too bad, but that is what happened. And after all, what was the white man to do? Should he have withdrawn from the North American continent?

It is not that the Indian is uncivilized. He has a very distinct and ancient civilization; a subtle and articulated one; but it is truncated and closed. Were he actually a savage it would be much easier to teach him how to be a white man. That you can never do except in the case of a rare genius or so. The best you can do is to make him a good Indian with what modern improvements are necessary. To make an Indian a white man, you have first to unteach him countless centuries, and then to teach him countless more. You have to undo before you do. Start down before you start up. Come from the tip of the thumb down to the palm before you ascend the index finger.

The white man treated the Indian terribly. The Indian treated the white man terribly. Nowadays it is the fashion to upbraid the white man for his treatment of the Indian, and justly, just as fifty years ago it was the fashion to hate the Indian—and justly. Neither attitude is fair. To repeat, like so many things in history, it just happened . . . the troubles between the Indians and the white men. And nowadays we have forgotten a little too much perhaps what it feels like to be scalped or burned by a small fire, or even worse, your hands tied behind your back, to stand and watch your wife or daughter or sons being burned.

The Indian and the white man did not even understand each other when both—according to their lights—were telling the truth. They thought each other liars. Neither were liars; that is, the best of them. The Indian's truth, like his bravery, is a question of face, of dignity. Great chiefs do not break their word, but they can couch that word at times in such a fashion as to fool their enemies and so gain even added honor among their own people. Good white men do not lie, but often they bind themselves for some future act. How in a changing white man's civilization can you predict the future or bind yourself to it?

One distinct virtue the Indian had. One we could learn from him, and a very important one, and one needed especially at present, and that is the Indian's love of his land and his ability to see it as something separate from himself; an entity. Something to which he belonged and which belonged to him, but with a life and spirit of its own, as a mother belongs to her child, or the other way around, although both are separate individuals. The Indian loved his land passionately. It was constantly in his mind. In fact it was the essence of the vague, never clearly defined Indian religion. The land was actually that misty figure, the Great Spirit.

It seems to me that we should be careful how we explain to the Indian our own faith. According to his lights, he led a wonderful life, for those who like such a life. We will have to show him something better than gasoline stations and the average white man's religion before we can convince him.

Hardly had the thunder of the Sioux ponies, along the Powder, the thunder of the cavalry died down, when over the southern horizon came a new army. An army of tossing horns, white in the sun; of lithe young men lolling in their saddles; riding at point, on the flanks, on the drag.

The Cowboy was coming to Wyoming.

PART FOUR

Cattle Country

*You mount your horses
from the left; white men
mount from the left*

CHAPTER TWENTY-SEVEN

As I Was Walking One Morning
for Pleasure

As I was walking one morning for pleasure
I spied a young puncher a-riding alone,
His hat was throwed back and his spurs were a-jingling,
And as he approached he was singing this song:

"Whoopee ti yo, git along little dogies!
It's your misfortune and none of my own.
Whoopee ti yo, git along little dogies,
For now Wyoming will be your new home.

It's only in spring that we round up the dogies,
We mark them and brand them and bob off their tails,
We round up the horses, load up the chuck wagon,
And then throw the dogies out on to the trail.

Your mother was raised away down in Texas,
Where the jimson weed and the sand burrs grow:
Now we'll fill you up on prickly pear and cholla
Till you're ready for the trail to I-di-ho.

Oh, you'll be soup for Uncle Sam's Injuns,
'Beef! Heap beef!' I hear them cry.
Git along, git along, git along, little dogies,
You'll be in Wyoming in the sweet bye and bye!"

THE tradition of the mounted man—the cava-
lier, the caballero, the buckaroo—is as old as history
and comes down to us with the ring of spurs and the

tapping of proud and delicate feet. Somehow or other a man on a horse feels different from his fellows. Somehow or other all he does is colored and accentuated by his position. A little above the ground; his mind, his voice, his hands controlling casually but instinctively the silken living thing between his legs. Whatever the horseman does is just a trifle more gallant, more swaggering than the gestures and actions of a footman; his vices are more dashing, his virtues freer. There's a fanfare to a horse.

And where the Far West is concerned, the horse has always been a "work" horse, first an Indian buffalo horse and war horse, then a cow pony, and this, it seems to me, makes the tradition even more gallant and integral. The Far Westerner lives with horses as the Arab does. The horse is part of him and of his country. He takes horses for granted; like breathing, like food. The horse is not merely a social hallmark, or a means of exercise or excitement. He is one of the colors of the background.

Up from Texas came the cow pony convoying as useful if not as gallant a creature as himself. A sullen, wide-eyed creature with horns.

It took a cow to teach Chicago how to build, and it took another "cow," a longhorned one, using the word cow generically and irrespective of sex as it is used in the Far West, to teach Americans what a fine country Wyoming was, and to teach the scattered residents of Wyoming in what the real future of their territory lay.

To begin with, men had thought that this future was beaver, then for a long while they had thought it gold, neither of them homemaking businesses, suddenly they realized that it was beefsteak on the hoof, and that the gold lay on the surface of the ground in the shape

of mountain and prairie grasses. Gold that waved in the
wind and turned brown in the fall.

Don Something-or-other—undoubtedly his last
name was Gomez, and his first Diego or José—began
the North American cattle business down in Mexico,
and Don Diego, or José, began it shortly after Cortez
had finally conquered the Aztecs. Don Diego, or José,
knew cattle country when he saw it. He had brought
the knowledge with him from Spain. It was in his blood.
And after Coronado, but slowly, a hundred years later
perhaps, the business spread across the Rio Grande. For
two centuries it remained Mexican-Spanish. With the
annexation of Texas in 1845 it became, on its outer
edges, American, with the subtle differences which that
implies. Saddles began to change a little, bits, clothes,
the breaking of horses, the texture and use of ropes.
Maguey and leather here and there turned to hemp. The
half-Spanish, half-American cow talk of the Southwest
emerged.

The Texas cattleman and the Texas cowboy, the
few that then existed, went to the Civil War; when
they came back they found that nature and their absence had made the west of their country a great cattle
state. Pretty soon they had more cattle than they knew
what to do with. Not the big, white-faced, sleek fellows
we are used to now on the northwestern ranges, but
little fierce creatures as swift as antelope, with huge,
absurd and dangerous horns. Nature had seen to that.
They had to look out for themselves—against mountain
lion, and bear, and wolves. Nor were the Texas ranges
the lush prairies of the North.

But they had ancestry, these Texas longhorns.
They were noblemen by descent just as were their constant companions, the little Texas cow ponies. So small,
the latter, that, just as nowadays in Mexico, a big man's

feet seemed to touch the ground; so small that men
boasted they could ride their bucking with the perfectly
straight stirrups then in vogue and hold a silver dollar
under the ball of a boot.

The longhorns were the distant descendants of the
black bulls of Andalusia.

With the building and finishing of the Kansas
Pacific in 1867 the Texas cattlemen had their chance
for the middle western market, and by now Iowa and
Nebraska were no longer frontier, and the middle western farmers wanted stock for fattening. Pretty soon
word drifted down that the still undeveloped Northwest wanted cattle as well.

Three new figures began to emerge in the cattle
business. The drover, the man who took the cattle up
the Texas trails to the shipping point; the buyer, the
man who met the drover and his cowboys at the railway; and finally, and unfortunately, the cattle finan-
cier, the man who organized the great cattle companies,
speculated in land and herds, sold stock, and often did
not know a latigo strap from a prairie dog.

The raising of cattle was no longer a "way of life"
as it by rights is and must be to be successful; it became
a "business." It is still a "business," and so is still a gallant and pleasant and picturesque way of losing money.
When it becomes once more a way of life, the American
cattleman will be as successful as his Mexican-Spanish
progenitor.

Texas had to thank a certain Colonel Maverick, if
the tradition is correct, for the spread of its herds and
for the foundation of several prominent cattle families.
The whole cattle business has to thank Colonel Maverick for a word, and a most important one; one that
caused a lot of trouble in Wyoming later on. The Maver-

ick clan, as you may have noticed, is still vigorous in Texas and, until recently, in Washington.

There are two stories about Colonel Maverick and the use of his name. The first is that he went to the Civil War leaving his cattle unherded, and that they increased fourfold, and since they were unbranded, when Colonel Maverick returned from the war he found that those of his fellow veterans who had been discharged early had helped themselves. The other story antedates the war.

This story claims that Colonel Maverick, a lawyer and not a cattleman at all, somewhere around 1855 found himself with a bunch of cattle in payment of a bad debt, and not wishing to be bothered with them, placed them in charge of one of his Negroes on the San Antonio River. The Negro, also not wishing to be bothered, neglected to do any branding, and so when Colonel Maverick sold the undesired cattle to Toutant Beauregard, Beauregard was the owner of a number of unmarked cattle and improved upon the situation by at once claiming and branding all the unmarked cattle on Colonel Maverick's range.

At all events, as you probably know, and this is the important thing, a maverick is an unbranded cow or steer or calf whose ownership is in doubt. "Dogie," pronounced dough-gie, actually means an orphaned calf, or, as the old saying goes, "A calf whose mamma has died and whose father has run off with another lady cow," but as in the song that heads this chapter, the word is frequently used to mean cattle as a whole.

The word "maverick" killed more men in the Far West than any other word.

And now, with the Texas longhorns coming north, we can see once more how the Oregon Trail, the Great Medicine Road, conditioned Wyoming history.

To begin with, the Oregon Trail had made Wyoming a thoroughfare and a way station; now it was to make Wyoming a home and a cattle country. Wyoming's earliest ranchmen were the traders along the Oregon Trail, although they didn't know they were ranchmen. They thought they were traders. The cattle business came to Wyoming slowly and naturally.

The early emigrant trains used a great many ox teams, and both they and the later trains brought with them numerous milch cows. The stationkeepers along the trail—Jim Bridger down in the southwestern corner of Wyoming, the men around Fort Laramie, and so on —not only had to be in a position to shoe the ox teams, but also to feed milch cows, horses and other stock. Moreover, by the time Wyoming was reached a great many oxen and milch cows were worn out or footsore and their owners were glad to trade them for supplies of various kinds. Presently the stationkeepers found themselves stockmen. For the sake of convenience they began to fence in the patches of wild hay and river-bottom grasses adjacent to their stores and stations.

The wild hay and the range grasses of Wyoming, selected by nature through untold ages of trial and error, nurtured by high altitudes and strengthened by cold winters, and in the mountain valleys watered by snows six feet deep on the level and six months in duration, were discovered to be unbelievably nutritious. One of Wyoming's favorite stories is that of the fabulous Texas cattleman who, migrating to Wyoming, lost his trail herd near the Chugwater in an early November blizzard and having settled gloomily down to bankruptcy in the then infant Cheyennes, found in the spring his lost herd, fat, saucy, and weighing a quarter more than when he lost it.

To this tentative business, begun by chance along

the Medicine Road, impetus after impetus was given by the increasing number of emigrants, the taking over of the forts by the government, and, much later on, the feeding of the Indians. Emigrants had to be fed, soldiers had to be fed, railway construction gangs had to be fed. The great Wyoming ranges were open and empty. Montana also was wanting cattle on its small, secluded, western mountain ranches. The Texas cattlemen began to divert some of their cattle from the Kansas shipping points and to extend the Texas trails farther north.

No one knows just when the first Texas trail herd came to Wyoming. Probably in '68 or thereabouts, for we have seen how two years earlier Nelson Story had gone up the Bozeman, straight through the Sioux and Cheyennes, with 600 head of longhorns for the Gallatin valley. But it took a while longer for the stock-raising possibilities of Wyoming to be fully realized. Once that was clear, the trickle of cattle turned into a flood. In 1871 over 600,000 Texas longhorns crossed the Red River in northern Texas headed north, mostly for the railway, but of this spate of cattle 40,000 came to Wyoming. Even this was merely a handful compared with what came later.

Meanwhile, Colorado had become a cattle country. Just as the Spaniards in the seventeenth century surely reached this half-southwestern, half-northwestern state, so the Texas cattle reached it first. The first northwestern cattle baron had appeared: John Iliff, a college-bred man from Ohio. Iliff took up his Colorado holdings in the early sixties, and at one time his herd was estimated at 40,000. In 1868, a year after that town had sprung full-armed from the brow of the plains, John Iliff drove a bunch of his Texas longhorns up to Cheyenne, but this was, of course, not a direct drive from Texas, like the drives that shortly were to follow.

The valleys of the Chugwater, of the Sibylle, of the North Platte and Sweetwater, all those lovely grasslands of southern and central Wyoming; the high summer pastures of the Medicine Bows and Sierra Madres to the south, began to see cattle, but over the divide of Teapot Dome, into the Powder River country, cattle could not go. That was forbidden country. Sioux coun-

try, made doubly so, and for good—at least that was the assurance—by the Treaty of 1868.

Even south of the dead line, life for that new Wyoming figure, the cattleman, was not always safe. Now that the buffalo were thinning out, nothing so pleased occasional marauding bands of Indians as to run off range cattle and slaughter them. This was both sport and an economic gain. The Great Spirit had no sooner restricted one form of manna than he had replaced it by a new. And so far as hunting was concerned, this new manna was as much fun as the old. These four-hundred- or six-hundred-pound creatures, with horns almost as long as their bodies and exceedingly pointed, ran as fast as buffalo and hated mankind, red or white.

The first Wyoming cowboys and cattlemen had to be scouts and Indian fighters in addition to their other duties.

Added to the risks of their ordinary life, the early cowman and cowboy had often, as Jim Bridger had advised, "to keep their scalps by thinking about them." There is a musical deprecation of this constant danger.

I saw the Indians coming, I heard them give a yell;
My feelings at the moment no tongue can ever tell.
And maybe you have a sweetheart to weep and mourn for
     you;
If that be your situation, although you'd like to roam,
I advise you by experience you had better stay at home.

As to what this new country looked like to the half-tropical Texan, there is another ancient lament.

Oh, I'm a Texas cowboy, far away from home;
If I ever get back to Texas, I never more will roam.

Montana is too cold for me, the winters are too long,
Before the roundups do begin, your money is all gone.

I've worked up in Nebraska, where the grass grows ten feet
     high,
And the cattle are such rustlers they seldom ever die.

And I've worked up in the Sand Hills, and down upon the
     Platte,
Where the cowboys are good fellows, and the cattle always
     fat.

But the badlands of Montana are the worst I've ever seen,
The cowboys are all tenderfeet, the dogies are all lean.

And work up in Montana is six months in the year,
When all your bills are settled, there's nothing left for beer.

Come, all you Texas cowboys, and warning take from me,
Don't waste your time in Montana, to spend your money
     free.

But stay at home in Texas, where work lasts all year round,
And you'll never get consumption from sleeping on the
    ground.

It wasn't all like that, however, and a good many
of the Texans saw Montana and especially Wyoming
and at once said, "This is home!" The grass and the
water and the snow mountains and the coolness delighted them, and it specially delighted the cowboy,
who intended to become a cattleman or the Texan who
was already a cattleman.

Nor was the cowboy always complaining of his
environment, although that is still one of his characteristics and he likes to travel south with the warmth, and
north with the spring. On the whole, however, he loves
country as much as the Indian does, and although he
has his favored sections, any country looks pretty good
to him so long as it isn't too crowded.

One of the loveliest of cowboy songs has to do
with John Iliff's Colorado country; it is called "The
Colorado Trail":

> Eyes like the morning star, cheeks like a rose,
> Laura was a pretty girl, God almighty knows;
> Weep, all ye little rains; wail, winds, wail;
> All along, down along, the Colorado Trail.

John Clay, a young Scotchman who became an
American and one of the great cattle buyers and stock
experts and ranch owners of Wyoming, describes in
his autobiography the approach of a trail herd months
out on the trail: "You see a steer's head and horns sil-
houetted against the sky line," he writes, "and then
another and another, till you realize it is a herd. On
each flank is a horseman. Along come the leaders with
a swinging gait, quickening as they smell the waters of

the muddy river. More cattle, more men, a small bunch of horses, a mess wagon with a tattered tarpaulin over it, drawn by four horses."

On the edge of the Powder River country, where the North Platte makes its swing to the north, in the Big Horn Basin to the west, along the Sweetwater, the cattleman waited during the first half of the seventies, adding his impatience to the impatience of the miner, the freighter, the stagecoach driver, the emigrant, the ordinary citizen, and the lusty and vocal Wyoming papers.

Across that dead line that encircled the Powder, the cattleman knew was some of the finest grass in the territory, and besides, the cattleman was being crowded. It doesn't take much to crowd a cattle country nowadays, and it took even less in the days of the open range with cattle pouring up from Texas and newcomers arriving daily from the south and east.

CHAPTER TWENTY-EIGHT

The Cowman! God Bless Him!

THAT used to be one of the favorite toasts, and
still is, at the annual dinners of Far Western Stockmen's Associations.

A marked peculiarity of the human race is its
ability to settle down to any form of danger and become used to it.

In 1914 the Stockgrowers Association of Wyoming asked for letters from its older members, and
those sent in constitute one of the most valuable of
frontier collections. Their persistent note—and it is not
merely the calmness of retrospection—is one of extraordinary and engaging sang-froid. And you must remember that the early rancher and cowboy was far less
protected than the emigrant or soldier had been. These
ranchers and their hands lived on isolated and increasingly outlying ranches and, except on drives or roundups, usually rode in twos or singly.

To understand how a man became a cowboy and
a cattleman, and what happened to him in those early
days if he settled in Wyoming, I can think of nothing
better than to quote from a few of these letters.

Here is a typical one from C. F. Coffee, dated
March 31, 1915, Chadron, Nebraska:

I consider myself about one of the oldest timers in the
cattle business. My start as a cattleman was very humble,

being a hired man, but a boss of other hired men. In 1871, when I was yet quite a young man, I hired out to D. H. & J. W. Snyder to drive a herd of cattle from Texas to Wyoming Territory. They were driving ten herds with about 1500 head to the herd. In those days driving through was a hardship, as we had to break the trail, fight Indians and scare buffaloes out of the way to keep them from stampeding our cattle. There were thousands of them [buffalo] after striking Kansas and Nebraska.

We had lots of fun with the early settlers while going along. They would catch us grazing or watering our cattle on their lands and would demand pay nearly every time. As I was stubborn, I got out of paying many times, but when I was met by fifteen or twenty men with shot guns, I would come through. Having but little money, I often settled with lame cattle—and didn't steal them back, either.

Well, we got through to Cheyenne along in August, after three months on the trail. As no one there wanted to try raising cattle on the plains, the herd, excepting about 1200 steers, fours and up, went on to Idaho. Those steers were picked from all the herds to get the number and John and Tom Durbin were the buyers. . . . The rest of those cattle went on to Ross's Crossing on Snake river, Idaho, and struck some nice snow storms. To a Texas cowpuncher who had never seen snow, it looked like "the other place" on the plains.

That winter I went back to Texas and in 1872 the same parties drove only three herds, one of which I had. We got through to Cheyenne all right and sold one herd to J. H. Durbin, one herd to Judge J. M. Carey and one to F. M. Phillips, who lived close to old Fort Laramie on the Laramie river. I had to deliver and turn over the cattle to him and I had a time with the tally, as the Snyders wanted him to take the Texas tally and he would not. So I tallied out and they did not tally with the Texas tally—less yearlings, more two-year-olds, and so on, making quite a difference when he had to pay for them. As they were fairly well classed I could do nothing but hold him to his trade. By the time I got the herd off my hands, the Snyders had bought about 10,000 cattle from the Dalton Brothers of Texas, and had to receive them at Ogalalla, so I had to go there and help tally them out.

When we sold to Durbin Brothers I had to deliver the cattle on Horse Creek. Durbin went through ahead with a wagon and planted some pine trees for us to drive by. He asked me to trail the cattle as long as possible so as to make a trail to travel by. We did, and that old road is there today.

One little incident I have never forgotten. When I was cutting ages, John Durbin wanted to know what I went by in telling a yearling from a two year old. I described the difference in their horns, so he said: "You go by the horns?" which I admitted. We were getting along fine until a big two year old came out and I called to him: "One two year old." Durbin says: "Hold, on, he has no horns and I call him a yearling." I had to let him go as such for I had lost my key.

I went back to Texas when the geese began to move. By that time I thought that I had better be getting into the cattle business myself. I hunted up a partner who had about as much money as I did, was a cow man and had been on the Chisum trail. A. H. Webb was his name. We bought a herd of cattle, about 1500 head, paid for part of them and gave notes for the balance. We made for Cheyenne in the summer of 1873. It being a panic year, we could not sell for as much profit as I wanted, so I held the cattle and wrote back to find out if they would hold our paper for another year. I was favorably answered—that they would if we would pay them two per cent per month or 24 per cent per year. That almost tickled us to death as we were paying three per cent per month for what we were getting at the Cheyenne banks.

So I located a ranch on Box Elder creek, 65 miles north of Cheyenne. There had never been a cow track in the country, so the grass was fine and cattle got fat. I got a contract to furnish about 60 cows a month and drive them to the post at Fort Laramie. I had a hard time but was paying up our notes. I did not know until then that I was so tough. I was from Texas but could wallow in snow at 30 below. By the next fall with what beef we had we paid off all our debts.

I remember that I sold steers to bullwhackers for work steers. As cattle men were afraid to scatter their brands in this way, I could get $25 more per head for them than they were worth. The road ran within about five miles of my ranch. I would go down when these bullwhackers came through, get the boss and ride among my cattle and he would pick out the ones he wanted. Then the trouble would begin. They wanted each wild steer necked to one of their tame steers. I would get a necking on a tame steer and rope a wild one and get my rope through the necking on the tame one and take a turn with my horse and pull them together—then they would tie the two steers together.

On that ranch the Indians kept us stirred up for five or six years. We carried guns on our saddles all the time and never thought of going to the spring after water without a gun in one hand a bucket in the other, and took guns along with us when we went to milk the cows. When I built the ranch house I made the windows so high that no one could shoot us in the night.

I stayed there until times got too tame for me, then sold out to Sturges & Lane in 1879 and bought a herd of cattle and moved north to where I now have a Hereford ranch in Hat Creek Valley, fifteen miles from Harrison, Nebraska. That was a fresh range and of course there were lots of hardships. We had to get all our supplies from Cheyenne, 175 miles away, and freight everything by wagons. As we had to bring heavy loads, sometimes it would take a month to make the trip.

Well, I have my ranch there yet, but I had to get deeds to the lands I occupy, as Uncle Sam and I could not agree. We came very near running together once. I thought I was the fellow who discovered that country but he sent a bunch out from Washington in 1883 and surveyed me out of house and home and told me what I could do. I wanted to treat with them but they would give me no red wagons so I had to take my medicine.

I lived quietly there until 1885. Then the Northwestern Railroad came poking in and brought the festive grainger. Then trouble did begin. It was not like the Indians for one couldn't shoot and the only way I could do to get even was to go into the banking business, so I am there. I also bought out a ranch on Raw Hide Creek in 1886 and am running cattle there now. I got so old that I have to have a partner, so the firm name of that ranch is Coffee & Tinnin.

Here is another letter, one from Hiram B. Kells, dated March 22, 1915, Denver, Colorado:

In '63 I quit the stage line and went back over to Fort Laramie and during the summer traded with the emigrants who were on their way to California and Oregon. I traded them well stock for lame stock, etc., and followed that up; until 1864. In the fall of '63 E. W. Whitcomb and I were putting up a lot of hay in Chugwater and cutting it with scythes, to feed our horses on that winter, right where the old station stands now. It was pretty tough, hard work, and I got tired one day, threw my scythe into a bunch of willows and told Mr. Whitcomb that if I could not make my living without cutting hay with a damn scythe, I would starve and so I quit my job.

In 1865 I went across to Fort Hallacker near Elk Mountain. In the fall of '65, E. W. Whitcomb and I came down the Cache le Poudre, Colorado and wintered.

In 1866 I went back over to Fort Laramie. In the fall of '66 I went down to Nebraska City, Nebraska, and bought six five-yoke bull teams and wagons, loaded them with groceries and provisions, and came back up to Horse Creek, forty miles below Fort Laramie, and bought out a man by the name of Tod Reynolds who had a little store there. I put my goods in it and fixed to stay there and winter.

That year Ed Creighton of Omaha was building the telegraph line across to Salt Lake from Omaha, and I got a contract for getting out telegraph poles for him. I sent my men up Horse Creek to Bear Mountain to get out the poles and hired two men with four-mule teams to haul them down to the store on the road. The Indians came along through the country up on the Laramie river and ran off a band of horses from different parties who were living on the Laramie at the time, and on their way across through Goshen Hole they ran across my two men loaded with telegraph poles. They killed and scalped the men, took their mules and went on. The next day after that there was a party of men from the Laramie river following their trail and they discovered where they had killed and scalped my men—it was winter time and the bodies were lying there frozen hard and stiff. They came down to my store and told me about it. I wanted to send word up to my men to pack up and move their teams and everything down to the store.

I had a little Indian boy living with me, so I wrote a note, gave it to him and told him to go up to the camp and I instructed him not to go by those wagons, for I knew that if he saw those dead men there he would come back without going to my camp so I told him to go around the wagons. But he had to go by the wagons and when he saw them he took the back trail and came back; so we got up a party and went up the next day to my camp and got my cattle and wagons and men together, and came back by the two wagons where the men were killed, loaded them on, brought them down to the store and buried them the next day. The Indians got so bad through the country that I had to move up nearer to the fort for protection, so I packed up, loaded everything on and left the store building standing by itself. It wasn't a great while until the Indians burned that down.

In '67 I bought some more teams from a man by the name of Kerr and took a wood and hay contract at Fort Laramie. That fall I sold my teams to Jim Porter and he loaded them with grain and stuff for the government at Fort Laramie, Fort Reno and Fort Phil Kearny.

In the spring of '68 I bought some teams, took a con-

tract for helping move the government posts Fort Reno and
Fort Phil Kearny down to Fort Steele in Wyoming. During
that time, just after I got back off that trip in the fall, I was
living on Horse Creek 25 miles north of Cheyenne. The
Indians came along and ran off 24 or 25 horses—all I had
except one.

In 1869, a man named John Richards and I took a wood
and hay contract for Fort Fetterman. We went up in the
spring and started in to work on our contract. He was to
put in the hay and I was to put in the wood. He had mule
teams and I had ox teams. During the summer he got drunk,
and riding along in front of the sutler's store at Fort Fetterman, he shot and killed a soldier who was sitting alongside of the store and then went with the Indians who were
on the war path. I was at that time camping on Deer Creek
above the fort some 30 miles. We were then working on the
hay. The Indians came along one day and got after my men
who were running the mowers and they all got into the
brush and willows and beaver dams and lay there two days
and came into camp at night as wet as rats. I could not get
them to cut any more hay, so I went to Omaha to the chief
quarter-master and tried to get the contract annulled, but
they needed the hay and he would not stand for it. The men
would not do any more work while I was away. I came back
down to the Chugwater along about December. I had to
hitch up my train and come over to Cache le Poudre in
Colorado, and bought the hay and had it baled and hauled
up to Fort Fetterman about 200 miles, all at $20 per ton.
I lost about $5,000 on the 100 tons of hay. I had William
M. Brown in charge of the train.

In July, 1870, I sold all my work cattle to a man by
the name of Pritchard. We loaded them right where the
Cheyenne depot now stands into the cars in one of those
little short chutes that they loaded and unloaded horses in.
They were the first cattle loaded and shipped out of Wy-
oming and went to Paris for beef, as it was the time of the
Franco-German war. I got $70 per head for them and
Pritchard got about $150 per head.

In the fall of 1870 came my first experience in the range cattle business. That fall I bought 200 head of two-year-old heifers on the Chugwater. I think I had about 10 Durham bulls with this bunch of cattle. The only range stuff in the country at that time was that of Bullock and Mills. Later Bullock and Hunton had a small bunch of cows below the mouth of Richard, known as SO ranch.

In the winter of 1871 and 1872 I got a government beef contract at Fort Fetterman. I bought my beef cattle to fill that contract from Ab Loomis, who lived on the Cache le Poudre in Colorado. They were mostly dry cows.

I stayed on the ranch then at Chugwater with this herd of cattle until 1884 and when I sold out to a Scotch company.

In February, 1873 the association was formed known as the Laramie County Stockmen's Association. [In 1879 this became the Wyoming Stockgrowers Association.] W. L. Kuykendall was secretary. The association was composed of the few stockmen in the country who had a number of herds in western Nebraska.

I will quote finally from a shorter and more atmospheric letter:

The business was very attractive in many ways excepting the risk and hazard of hard winters and Indian raids, which did occur in the early days. The winters were very severe on the herds of cattle and in 1884 the range losses were considerable, but with free grass and water, good shelter and no taxes, it took but a few years to work out of our losses and still have a profit in the business.

The calf-branding season was very interesting, and it took considerable riding to round up the cows and calves. When the large herds were brought from the south, they were all rebranded with the brand that belonged to the ranch. This was quite an event as it took many days to brand the large herds that were bought in those days and turned on the range.

The season for shipping beef cattle was also very exciting. Cutting out the beeves from the herds and driving them
to the railroad for shipment required considerable time. From
two to three months were consumed in the shipping of
beeves to Chicago, to which market most of the cattle went
at that time, although some were sold in Omaha.

CHAPTER TWENTY-NINE

Leather Pounders

So I'll sell my outfit as fast as I can,
And I won't punch cows for no damn man.

THAT's what he said, the combined and epitomized hero of "The Old Chisholm Trail," the greatest of cowboy classics, and he said a lot of other things as well, too many to quote.

He has left us . . . they have left us, for "The Chisholm Trail" was composed by any number of different shadowy waddies on the long trail up from Texas to Kansas . . . about a hundred quotable and respectable verses, and no one knows how many others. Even now, sitting around a campfire at night, men will make up new verses, that never reach publicity, pointing out the peculiarities of those in the circle, or referring to some incident, usually embarrassing, in their lives.

Sometimes the song becomes a round, each man taking it up as the other finishes.

And at the end of every couplet the chorus is supposed to come in, accentuated, tapping, like the fast trot of a horse or the stamping of boots.

223

Come-a ti yi yippy! Come-a ti yi, yeh! Come-a-ti yi yippy
　i-yeh!

or any other way you want to spell it.

All cowboy songs, except the sad, drawn-out
ballads, which usually celebrate the unfaithfulness of
women or the loneliness of the cowboy's life, have the
rhythm of a trot, a lope, or a pace; the last swaying and
overreaching a little.

"I went to my boss to draw my roll, he figured me
out nine dollars in the hole" sang the victim of "The
Chisholm Trail." He was constantly subject to man's
injustice and nature's uncertainty, also the vagaries of
livestock. For example: "he woke up one morning on
the Chisholm Trail, with a rope in his hand, and a cow
by the tail," and before the day was over, owing to a
thunderstorm and the subsequent stampede, "the tail
cattle broke, and the leaders went to hell," but the then
boss, who seems to have been an unusually just and patient man merely said, "Never mind, boys, you done
very well."

Nice of him, wasn't it?

Perhaps he was the famous "old Ben Bolt," who was
"a blamed good boss," although he had a habit of "going
to see the girls on a sore-backed hoss," and was a trifle
too "fond of his licker," for he "always had a bottle in
the pocket of his slicker."

Especially when he got to town, the drive over, was
the cowboy misunderstood. Two diverse elements met:
the cowboy and the gambler and other sharks who had
followed the railroads west. The latter were waiting for
the cowboy's pay. Even the so-called "forces of justice"
were inclined to resent the cowboy's pent-up exuberance
and the manifestations of lusty health and long ab-
stinence. It didn't matter, however, according to "The

Chisholm Trail." When the hero got drunk and "they
fined him ten," he "borrowed twenty and got drunk
again." And there was always some sympathetic girl
whom he knew and saw at long intervals; usually once
a year. This generic and epic female has been memoral-
ized.

> And I'll drive those cattle to the top of the hill,
> And I'll kiss my girl, by God I will!

Again and again, as in the verse that heads the
chapter, the cowboy was going to pull off his saddle and
sell his outfit, and quit for good. The idea that he could
. . . the idea that he was completely independent and
self-sufficient and could change his country and change
his outfit at will . . . was the mainspring of his character and philosophy, what had attracted him to cowpunching in the first place and often kept him there
long after, as a mature and sensible man, he should have
quit. But while he was young he didn't quit as a general
rule, and later on he seldom quit the country or some
connection with his former life. Either he settled down
and became a cattleman and rancher, provided he had
had enough sense to save some money, or, let it be stated
regretfully, enough adroitness and lack of conscience to
run his brand on a small bunch of someone else's cattle,
or else he went into some local business. Every now and
then he just dried up like a stand of good hay, that nobody had cut, and disappeared.

John Clay asks the question "has anybody ever seen
an old cowboy?" By that he meant that cowpunching
was a young man's job and that as men grew older they
usually drifted into something else. You do see them,
however, occasionally; old fellows who wouldn't do anything else no matter what opportunity offered. And invariably they have become very gentle, very ruminative,

very quiet and very philosophic. Long days of loneliness make a man that way, and the intimacy of stars at night, and the level suns of noon on the hills and the ranges. I once had an old cowpuncher working for me who was seventy-two and who, three times a day, out on the range summer-herding alone, had to stick a hypodermic needle into his arm for diabetes.

These old men have even got over being angry with the indecent obstinacy of cows and horses, with the wiles of men, and the profound if unsympathetic sense of humor of thunderstorms, snow, drought and freshets.

In the beginning no one in Wyoming or Montana knew what a cowboy was. By the late sixties those states had known every frontier type except the cowboy; trapper or mountainmen, miner, scout, soldier, bull-whacker, mule skinner, stagecoach driver, storekeeper, settler, but no cowboys. The small ranches springing up along the Oregon Trail and in the mountains of Montana were owned and run by men new to the cattle business, none of whom had begun as cowboys, and the lore of the open range, the technique of handling cattle on the open range, was totally unknown. And then startlingly up over the border rode this picturesque addition to the northwestern portrait gallery, this bucka-roo, with his traditions, his manners, his technical terms, his especial way of talking, and his knowledge of a hard-bitten and intricate profession. Diaries and letters of the time speak of how alien these young men from Texas seemed at first to the Northwesterner. The Northwest-erner didn't like them much. Presently a number of these strangers, seeing the good grass and water of the Northwest, settled there. Others, the less thrifty and perspicacious, hired out as hands in this new country, or drifted back to where they had come from. They taught

the little ranchers already on the ground how to run
their business and helped to build up the huge ranches
that followed the little ones, training the new generation
of native cowboys. For a long while the name "Texan,"
with the especial characteristics it was supposed to
imply, clung to these newcomers. In the Northwest it
is still the belief that a "Texan," despite his virtues, is
a bad man when drinking; a fiery man, a "knife man."
And from what I have seen, the belief is not without
foundation.

At all events, fifty per cent of Wyoming was built
by Texans and among its older inhabitants you can still
catch that slow, exciting drawl; gentle, a trifle edged,
like the small desert winds that often whirl unexpectedly into troubled weather.

And now for a final word about that perpetually
described, and usually wrongly described, professional
and craftsman of whom we have been talking.

The cowboy is almost as old as his companion, the
horse. He is as old as the tradition of the horseman, the
caballero, and he, too, has ridden straight down to us
through the centuries.

You can trace the cowboy—the cattle herder—
back to the Jews and Judea, back to "cattle on a thousand hills." Beyond that the cowboy is lost in the mists
of time.

From North Africa he moved with the Moors into
Spain; from Spain he moved with the conquistadores
into Mexico; from Mexico he drifted north to Texas;
and from Texas he drifted to our Northwest and into
Canada. Always he works with a horse, and in Mexico
and Canada and the United States with a rope. His
saddle rig and his clothes, however much they may
change in surface details, are based on use and experi-

ence and are as traditional as his calling. His saddle with its leather strings instead of buckles is made so that he can repair it easily with the leather punch that is part of his stockman's knife. His high-heeled boots are worn so that if his horse falls he will not be caught in his stirrup and so that, if he is roping on foot in corral, he can lean back on his rope and dig his heels in. His sombrero is the most practical hat ever worn; cool in summer, warm in winter, and waterproof. A thermos bottle of a hat. There are cowboys in Hungary, there are cowboys in France—in the Camargue, that strange country at the mouth of the Rhone—there are cowboys in Andalusia, just as there are cowboys in South America, in South Africa, in Hawaii, and lots of other parts of the world. Their costumes, their horses, their way of riding, their sombreros, are all so similar that at a distance you can hardly tell them apart.

The cowboys in the Camargue use a long pointed stick instead of a rope to handle their cattle; the cowboys in the Argentine use a sort of rope with weights on the end of it, called a bola. The cowboys in the Southwest and Mexico are still inclined to braid their forty-foot rope to their saddle horn. The cowboys in the Northwest use a free rope and take dallies when an animal is caught. But cowboys everywhere are very much the same; just as sailors everywhere are much the same.

They are profane because they deal with the incalculable idiocies of horses and cattle. They are narrow-hipped, even when they are fat, because they constantly ride. They are clannish. They are proud because their way of life, their secret expertness, makes them that way, and, even if they don't know it, because in the United States the Spanish influence is still strong with them. They are proud because they are completely independent, self-sufficient young men. They are feudal in their loyalty to the outfit they are working for, but it is the outfit, not the owner, to whom, as a rule, they are loyal. They speak of themselves as Bar H men, or Tumbling L men; and if they leave one outfit, within two days they are as loyal to the new one as they were to the old one. There is a famous Wyoming story of "Bar Y Harry who married the Seven Open A Girl."

They are vain, egotistical, sensitive, and uncertain temperamentally; they are polite, soft-spoken and trustworthy physically. In a physical crisis they will never quit you.

Everything about the cowboy is the result of a young man's having to be watchful, adroit, and self-preservative in a big country where a great deal of the time he is by himself. And this alertness, this necessity for close observation, before and behind and all around; this working with stock; this closeness with nature make the cowboy exceedingly witty. They are the wittiest Americans alive. Not wisecracking like the city man, but really witty. One of the chief delights of the Far West is its deep and pervading laughter, which, like all real laughter, is sometimes close to grimness and often related to the sardonic.

The cowboy—the Far Westerner as a whole—is one of the great storytellers of the world. He has had time to think, he has trained himself to observe, and his life has trained him. The country with its clear-cut details makes him see character clearly and perceive the underlying humor in most people and most incidents, even when both are a little horrible. And because he lives with animals, tame and wild, he has that subtle, hair-raising final perception of the sameness and unity, and yet diversity, of life that makes the genius of a fairy tale or a Disney cartoon. He sees that horses are people, and people are horses, and that both are queer.

Listen to a far western story: so filled with atmosphere, with touches of character; so apparently casual and rounded; but never a detail too much; and then wait for the sudden tying of it all up with the pointed, unexpected climax!

Nor can the cowboy disappear, nor change very much—not in essence. Not so long as cattle and horses are handled as they have to be handled in a big country. Cowboys are an essential part of an old and carefully graded and articulated business. To believe that they have disappeared, or will disappear, is like believing that jockeys will disappear, or bank clerks.

It is quite possible not to admire or like the cowboy as a class. As a class, his faults are as obvious as his virtues, especially to those ranchmen—the vast majority—who have been cowboys themselves. But the cowboy, at all events, has definite character; he is a person. A man of color and charm.

In a world that has lost its sense of good and evil, that has become gray in too many respects, the cowboy retains a great and reassuring far western virtue. Things, people, are blessedly black or white to him. Bad or good. If he says that So-and-so is "a so-and-so," he means it.

The "Senator" was as typical a son of Wyoming as ever lived, or ever will live, for that matter, although he, too, had started in Texas. He ended up as the biggest cattleman on the Powder—he owned a principality—and the most adored man in his state.

A tall, lean, sunburned man, so graceful that you hardly knew he was tall, and one who to the end of his days—I have already spoken of it—never lost the walk of a cowpuncher, quick and swaying.

The Senator had a small gray mustache, and gray direct eyes.

The Senator's father had been a Confederate officer from Virginia who after Appomattox became a southwestern cattleman, and when he was sixteen, the Senator first saw Wyoming. In 1879 he worked as a cowboy on a drive from Matagorda on the Gulf of Mexico to Powder River . . . in those days they never spoke of "driving" cattle, they always "trailed" them. Two years later he was back again, this time as trail foreman. He was only eighteen and had charge of about four thousand head. "And we were the only outfit," he insisted, "who never made up our losses."

A significant and technical note.

Trail foremen were supposed to report at the end of their journey just as many head as they had started with. You lose quite a lot of cattle on a drive like that. When the big Texas trail herds went through like sluggish rivers, the cowboys calling and chirruping and occasionally bursting into profound range profanity, the little scattered ranchers and the local cattlemen lay out at night with rifles.

There was just one way of making up your trail losses.

This time—the second time he came up from Texas—the Senator found himself with a fever. He nearly died. He lay in a chuck wagon, the flap tied back, and directed things from there. His second time on the Powder convinced him. The Powder had just been opened up. From then on, with a short interval in Colorado, he belonged to Wyoming. It was fine to watch his face when he talked of Wyoming.

The Senator had got his start by being different in some ways from most cowboys. For one thing, he didn't gamble; for another, he saved his money; for a third, he

studied around the campfire or in the bunkhouse, reading everything he could lay his hands on. In 1883 he
borrowed $150 and brought his own small herd up from
Texas, and settled in the Powder River country. The
final home he built there was called "Trail's End."

The Senator was considerably worried by eastern
manners. He thought them too abrupt, too brutal, too
crowded. Once I asked him if he got any exercise in
Washington. I suggested riding. He was amused. Most
old cowboys never think of riding as exercise. They
don't know what a "brisk canter" or "hacking for an
hour" means.

He was standing at the window of his office, looking out at the park that stretched to the Capitol.

"Well, Ah'll tell you," he said. "Ah always take
Saturday afternoon off, and Ah drive around in my car,
and every now and then Ah make just the smallest traffic
infraction. Nothing serious. Just a small one. And then
Ah wait and see how the traffic cop behaves himself. If
he's a nice young fellow, Ah tell him who I am, and
write a note to his chief. If he's a bully, Ah give him a
little lecture on good manners, and how much they
help." He sighed. "Most people are all right," he decided.
"They're just bothered. They're like livestock. Crowd
'em—they're mean. But if they'd just be quiet, it would
help a lot."

There's a story that the Senator wishing, upon a
certain occasion, to teach one of his outfits not to waste
its money, and having heard it was doing so, strolled into
a bunkhouse and to the surprise of everyone joined
quietly a game that had been going on for a week of
nights. The Senator didn't gamble, but if necessary he
could play cards as expertly as he did everything else.
By dawn he had cleaned his outfit down to its last dollar.

"There!" he said, getting to his feet. "You boys

are going to be sure sleepy today! . . . Well—Ah hope Ah've taught you something."

It was the year before the Senator first saw Wyoming that the Powder River country was opened up. The dead line had at last been swept away. The cattleman and his cowboys began to drift north across the Teapot Dome Divide. The Sioux, with the exception of a few remnants left in Montana, were back on their reservations in the Dakotas. The Cheyennes were tamed. The buffalo were almost gone, even from eastern Montana. By 1882 they were gone from eastern Montana as well. The Powder had become a white man's country, and was entering upon its second epic period.

The Wyoming cowboy, the northwestern cowboy, began to build his own customs and traditions. Began to have his own songs. All of them based on the same general faith and the same general habits, but altered by local conditions, and then, within the circle of the Northwest, altered again. The Northwesterner is different from the Southwesterner. Looks different, dresses differently, talks differently. But by the same token, the Oregon cowboy is different from the Wyoming cowboy. And in Wyoming, the western mountain cowboy is different from the cowboy of the east and the Powder. Just as the Montana cowboy is different from the Idaho cowboy. And the Arizona cowboy is different from the New Mexican.

For ten years the drift from Texas, after reaching Cheyenne and spreading out north to the Platte, had paused. Now it began to flow again, and Cheyenne took its place in chronicle and song. Became in its turn a point of departure; a starting place.

CHAPTER THIRTY

I'm Leavin' Cheyenne

TEXAS taught southern and south central Wyoming; southern and south central Wyoming drifted over
onto the Powder when that country was opened up, and
on the Powder more than anywhere else, perhaps, the
northwestern cattle business reached its epitome. Wyoming and the Powder taught Montana when, in the
eighties, eastern Montana also ceased to be a buffalo and
Indian country and the small mountain ranchmen of
western Montana spread down through the plains and
had to learn the ways of the open range.

There were cattle in Montana before there were
cattle in Wyoming, but mountain ranches are different
from big, open-country ranches, and when Wyoming
became a cattle state, because, as I have said, it is such
a single-eyed, lucid state, it became the leading cattle
state of the Northwest, and still is. Not in actual numbers. Wyoming never has had as many cattle as some of
the other northwestern states, but Wyoming became
the symbol of the northwestern cattle business and the
northwestern cowboy. Consequently the Wyoming
Stockgrowers Association, when it was organized in
1879, speedily became the most powerful stockgrowers'
association in the Northwest. There were no other interests in Wyoming, mining and so on, as there were, for
example, in Montana, to interfere with the stockman.
The Wyoming railroads and the Wyoming stockman
worked hand in glove.

Only nature, and man's cupidity, and man's dishonesty, interfered with the Wyoming stockman.

The open range didn't last long; it couldn't. The interest on your money was too high; the life was too alluring and, in most ways, too easy; the handling of cattle was too negligent and grandiose.

A bonanza is nothing more than a discovery plus a couple of delusions. The discovery is that somewhere someone is making more than the ordinary per cent. The first delusion is that without experience, without thrift, without qualifications, and without work you can make money in the same way too. The second delusion is that there is no such thing as the law of diminishing returns. The latter is based on what lawyers call choplogic. If one egg is good for you, then twenty-four eggs are twenty-four times better. But they aren't!

No matter where a man goes, no matter how far off he settles, if he does well, before long he's crowded. You can crowd a big country with much fewer people than you can a small country. A big country is made for big business.

For a little while—for ten years perhaps; from somewhere around 1868 to 1878—there was a sort of paradise between the Colorado line and the North Platte; and then—for five years longer—there was another paradise along the Powder. Here was all the space of Texas with luxuriant grass and abundant water thrown in. Presently the whole world began to hear about this.

And what a life this country promised, especially for young men who didn't know what to do, or whose families wanted to get rid of them! And what a return on their money it promised to old men who wanted to invest with the chance of fabulous and quick returns!

All you needed was a ranch house, a couple of bunkhouses, a few corrals, a field or two of wild hay to cut for your work stock in winter. As for the rest of it, the horizon much farther than you could look was yours. You turned your cattle loose and saw them only twice a year: at the spring roundup when you branded your calves; at the fall roundup when you branded what had been missed in the spring, and cut your beef and shipped it. And, miraculously, each spring your herds had almost doubled.

Nor did you have to live on your ranch except at the pleasantest and most exciting times of the year. You could go where you wanted in the winters, and in summer, after the spring roundup, you could retire to the cool porches and cooler bar of that delightful organization, the Cheyenne Club, while back on the ranch there were always experts, frequently Texans, to do the real work. Finally, as if to lead men on, for a while the winters were mild.

No one unless he has figured the increase of a herd of cattle realizes, barring accidents, the arithmetical progression involved. Compound interest is small potatoes in comparison.

For fifteen years the stockman of southern and eastern Wyoming, like Adam in the Garden of Eden, pursued his profitable and spacious life. The great days of the open range were on; the handful of cattlemen who were first on the scene were making thirty and fifty and seventy-five per cent. You could buy a Texas steer delivered at $5 and in four years—no selling of two-year-olds then—the same steer was worth around $45. A $40 net on an original investment of $5. At least, that's the way it figured out on paper.

By the eighties the bonanza was in full swing. Adventurous young men from all over the world, from

New York, from Boston, from Philadelphia; from every part of the East and Middle West; the younger sons of English earls; the second sons of Scottish lairds, even adventurous young Frenchmen, were pouring into southern Wyoming and the Powder River country. The Powder, that only four years before had been Sioux country, began to see feudal estates.

Cheyenne resembled a mining town and Wall Street combined. The Cheyenne Club buzzed nightlong with excited talk. Young men with prominent names from all over the United States, from half a dozen European countries, dreamed visions, piling them one on top of another like poker chips. And moving among these young men, quiet and watchful, was a nucleus of solid and experienced cowmen.

By 1884 there were twenty great cattle companies operating south of the North Platte or along the Powder, half of them of Scotch or English origin, their capitalization somewhere around $12,000,000. Here are the names of a few: Anglo-American Cattle Company, North American Cattle Company, War Bonnet Live Stock Company, Belle Fourche Cattle Company, Horse Creek Land and Cattle Company, Powder River Cattle Company. By 1886, the last year of the bonanza, not counting the more numerous American companies, there were eleven English and Scotch companies in full bloom throughout the Far West, controlling 3,391,072 acres of owned or leased land, capitalized at $19,000,000 and running over 700,000 head of cattle. For a year or two these companies, if at all properly managed, paid dividends ranging from twenty to ten per cent.

To quote John Clay again, speaking of the Scotland of that period—hardheaded Scotland!—"Drawing rooms buzzed with the stories of this last of bonanzas, staid old gentlemen, who scarcely knew the difference between a steer and a heifer, discussed it over their port and nuts."

The English with their national desire to obtain something for nothing—not to mention Americans—were engaged upon one of their periodic South Sea Bubbles, from which, with their equal genius for self-justification, they would eventually emerge with the solace, at least, of blaming somebody else.

The prospectus of the Ranche 71 Quarter Circle, an English company, began in this fashion:

Wyoming is termed the Bonanza cattle territory, and cattle are driven to it from every pasture district in the Union, even from a distance of twelve to fifteen hundred miles. Here they attain the maximum of growth and fat and the perfection of quality on the native grasses alone (for they are supplied that food at every season), and when fatted they are already within the area of the market, and subject to no deterioration in weight and quality from prolonged transit prior to sale.

Watching all this were the usual, but as always, rare, tongue-in-the-cheek observers, including Bill Nye, at the moment running the Laramie *Boomerang,* now the *Boomerang-Republican.*

The original Texans, the handful, that is, that had brains and ambition; the few survivors of the Oregon Trail; the men who had come out from the East or from Iowa or eastern Nebraska in the sixties and seventies, some of these lost their heads too. Others sold out at exaggerated figures and pocketed their gains and left the state. But a number stayed and weathered the bonanza, like the Carey family of Wyoming and the Kohrs of Montana. The Kohrs and Careys are still ranchmen. Conrad, the first Kohr, began as a small butcher in Alder Gulch in western Montana and by 1866 he was beginning to buy cattle. When he died he was one of the mightiest cattlemen of the Northwest. The Careys became a great feudal family and went in for politics, governors and senators almost by divine right. The Senator, too, weathered the bonanza. He was just on his road to success. As is always the case, a number of other practical ranchmen were better off when the bonanza ended than when it began. Bonanzas are winnowing-out processes, but they are hard on the majority.

The Careys, the Kohrs, and people like that stayed on their ranches, or at least were in constant touch with them, winter and summer.

Very early in life I saw a bonanza—an apple bonanza. I saw a magnificent cattle country plowed up—almost every acre of it—and turned into fruit farms. For months, wanting to be a cowboy, I lay on my stomach and helped plant thousands of seedling apple trees. My eyes were filled with dust.

Fruit is all right, but there can be too much of it, and even with fruit you have to be a fruit man in order to raise it. At all events, early in life, because of fruit, I learned that no man can make solid money without

someone working for it . . . invariably, unless he's
rich, himself. I learned also that long-distance ranching
doesn't pay. Furthermore, I learned that even in fruit
communities a certain degree of space is necessary.
Finally, I achieved the conviction that the ultimate and
only salvation of the world lies in an intelligently self-
restricted population, properly informed as to where it
should go and how it should live.

Through all of this . . . through the tumultuous
and seething small town of Cheyenne, up and down the
great cattle baronies of the Chugwater and the Sibylle,
the Laramie and the Sweetwater and the Powder . . .
moved the insouciant figure of the cowboy, content,
unless he was troubled by the maggot of ambition, if
he could work for a good outfit in the summer and had
a friendly ranch on which to spend the winter.

Cheyenne was his jumping-off place.

One of the most haunting songs of the West, that
is, the curious music of it and the shuffling single-foot
rhythm, takes us out of Cheyenne and north:

> Good-bye, old Paint, I'm leavin' Cheyenne,
> Good-bye, old Paint, I'm leavin' Cheyenne.
>
> I'm leavin' Cheyenne, I'm off to Montan;
> Good-bye, old Paint, I'm leavin' Cheyenne.
>
> Old Paint's a good pony, he paces when he can;
> Good-bye, old Paint, I'm leavin' Cheyenne.
>
> My foot's in the stirrup, my bridle's in my hand;
> Good-bye, young lady, my horse he won't stand.
>
> Good-bye, old Paint, I'm leavin' Cheyenne;
> Good-bye, old Paint, I'm leavin' Cheyenne.

CHAPTER THIRTY-ONE

Castles on the Powder

"I fell asleep in the very act of building castles in
Spain."—Gil Blas

Bᴜᴛ bonanzas are glamorous while they last.

And this was a particularly glamorous bonanza
because it was based on a hardy and multicolored life.

These young men from the East, from England,
from Scotland, even from France, were adventurous
and sunburned and laughed easily and were filled with
life. And the young Texans, if grimmer, were also filled
with life. In the early spring the rich young men turned
up in Cheyenne, spent a glorious week or two in the
Cheyenne Club with its famous engraving of Albert
Bierstadt's "In the Heart of the Big Horns" and its
copy of Paul Potter's "Bull," a bullet hole through its
stomach, and then drove, sometimes two hundred and
fifty, sometimes three hundred miles, to their ranches.
Once there, they rode for a month or so on the spring
roundup at the head of their cowboys and foremen like
Arabian princes on the march. Then they came back to
Cheyenne for a summer of tennis, flirtations, and endless talk and dinners. In the fall they went to their
ranches again for the beef roundup and the hunting
that followed.

Bronzed, big checks in their pockets, they de-
scended upon the Cheyenne Club for the third time
when the plains were gray with frost and the moun-

tains stripped of leaves, and after a week or so of re-
union, departed for the East or England or the Riviera.
No wonder they were figures of admiration and enchantment to their families, their sweethearts, and especially their youthful male relatives. The uncle I have
referred to was like that. I remember him well. A tall,
graceful young man with a short beard.

Presently the cowboy, too, became almost anyone.
He was no longer exclusively a Texan, or a boy brought
up on the frontier when the frontier was Nebraska or
Missouri. Sons of dukes, sons of millionaires, might be
cowboys. Some young men preferred to work as cowboys, in the way that, during a war, there are always
a number of men who prefer to be privates. Other
young men lost their capital and were ashamed to go
home. Still other young men, mature ones as well, had
fled from home and were hiding their identities. The
wisest of the lot were young men who, starting with
or without capital, realized that to become a cattleman
it was better first to be a cowboy and learn the business
from the ground up.

There are still plenty of young men who don't
want to be anything but cowboys. I had a young man
like that working for me several years ago. He was the
son of a rich ranchman farther to the west, an ex-
United States senator, but he didn't want to be anything but a cowboy, although he was married and had
a couple of children. The life suited him, and he was
entirely content with the forty dollars a month a cowboy draws down.

Well—there's something to it! Like being a private
rather than a general! You have all the fun—if there
is any—and none of the responsibility. It's nice to wake
up in the morning with nothing on your mind but a
cow, or perhaps a small and docile party of dudes.

I wish there were words to convey the extraordinary metamorphosis that had set in. Twenty years before, the Medicine Road had been the dusty path of sweating and bearded emigrants. Only around Fort Laramie and the other bigger forts, with the officers and their wives, had there been any sort of urbane existence. In 1867 Cheyenne was a clapboard railway miracle. Thirteen years later, with the coming of the great cattle companies, Cheyenne was one of the most cosmopolitan small towns in the world. The Cheyenne Club boasted that it had the best chef and steward in the country and that its club book was a roster of eastern and European aristocracy. The Cheyenne Club was the first club in the United States to have electric lights; Cheyenne, the second city.

On those dark-blue, soft Wyoming summer nights, Capella rising to the east, the planets large and still, the young men down from their far-flung ranches, the porches and the bar and the dining room of the Cheyenne Club must have been something. Different from other clubs. Back of all the talk was the impetus and eagerness of youth. Back of all the nonsense was strength and adventure.

Nowhere did this life reach a more spectacular height than on the Powder, once the dead line was down; once the cattle moved. The Powder was a lovely, virgin country. It had everything; grass for its stock, mountains in its back yard, lots of game. The little towns of Buffalo and Big Horn were beginning to function; in 1882 Sheridan was founded.

Englishmen were especially fond of the Powder. Perhaps that was partially due to the fact that the Powder was opened up just at the beginning of the bonanza when young Englishmen and Scots were pouring into the West. The West would have lost a lot of its

best ranchmen, and considerable amusement and un-
diluted joy, and not a little irritation, if it hadn't been
for Englishmen.

Moreton Frewen and his brother, Richard, quietly
spectacular and assured, appeared. Moreton Frewen,
the father of Clare Sheridan. Moreton and Richard
Frewen managed the Powder River Cattle Company.
In 1885, the year before it began to go under, the Powder River Cattle Company, whose brand was the famous 76, still a Wyoming brand, ran sixty thousand
cattle on the Powder, the Tongue, and on Rawhide
Creek. Moreton Frewen and his brother controlled a
kingdom; a huge tract of land that ran down almost to
the Teapot Dome Divide and took in what was to become the notorious Hole-in-the-Wall country. They
had their line camps out all along the Middle Fork and
South Fork of the Powder. The Frewens, with their
sense of heraldry, named, because of its neighboring
formations, Castle Creek near Teapot Dome, and a
rock there is called "Frewen's Castle."

The Frewens, like a good many of their magnifi-
cently distant neighbors, built log cabin home ranches
that were like royal hunting lodges. They gave a number of hunting parties in the fall, and house parties in
the summer. In order that their guests might reach the
ranch quickly from the nearest railway station, two
hundred and fifty miles and more south, they kept relays of horses on the road up to the Powder and brought
their guests in on a gallop. They used these same relays
to bring hothouse flowers up from Denver so that their
lady guests could have corsages for dinner. The more
imaginative guests must have paused every now and
then and looked about them.

Candles on the table, and women in evening dress,
and the shining walls of the big log rooms, and then,

to the west, the shadow of the Big Horns, and all about the endless Wyoming night!

Seven years before, Sioux and Cheyennes had camped on the very spot. Seventeen years before, Carrington and his men had marched up the Bozeman Trail, and a little later through the desolation of a December blizzard, Portugee Phillips had ridden. Those white-faced ghosts shoveling on the snow-swept stockades of Fort Phil Kearny would have been astonished had they foreseen the lights of the 76; of the Powder River Cattle Company.

All those great original ranches are gone now. Hardly a trace of them is left. Clare Sheridan, the well-known English sculptress and writer, came to the Powder River country looking for the site of her father's ranch house. She had difficulty locating it.

Around Goose Creek, in a lovely fold of the Big Horns, a little north of the site of Fort Phil Kearny and the Fetterman massacre, a colony of young Scotchmen and Englishmen took up ranches. Many began as cowboys or sheepherders, taking any job that offered. Most of them are gone now; a few, either the original owners or their descendants, are left; Americans by this time and, because of virtues which survived bonanza, open range, and the winter of '87, nowadays among the most prominent of Wyoming citizens.

On the Powder—that is, in the Powder River country—there was an Englishman, a big cattleman, who was supposed to be the son of Edward VII, then the Prince of Wales. Certainly he resembled him. On the Powder there were the thirteenth and fourteenth sons of a Scotch baronet, uncles of a Scotch duke. The thirteenth son had gone to Oxford; the fourteenth son, the family educational budget being exhausted by that time, had to go without an Oxford degree. Both came

to the Powder as young men; the fourteenth son is still
there, a leading ranchman. The thirteenth son, after
years in Wyoming, went back to Scotland to write the
history of his clan. To the Powder as a young man came
an Englishman who started as a cowboy, became an
American citizen, served in the Wyoming legislature,
and years later, through the death of an elder brother,
rather against his will became an English earl. He discovered that once an earl you are always an earl, and
that trying to resign from being an earl is like trying
to resign from having been born. He is now an English
earl, but he spends a great deal of his time in Wyoming.

On the Powder today, that is, in the territory
around Buffalo and Sheridan, and all along the Big
Horns, are some of the loveliest ranches in the West.
Astonishing ranches! Some of them have Italian gardens.
Back of them are the great shaggy peaks, clouds about
their summits.

On the Powder for a number of years in those
early days, as the country's leading peace officer, was
the nephew of an Oklahoma senator. A tall, dangerous,
handsome fellow who had left the Southwest for excellent reasons and was not using his own name. Years
later, after any number of adventures, he died down
in Oklahoma as one of its most prominent and most
respected citizens.

Over in the Big Horn Basin was an Austrian arch-
duke, using a short and simple German name, who
became a big cattleman and eventually shot himself by
accident while carrying a shotgun over a fence. Up in
Montana, Pierre Wibeaux, the Marquis de Mores, that
odd dreamer, was laying his plans for a great cattle
kingdom and packing industry, and building his fantastic castle that still stands grotesque and lonely on its
naked plains. In Colorado, the Earl of Dunraven was

also planning a principality which, because of his arrogance and restlessness, came to no more successful end than his determination, decades later, to lift the America's Cup.

Sir Horace Plunkett, who became Ireland's most famous agriculturist and land reformer, owned the E K ranch. William Haywood, an English writer, the L 7. Stewart Wortly, the son-in-law of Admiral Schley, the Bar C. There was hardly a city of the East or Middle West whose better known families hadn't a representative somewhere around Cheyenne, or on the North Platte, or on the Powder. In the list of owners, managers, or stockholders you come across such names as Oelrichs, Agassiz, Teschmacher, Quincy Shaw, Higginson, Henry Cabot Lodge, Blair of Chicago, de Billier; dozens of others.

Englishmen, Scotchmen, graduates of eastern universities, Texas cattlemen, a few old-timers from the Oregon Trail, young quiet businessmen, youthful lawyers and bankers and merchants, were pushing in; Texas, Wyoming, and Montana cowboys; a sprinkling of badmen; speculators, buyers . . . that was the Powder during the bonanza.

A friend of mine—although this was up in Canada, not on the Powder—once had as cook a mature, unshaven, gruff fellow who hardly ever spoke a word. One day my friend came back from town with a packet of peculiarly good tea and gave it to his cook. The cook—forgetting himself—looked at the packet and said, in the then accent of the Guards, "By Jove! That's the first decent-looking tea I've seen for yeahs!"

Another friend of mine told me that when he was working as a young cowpuncher there came to the ranch house on foot a tall, dusty Englishman, under his arm a little sewing machine. He asked for work.

"Ranch work?" asked the owner.

"No," said the Englishman. "I'm tired of that. Sewing is what I want. I'm rather good at sewing. I'll keep all your clothes, and saddles and things, and everybody else's in order."

And he did, with contentment, for five years—

mending bridles and saddles, and torn overalls, and shirts, and towels.

At the end of five years he turned up for supper one night and said, "Sorry! I got a letter this afternoon, and I'm afraid I'll have to be going. My father's dead, and I suppose I'm in for a title or something."

The Powder is knee-deep in stories.

The cowboy reached his apotheosis on the Powder. He retained his pristine attitude for a number of years. He still has a touch of it. But it never again reached the level it reached then. The real "waddie" would lift his hand to nothing but cowpunching, and if asked to do anything else, saddled his horse with quiet dignity and rode off to find some other outfit that wouldn't insult him by asking him occasionally to pitch hay or dig a fence hole or carry a stick of wood. The bona fide cowhands wore heavy gloves not only to protect their hands from rope burns but in order, as proof of their profession, to be able to take them off and show what was underneath. White hands and uncalloused palms were the signs of a cowboy, as much the symbols of caste as the present long Manchu fingernails of idle women. In the winters of the open range there was manual work for only a few cowboys, the rest drifted into the towns or else to hospitable ranches.

Moreton Frewen, unless I have been misinformed, is still living in London. At all events, until recently, in all the clubs of the East, and in London clubs, and every now and then a club in Paris, you ran across old men who had known the Cheyenne Club, and the North Platte, and the Powder.

Old men whose voices would kindle when they talked, as if they heard again, faint and far off, the jingle of spurs and the speech of ranches. Old men who for a moment saw again campfires in the high starlit dark, and heard the faint sounds and rustlings of bedded-down cattle. At the back of their eyes you could see, like little lanes of distant fire, the broad and lighted streets of Cheyenne.

CHAPTER THIRTY-TWO

Frozen Death

GARDENS OF EDEN, however, don't last long. Whatever goes up has to come down. You cannot have an open range, in the old sense, and have many neighbors. You cannot have any fences to speak of, or your cattle will drift against them in blizzards and die. Without fences cattle can drift for a couple of hundred miles and be all right in the spring. With fences, even a few, they pile up against them and stay there.

Any range, no matter how good, can be overstocked and fed off. Water in any far western country, except in the mountains, is small and far between. If there are many brands on the same range, or even a few, you must herd your cattle fairly closely during the summer and arrange for neighboring roundups that occur on the same date. If, in order to have fine and more valuable cattle, you eradicate the old range stock, wild animals not worth much but able to take care of themselves, and substitute blooded stock, Durhams, or white faces—Herefords, you have cattle that have to be well looked after and fed for part of the winter. And the more you take care of any kind of range cattle, the less they are able to take care of themselves.

If your cattle are more valuable, then you cannot afford winter losses, or occasional rustling, or any of the old, generous, spendthrift ways. And especially, as things tighten up, you cannot afford nonresident ownership.

These were a few of the problems that began to confront the cattlemen of eastern Wyoming and the Powder as the country became more crowded. . . . Crowded? Well, you know what I mean. The country is still uncrowded. But it takes only a few people, as I've said twice before, to crowd a cattle country.

A cattleman's idea of heaven, just plain ordinary heaven, is a range where everyone's stock except his own exercises continually an intelligent birth control. His idea of a seventh heaven is a range where there isn't any stock except his own. But the latter is hard to come by except in a country newly opened up, and then it is temporary.

The great ranches for the most part were run by managers and foremen, and one of the especial causes for the downfall of the big companies was the necessity their hired men felt for paying dividends, and exorbitant ones at that, in order to keep their jobs. A curious custom of the time, indicative of a bonanza, was what was known as the book count, or book tally, we have already come across. A man, or a company, bought a ranch with the stock on it, or, having a ranch, bought a bunch of cattle on the say-so of the owner without making an actual tally. As a result, the man, or the company, often paid for more cattle than they got. Left largely to their own devices, and well aware of the fact that they would be dismissed if they failed to meet dividends, the managers and foremen began to fall into the habit of selling off their seed cattle—the breeding stock —and the young cattle, in order to make their supposed profits, which, of course, is using your capital to pay your interest charges. Nor did it stop there. Some of the foremen began to acquire mysterious herds of their own. The business was overextended, overorganized, and overcapitalized. The range was crowded. And all that had happened in twenty years, and, where the Powder was concerned, in nine.

As if tired of man's foolishness, in the winter of '87 Nature spoke.

Old-timers still talk about that winter.

The summer had been a dry summer. Not much rain and little grass, and so the cattle came into the winter thin and in poor condition. The winter began

early. In October it snowed so heavily that a number of the smaller streams were feet deep in snow, and the snow never left them. December was a month of blizzards, and sometimes a blizzard, in the Far West, can last for twenty days or more. In January came the most fatal event of all, a chinook, one of those great soft wet southern breezes that blow unexpectedly for a couple of days and leave the range covered with a foot or two of water. Chinooks are exciting and delicious, but unusually deadly, unless they come late and there's an early spring. The water freezes above the snow and the most persistent steer alive cannot get down to grass. After that, blizzards, worse than the December blizzards, once more blotted out the world, and now a terrific wind blew night and day.

The thermometer at night was 40 and 50 degrees below zero. Even by day it was below zero. It was so cold, the wind so terrific, that often men did not dare

venture out for a week or so at a time. Sitting around
their fires in their snow-banked ranch houses, they tried
not to hear the sounds that occasionally came to them
from their corrals where range stock had drifted to find
the feed that wasn't there.

Among these dreadful memories there is a real
ghost story. A tale of ghostly cattle.

Little Falls, Montana, was a small village at the
time; a village beleaguered by the blizzards. One afternoon a storekeeper looking out of his window at the
endless snow, driven by the wind, saw coming down the
main street of the town, weaving and staggering from
weakness, falling occasionally not to get up, dark moving blotches in the eddying whirlwind. A hundred head
or more of range cattle! Drifting without knowing
what they were doing except somewhere near were those
mysterious creatures, men, who might in some way help
them, these survivors had struggled in from the blind
white range.

They were all that were left of a herd of five
thousand.

In the spring the cattlemen of the Northwest—the
Americans, the Canadians—found themselves in most
instances wiped out. The lucky ones sustained losses of
seventy and eighty per cent. Men who had entered the
winter with 10,000 head now had only 2,000. Companies with 50,000 head were lucky if they had 10,000.

The winter of 1887 would have killed the open
range even if speculation and crowding and dishonesty
and cupidity had not done so.

I know some old-timers who rode in the Powder
River roundup that spring. They say it was the quietest
roundup they remember. No joking, no singing, not

much talk. In every draw and along all the streams the cattle by the thousands were piled up.

Bones and hides and distorted, heaped-up carcasses . . . that was the Powder when the snow melted.

"I never again want to hear of the open range," wrote one great cattleman.

CHAPTER THIRTY-THREE

Lost Cabins

I SUPPOSE in all this talk of cattle, of cowmen and cowboys, it would be unfair not to mention the other types of men who were making the Powder.

That's the trouble with cattle . . . once you begin to talk about them, you don't want to talk about anything else! There are, however, always a number of men on every frontier who have nothing to do with cattle, who have no interest in them. And who, if they have to do with horses, don't ride them.

If it hadn't been for the freighters, the mule skinners, the two- and four- and six- and eight-team drivers . . . the bullwhacker and the ox team of the Oregon Trail, were already disappearing . . . the Powder wouldn't have got its supplies. And if it hadn't been for the stagecoach drivers, men who handled their two-span or three-span with the delicate finesse of someone winding an expensive watch, most newcomers to the Powder wouldn't have got there. In addition, the West would have lost a great deal of its accumulated philosophy and a number of its best stories, some true, the majority not, but all of them based on some absurd fourth-dimensional expansion of the truth.

If you trudge all day alongside of four or six or more mules, or if you sit up on your wagon seat guiding and talking to them, you have plenty of time to ruminate and to survey the landscape and reflect upon the peculiarities of nature, man, and beast. If you drive through the country at a steady fast trot or lope, passengers, many of them tenderfeet, beside you, your imagination is stimulated. You are likely to become not only the prize storyteller of your district, but you also collect the news in transit, observe how the ranchers are getting on, with their wives and in other ways, and day by day carry the open country into the town and the town into the country. The old-time stagecoach driver was a sort of Mercury, newspaper, minnesinger, first-aid and Homer rolled into one. The desire of the West to take facts and swing them about your head until they straighten out into something interesting found in the stagecoach driver its widest expression.

They are gone now, the stagecoach driver, the mule skinner, the horse freighter, their places taken by silent young men who drive trucks or talkative young men who drive automobile stages. But some of what was precious has been preserved. Machines also, in their own way, make you philosophic, and newcomers are newcomers, and the country remains wide enough for rumination.

An old stagecoach driver of my acquaintance died recently. His last words—he was delirious—were, "Turn 'em loose! It's all downhill and a shady road!"

The miner, however, hasn't gone, nor the mountainman. They are perennial types. Despite the fact that no real gold has ever been discovered in the Big Horns, there are always prospectors wandering about them, and in the recesses of those great hills there are still mountainmen. Farther to the west, in the wide mountains of western Wyoming, and in Idaho, there are plenty of mountainmen. But, after all, the Big Horns are over a hundred miles long and so even if three highways nowadays run across them into the Big Horn Basin, there's still room for mountainmen.

All miners are in a way mountainmen, and most mountainmen at one time or another have been prospectors, but there's a difference. Prospectors are looking for gold, even if their real purpose is not that but the pursuit of some lost crock at the foot of a rainbow. Mountainmen are hunting loneliness and independence. Usually they are bachelors, or if they have a wife, no one knows it; not even to any great extent the wife. Usually mountainmen live in a little cabin by themselves. Usually they are suspicious on first sight, a suspiciousness that hides a pathetic desire for conversation. They trap a little—that's their real business; hunt for meat, fish for dinner, go to bed at dark and get up incredibly early. They regard anyone who takes more than a temporary job as some sort of fool. If their suspicions are removed, their desire for conversation roars through like water breasting a broken dam.

If a mountainman can become the caretaker of an abandoned mine his life is complete. Mountainmen are, however, the direct descendants of John Colter and Daniel Boone.

All western mountains, gold-bearing or not, have their miners, and most western mountains have their tales of a lost mine. Like the trolls who haunt the Catskills, making thunder with their ninepins, so the story of a Lost Cabin Mine, or a Lost Gulch Mine, or a Lost Canyon Mine haunts most far western mountain countries. These stories are like the belief in a mother lode. Most prospectors believe in mother lodes even when they know perfectly well there are no such things. The details about lost mines are usually the same.

A lone prospector, discouraged, about to give up, starving, stumbles upon a stream or ledge shining with precious metal, or kicks with his foot a huge nugget. Worn out, almost unconscious, he manages to make the nearest town, fifty, a hundred miles away. When he is restored to health . . . sometimes he dies, which makes the search even more perplexing . . . he leads a party back to his golconda, but he is never again able to locate it.

Powder River has its "Lost Cabin." Powder River's Lost Cabin was supposed to have been found by seven Swedish and German miners somewhere near the South Fork of Crazy Woman while the Swedes and Germans were on their way south from the Black Hills in 1865. They shouldn't have stopped to prospect in the Powder River country in those days, nor would they if they had had any sense. Within a week—so the story goes—the Swedes and Germans had pickaxed out $7,000 worth of gold, and then the Indians discovered them and killed all but one. There must always be a survivor, of course. In this case the survivor was one of the Germans, and eventually this German made his way to the Montana gold fields, and in his pouch was the evidence of the strike.

Just as soon as possible the German led a party back to the base of the Big Horns. It isn't especially difficult country. The Big Horns are huge but they are self-respecting, tall-standing mountains, not interminable and jumbled. The party might have found this particular Lost Cabin if, just as they reached its vicinity, the German hadn't gone mad. Quite mad; waving his hands, laughing, running around in circles. His insane laughter has added itself to the tales of Jim Bridger, to Father De Smet's unfortunate remark, to old La Pondre's well-stuffed wallet.

The echo of the laughter still clings to the canyoned headwaters of the Crazy Woman. There's a little town in the Big Horns called Lost Cabin.

The windows of the ranch house were black opaque squares. Five miles from the western-facing windows were the Big Horns, but the night was so dark that even their huge shadow, except at the very crest, was lost. It was one of those portentous nights, edged with sheet lightning, that come in the Julys and Augusts of high mountain countries. Just outside the door, to the east, was the road up which Carrington had marched; the

road down which the men from Fort Kearny had retreated; the road up which Crook had pushed his way in the winter of '76.

The old-timer was quietly amused and sardonic as most old-timers are . . . either that, or else loudly and profanely sardonic. We had been discussing Lost Cabins in general and had come to the conclusion that the folly of mankind is incalculable. Then I asked about the Lost Cabin of the Powder.

The old-timer was leaning back in his chair, a pipe in his mouth. He sat forward and looked at me keenly. The old-timer was tall, thin, blue-eyed, and his white hair grew in a thick, vigorous patch. He was no longer smiling.

"I knew a lot of men who knew that Dutchman," he said solemnly. "I knew two of the men who came back with him. They'd have found it all right if he hadn't gone crazy. There's a party up looking for it now. Most every summer there's someone out."

His eyes were remote. He was looking over my shoulder at nothing.

"No," he said, "there's no fake about that mine."

The queerest little frisson went across my cheeks and up the back of my neck. I could feel my hair stir. It was a portentous night. Sheet lightning played along the summits of the Big Horns.

Had the old-timer proposed at the moment that we go to look for the local Lost Cabin, I think I would have followed him.

CHAPTER THIRTY-FOUR

Under the Earth and on Top of It

Bill Menor was tall and thin and had a drooping, sunburned mustache that once had been yellow. He was a retired cowpuncher who had ridden the Kansas and Texas trails. Across the river from him on an equally neat small ranch lived his younger brother Holiday, who had chosen his first name himself because his parents, in an unfortunate moment, Holiday having been born on that festival, had called him Christmas.

Holiday, naturally, hadn't liked that and so had substituted the nearest thing.

Holiday had a long black beard and was as excited as Bill was dour. Holiday was always finding something wonderful to plant or do—a new grain, Chinese, Siberian, or African, that would stand any amount of frost and needed not a drop of water. . . . "By gum, yes, Burt! You betch-you! Yes, sir, you bet!" . . . or else the exploration of a canyon no white man had ever seen. Bill wasn't afraid of any horse alive and would creep on, or over, or under them as if he and they were a lot of kittens frolicking. Holiday dreaded horses. He rode something so old and fat that it ought to have been in the opera, and when Holiday harnessed his equally fat and gentle team it was a ceremony of deft approach and respectful salutation on both sides. This caused Bill immense and Jovian mirth. On the other hand, Holiday, thanking God he had never been silly enough to be a cowboy, loved the bowels of the earth. Nothing pleased

261

him so much as to dig a well for a neighbor, his slowly descending bald head in constant danger of slipping earth and rattling stones despite the growing casing he put in as he went down.

Bill used to come and lean on the edge of the casing and regard Holiday's labors with amazement and alarm. Bill hated mining as much as he liked livestock.

After a long silence, Bill would take his pipe out of his mouth, and spit, and shake his head, and say:

"That dummed young fool is going to get hurt someday."

Holiday was well over fifty.

Into the country in which I live there arrives every summer a charming old gentleman with a square white beard. He comes in every June, and is rowed across a big lake, his supplies with him, by a forest ranger, and settles down until October in the neat cabin he has built in the loneliest spot in the world. It's a nice cabin, a good spring near by, and there are lots of books, especially Shakespeare. The old gentleman never sees anybody. There's nobody to see. Right back of him are huge mountains. The old gentleman is driving a tunnel into them. If you go over, the forest ranger says, you can hear him pickaxing at the end of the tunnel like one of the dwarfs in *Snow White*.

The old gentleman is well-to-do. Most prospectors aren't. They say the old gentleman has a fine house in California, and a wife, and a couple of daughters who travel about and often go to Europe. Also the old gentleman is well educated. He knows there's no real gold where he's prospecting, at least, none you can get at, any more than there's any real gold in the Big Horns.

But that doesn't bother the old gentleman. He comes into our country every summer. By now he has dug a tunnel three hundred feet long, straight into the living, but barren, rock.

The cattlemen of the Powder before long were to meet enemies more persistent and even more dangerous than blizzard and drought. First they were to meet men more or less of their own kind who preyed upon them, and then, when they had partially settled this question, they were to meet men of another kind who took up little farms right on their ranges and fenced their water holes and streams. After that they were to meet men who drove before them dirty-white, slow-moving animals with whom horses and cattle could not live.

PART FIVE

Next-door Neighbors

"*Here's talk of the Turk and the Pope, but it's my next door neighbor who does me harm.*"
Thomas Fuller, *Gnomologia*,
1608-1661

CHAPTER THIRTY-FIVE

The Fine Art of "Rustling"

RUSTLING," as used in the West, is a queer word. Like a good many far western words, it has several opposed meanings. If you say a man is "a good rustler," you mean he is energetic, a good worker, a good provider for his family. If you ask a man "to rustle" something, a log of wood for the fire, for instance, you mean will he go and get it. But if you say a man is "a rustler" and leave out the adjective you mean he's a thief.

A "cattle rustler" is a cattle thief; a "horse rustler" is a horse thief. And wherever there is wealth there is rustling, and wherever there is rustling there is trouble.

Cattle raising and horse raising are among the oldest businesses in the world, and almost as old is the business of stealing them.

In the generous, careless, and magnificent days of the open range there had been plenty of cattle rustling, and as John Clay states candidly and Bill Nye humorously, several proud families of the Northwest began, as in an earlier Texas, with nothing more than a running iron, a rope horse, an urge on the part of some young cowpuncher to prosper, and a couple of expert assistants plus a number of close-mouthed friends. No form of crime can survive, of course, without either the carelessness or the co-operation, usually both, of honest people.

So long as the valuables purloined were Texas longhorns and so long as there was plenty of room, it didn't make much difference. Nobody knew within several hundreds, and, with the big outfits, thousands, how many cattle he had anyway. And when cattle drifted across a range a hundred miles or more square, it was impossible to keep accurate count of winter loss, poison in the spring, and the depredations of wild animals. A certain amount of your cattle disappeared, and that was all there was to it. If some earnest and well-liked young fellow who had worked for you at one time or another suddenly emerged as a cattleman, you shrugged your shoulders and wished him luck so long as he settled at a discreet distance. It wasn't worth bothering about unless the young man got "too strong."

"Three years ago," wrote Nye in his Laramie *Boomerang*, "a guileless tenderfoot came into Wyoming, leading a single Texas steer and carrying a branding iron; now he is the opulent possessor of six hundred head of fine cattle—the ostensible progeny of that one steer."

Bill Nye made two mistakes. You didn't "lead" Texas longhorns. They either led you or else hooked you where you fitted your saddle, and it was no "tenderfoot" who did the supposed leading. The rustling of cattle in those days required expert knowledge; of cattle, of roping, of changing brands, of the habits of the outfit you were stealing from, and the topography of the country you were working in. The old-time cattle rustler was a top cowhand.

With the end of the open range, however, and the breeding up of cattle and the general tightening up of the business, the carelessness toward the rustler ceased. Even before the end of the open range the wiser and more far-visioned cattlemen had been buying their own land, and leasing their own range, and pre-empting water holes and streams. The longhorns, poor beef, subject to Texas fever, infested with ticks, hard to handle and ship, now that cattle cars were in use instead of trailing, were being replaced by thoroughbred stock. Moreover, the driving of cattle up from Texas was becoming more and more difficult. The farmer was spreading west; into western Kansas, into eastern Colorado. The old trails were being fenced off or marked with "No Trespass" signs. Legislatures were passing laws against the trailing through of the great herds. Each cow and calf and steer began to have its individual value.

And yet . . . and here is the catch . . . even today the range cattle business is a large and generous business and cannot be run without co-operation and mutual trust and an unwritten code.

There is the matter of estrays, for instance. Estrays are stock that have wandered from one range to another and are picked up in the fall and shipped to the market. It would be too much trouble and expense to return them to their own range. But at the market their brand is taken and presently a check arrives for their rightful owner. Cattlemen, for the most part, have always been honest and co-operative. Otherwise they couldn't exist. No matter how well guarded they are, range cattle have always been easy to steal and always will be. As a final hampering factor, there was, and still is, the code of the cowboy.

One of the oldest laws of the range is that you mustn't give away a friend; mustn't "sell him out." One of the oldest of cowboy beliefs is that friendship doesn't mean much when a man is riding high, wide, and handsome; it's when he's being trampled on that it counts.

In addition, and as always, there was a tendency to romanticize the criminal, and at least this can be said for the old-time rustler, he took his life in his hands; he had the outer trappings of a caballero. Besides, as a rule, a number of his enemies, not to speak of his neighbors and friends, had at one time ridden with him, been out—just two men—in line camp all winter, summer-herded with him, spent night after night with him in bunkhouses or playing cards in the nearest town. You hate to hang or shoot a man you've known so intimately.

Two incompatible loyalties and codes were meeting. The code of the loyal cowboy toward his outfit and its owner; the code between cowboys as cowboys.

But the cattlemen didn't romanticize the rustler, he set out to get him.

In popular esteem, horse stealing has always been different. It is too easy. A man turns the horses he is not using out on the range and doesn't see them from the beginning of summer until its end. Anybody can run horses off and they travel fast and far . . . clean out of a country. Horse stealing was looked upon as a lower order of crime, unless, as was often the case, it was merely a symptom of youthful exuberance as, in more civilized communities, undergraduate intoxication is. But in its more serious aspects horse stealing was very close to murder. To set a man afoot, if that was what you had done, in a lonely and sparsely watered country is to show a bland contempt for his existence. Horse thieves got hanged quickly and their profession was a term of contempt, which the term "cattle thief" has never quite been.

The history of Powder River during the eighties and the first half of the nineties was largely the history of the fight between the cattle thief and the cattleman; a guerrilla war to begin with, piling up until it flared finally into one of the most tragic and dramatic fiascoes in the history of the West. And as usual, this fight became confused. Became involved with issues that had little at the start to do with it.

The implications widened as the causes receded into the past.

Economic and social and political factors entered in. The fight became one between the man in possession and the newcomer wishing to possess. Between the man whose fortune was made and the man wishing to make a fortune. Between the small cattleman and the big cattleman. Between the ranchman who had a score of cowboys and the ranchman who had only himself and a son or two and maybe a hired hand. The fight, in short, became a class war, and when that happens the fat is in the fire and for a while all good sense is lost.

The moment it became a class war, this guerrilla war also became a political fight. That is bound to happen. Where economic and class issues enter in, political parties are eager to take sides.

The big cattlemen, the railways, most of the time the territorial government, were Republican. When the Democrats captured for a short while the territorial government and the unfortunate former Indian fighter, Moonlight, became governor, it only added to the confusion. The little cattleman, the homesteader, the federal government in 1885 and in 1893 under Cleveland, were Democratic. But the federal government, even when it was Republican, did not dare go back on the doctrine of "free land for everyone."

The doctrine of "free land for everyone," embodied in the various homestead laws, was the cruelest joke ever played upon innocent citizens by a timorous government. It was especially crippling to the West. The West is still staggering under this hypocritical burden. The myth of free land has complicated all far western policies and politics; has almost ruined the cattle business; and has made drifting paupers of thousands of American citizens. Had the government sold its land cheaply in the beginning and encouraged the thrifty settler to buy its own range, half the problems of the West, including erosion, would have never arisen or would, at all events, have been considerably less threatening. Nothing is free.

The Wyoming Stockgrowers Association invariably claimed that it was entirely a democratic organization, membership in which was open to any honest stockman however small his holdings, and that is absolutely the case today, but as a matter of fact in 1891 there were over five thousand brands in Wyoming and at the meeting of the association held in the spring of that year, a meeting we are coming to shortly, the most momentous meeting in the association's history, there were only forty-three names on the roll call and of these all but eight represented big outfits.

To add to the confusion the guerrilla warfare of the late eighties and the early nineties became a sectional war as well. Eastern Wyoming was divided into two hostile camps.

The word "rival" comes from the same root as the word "river," and it means no more actually than that people hate and fear each other because they live on opposite banks of a river. That shows about how much sense there is to most hate and dread. But the rivalry between southeastern Wyoming and northeastern Wyoming, between Cheyenne and the Powder, had back of it more valid reasons.

The winter of '87 had wiped out most of the big outfits up on the Powder. Not all, but the majority. The gay young men were gone. Southeastern Wyoming had, on the whole, been settled by earlier comers and more practical cattlemen. A good many of these survived the winter of '87 and the end of the open range. And they, and the few men like them left up on the Powder, were the elite of the Stockgrowers Association.

The North Platte was the dividing line. On one side you had the Powder River country; on the other you had the older country around old Fort Laramie and Cheyenne. Johnson County was arrayed against Laramie and Albany and Converse, and the other counties south of the North Platte.

Cheyenne was the capital of the south, the new little town of Buffalo was the unofficial capital of the north. The Cheyenne Club and the Stockgrowers Association were aligned against the general stores of Buffalo, Big Horn, and Sheridan.

With the majority of the big outfits out of the country, Johnson County as a whole was being settled by small men, many of them former cowboys of the big companies. Some of the louder mouthed of these boasted, and not always without justice, that they had been taught to be careless concerning brands and mavericks by their former employers. The big outfits still left up on the Powder were in a particularly parlous position.

More and more the small men, along with the newcomers, resented the attempt to hold the range and the water. As Johnson County became more powerful, the

machinery of the courts fell into the hands of the small
settlers, and the big stockman, local or otherwise, found
it almost impossible to convict a rustler, no matter how
clear the evidence. The less discreet residents of Johnson
County proclaimed this fact with much satisfaction.
Not a tactful thing to do.

Unless you have been a stockman, you do not know
what this constant preying upon you means, especially
if you can obtain no justice. It is like a gnawing illness.
Sooner or later, unless you are a very calm man, something is bound to happen.

In a letter of 1887, Harry Oelrichs, president of
the Anglo-American Cattle Company, writes: "The loss
through farmers on Hat Creek has been something
frightful. They have not confined themselves to killing
for their own use, but have killed wantonly. On one
stretch of a mile and a half on Hat Creek there were
over thirty dead cattle, each of which showed rifle or
pistol wounds." There were even instances where a
group of heavily armed men would ride into a camp of
one of the big owners whose cattle were being held for
branding or some other purpose and, before the eyes of
the cowboys in charge, would calmly drive off stock
claimed by the intruders as their own.

Most of the small men of Johnson County were
honest. Most of the big cattlemen were honest, but
on both sides there were men, of course, who were
not honest at all. Allied with the Johnson County
men, to their own hurt, were a number of former cowboys of more than shadowy reputations. It was not so
much that these men took advantage of the new conditions, as that the new conditions made their depredations more noticeable.

The most notorious of these men of shadowy reputations were two ex-cowboys, Nate Champion and

Nick Ray, or Rae. Just how much is true about these men, or how little, will never be known, but the big cattlemen around Cheyenne and the big owners on the Powder looked upon them as the leaders of what had now become known as the "Rustlers."

Champion, it was claimed, had been run out of Colorado for rustling. Ray was said to have killed two men down in Texas, and the story was that he had followed the big Irvine outfit from Nebraska into Wyoming when William Irvine decided to move his forty thousand head of cattle across the line. Ray, so it was said, had harried William Irvine for years, picking up unbranded cattle and driving off, where he could, small bunches of steers. Ray and Champion were accused of being leaders of a group of ne'er-do-well Texas cowboys who called themselves the "Red Sash Gang" because they liked to wear red sashes at dances.

Champion was a likable fellow, however, fearless, and the best gunman on the Powder.

The fact that the Northern Pacific was by now building its transcontinental line up in Montana did not help matters. The construction crews of the Northern Pacific needed beef just as much as when William Cody had been shooting buffalo for the construction crews of the Union Pacific. Stolen beef is as valuable as honest beef.

CHAPTER THIRTY-SIX

Cattle Kates

MYSTERIOUS "necktie parties" began to break
out sporadically on the ranges of eastern Wyoming, also
"dry-gulchings," as the expression goes when a man
leaves his ranch and is found dead several days later up a
canyon or a draw.

In 1889 Ella Watson and her man, Jim Averill,
were lynched . . . hanged, both of them, to the same
small cottonwood tree in a narrow rocky coulee down
in Sweetwater County near Steamboat Rock. Averill
ran a small saloon and store that was a rendezvous for
the tougher element among the cowboys. Ella Watson,
who had changed her name to Kate Maxwell, had a small
ranch near by, and it was the common belief, well sub-
stantiated, that her increasing herd of cattle was due to
the admiration of the cowboys who frequented Averill's
saloon. Kate Maxwell was supposed to trade her favors
for beef on the hoof. Both she and Averill were repeat-
edly warned, but it did no good. And so one bright
July morning a number of masked men took them out
and hanged them.

But it didn't end there. Averill was an educated
man and he was in the habit of sending open letters to
the Casper *Weekly Mail* denouncing the big cattlemen
as land-grabbers and range tyrants. Just four months
before his death he had written:

They are opposed to anything that would settle and im-
prove the country or make it anything but a cow pasture for

Eastern speculators. . . . They advance the idea that a poor man has nothing to say in the affairs of his county. . . . Is it not enough to excite one's prejudice to see the Sweetwater owned, or claimed, for a distance of seventy-five miles from its mouth by three or four men?

At once a certain element in Wyoming announced that Averill and Ella Watson had been hanged because, bravely and honestly, they had defied the big owners. The lynching led to several deaths. George Henderson, range manager of the 71, who was supposed to have been one of the leaders of the vigilantes, was shot by a cowboy named John Tregoning a few months later. George Henderson had been an "iron and coal" policeman back in Pennsylvania during the Molly Maguire troubles.

The fact remains, however, that both Averill and Ella Watson were bold and unrepentant cattle thieves.

Ella Watson . . . Kate Maxwell . . . gave her assumed name to the occasional ladies who, sisters in spirit to the present-day gunmoll, went in for cattle rustling. These women were called "Cattle Kates." There were none worthy of note on the Powder, but down in Colorado there was a very famous lady, a Mrs. Richey, known as "Queen Anne," daughter of a former prosperous cattleman and the divorced wife of a Wyoming school superintendent, who operated in a big way as late as 1922. Queen Anne, unlike most Cattle Kates and gunmolls, was an extremely beautiful woman, imperious and cultivated; only thirty years old. She was supposed to have been poisoned by a neighbor who just couldn't stand his losses any longer.

Another famous Colorado lady, operating on the Colorado-New Mexico line, was a Mrs. Green Newton. A more forthright lady than Mrs. Richey, although not so charming, Mrs. Green Newton was in some ways better equipped to face a wicked world. At the trial where she, and her son Orlando, and three fellow conspirators were finally convicted, court on one occasion had to be adjourned "until such time as Mrs. Green Newton can testify like a lady."

During the sixties, seventies, and eighties another famous woman, Martha Jane Canary—Hickok-Steers-King-Burke by marriage or courtesy, no less a person than "Calamity Jane," was in and out of the Sweet-water valley, the Black Hills, the country around Cheyenne, and the Powder River country when that was opened up. Calamity Jane was no rustler, that is, no rustler of cattle, although she took what she wanted when she needed it. It is a pity the motion pictures have made her out a beautiful woman. She was not beautiful, but in her own way she was most certainly somebody.

As early as 1872 a few men had met in Cheyenne to see what could be done about the increasing menace of horse and cattle stealing. In 1873 the Laramie County Stockman's Association was formed. In 1879 this became the Wyoming Stockgrowers Association.

The Wyoming Stockgrowers Association began immediately to organize the cattle business and the range. One of the first steps taken was to divide the cattle country into roundup districts and set dates on which these roundups were to occur. The "sooner," the man who jumped the accepted date, became an unpopular person, outside the law. To hold a private roundup ahead of the other owners of your district meant that you had an advantage where unbranded calves and other mavericks were concerned. You were regarded as a potential rustler, a possible "mavericker," and quite rightly. To the accredited district roundups the stock association sent its representatives who were the judges of any disputes.

The carrying of a running iron . . . a straight iron, usually with a small curve to its tip, capable of forming any brand . . . became an *ipso facto* proof of guilt. As a general rule a rustler, when he settled in a country, adopted as his brand one that would easily embrace several of the brands of the neighborhood.

The maverick question, which had grown to be a very vexing one, was settled, as far as it could be settled, by instructing the foreman of every roundup district to hold all mavericks found and sell them at auction every ten days during the roundup. The money obtained was turned in to the stock association to help pay its expenses. A maverick when sold was branded with the brand of the purchaser and the brand M, the maverick brand of the association. It was illegal to brand any stock between the middle of February and the date of the spring roundup.

The old excuse that you couldn't help it "if someone else's calf sucked your cow" or you couldn't bear to see "little fellows wandering around unclaimed and untended" no longer worked.

In the comparatively peaceful, uncrowded days when the stock of only one outfit ran on a certain range, the maverick question had settled itself. It was taken for granted that calves followed their mothers, and in the case of dogies, or orphan calves, that the calf would follow its herd. The unwritten law of the "accustomed range" was in effect. That is, you branded all calves on your own range. But as soon as two or more outfits began to use the same range this unwritten law no longer worked. The herds got mixed, and maverickers, dishonest owners, or rustlers, or ambitious cowboys, found things too easy for them. You could separate calves from their mothers and hold them until they could no longer find their mothers; you could slit the tongue of a calf so that it would no longer suckle and so, eventually, would stop following its mother. And even honest owners found themselves in dispute as to the ownership of strays.

In addition to the inspectors sent to the roundups, the association, in co-operation with other state associations, instituted an elaborate system of inspection at shipping points and at the markets in Omaha, Chicago, and Kansas City. To this was added a state brand book in which all brands were registered. Nor could you register a brand without the permission of the association, or, later, the State Stock Commission. Brands that were too similar and too easily changed were not encouraged, especially in the same locality. A man who applied for a B C, for instance, in a country where there was a C, was told to think up something else. An O F Quarter Circle was regarded askance in a C F district. A Ladder W was not considered good manners, nor was it registered, where there was an H W. Brands became more and more elaborate. There was one in Texas known as the Backhouse. A famous changing of Wyoming brands was from the 71 to the Rocking Chair. A well-known western Wyoming brand was obtained in the following manner:

The owner having sold his former brand wanted another one in a hurry. Three times he sent brands in to the state board and three times they were rejected. Finally he telegraphed, "Please send brand of your own selection P D Q." The answer came back, "P D Q fine!"

And now there began to appear on the ranges these mysterious and sometimes sinister figures, the stock detectives, men employed by the stock associations or private owners, who anonymously, usually singlehanded, went out among the ranches and on the range to gather evidence. Many of these men were fine fellows; a number were not. Some were "killers." Often they worked as cowboys for the big outfits, their real purpose unknown to the other cowboys.

But no matter what your organization, certain people will beat it. Rustling continued to flourish. The Wyoming Stock Growers Association, increasingly powerful, met force with force; became increasingly arbitrary. It would receive no members who had even a hint of a black mark against them. It black-listed suspected cowboys and black-listed cattlemen who for any reason, and no matter how sincere their repentance, hired these cowboys. And if you were a black-listed cowboy it was hard to find work in Wyoming, and if you were a black-listed owner you not only received none of the benefits of association membership, but you were treated as an open enemy. You couldn't round your cattle up under protection and when you shipped them they were likely to be impounded and questioned by the inspectors either at the end or at the beginning of their journey. Even if sold, if there were any individuals claimed by the stock association, the checks for these were sent to the association and not to you. This meant ruin, of course.

The farmer, the newspapers, the local politicians, began to turn against the big cattleman. The little cattleman was already against him.

The association carried life and death in its hands. It could refuse membership to whom it wanted, black-list on a hint of suspicion. Most of the members were honest men, but such power as was theirs cannot help but lead to abuses, and if you came, let us say, from the Powder, and a man you knew from the Sweetwater, or the Laramie, accused some neighbor of stealing his cattle, how could you tell whether he was stating the literal truth or whether he merely wanted to get rid of an intrusive rival? You knew your own country, but not the details of someone else's. Moreover, the same code applied to the big owners as applied to their cowboys. They stuck together. The majority had been cowboys to begin with.

Above all, cattlemen want room . . . plenty of room. If you black-list little fellows, pretty soon they pull out and go somewhere else. That is a temptation even to the most fair-minded. Unconsciously you think up reasons for disliking a man. The Far Westerner has a passionate love of space and loneliness. Presently this matter of life and death extended itself, where a certain element of the association was concerned, from the economic realm to the physical one. Suspected rustlers began to be found near their corrals, rifle holes in their heads. A few of the stock detectives were appointed, or appointed themselves, sub rosa judges and executioners all in one.

It couldn't have been very pleasant to have to go down to your corrals at dusk on a cold October night with the thought that possibly someone was watching you from the bushes across the creek, or from the top of a near-by hill, your head between his sights. Nor did this increase the amiability of a neighborhood.

Rustling is not over in the West. For a decade or so the cattleman thought he had the situation under control, but he was mistaken. It is true, the old days of the running iron and the changing of brands are about done. There is too much inspection nowadays at shipping point and market to make these older methods safe. Cattle are no longer stolen on the hoof; nor do you have to be a cowboy any longer to steal them. All you need is a truck, some butcher knives, and a .22 rifle with a silencer.

Like everything else, cattle rustling has been stream-lined and brought up to date.

A new ghost, a new uneasiness is riding the range. The ghost is known as "rubber-tired rustling," and so far nobody knows who these "gasoline cowboys" are. All anybody knows is that they strike unexpectedly, steal ten or fifteen head of steers from a range, and are gone. By dawn they are a hundred, two hundred miles away. Noiselessly they shoot the steers they want, dress them out where they lie, bury the hides and entrails, load the carcasses on trucks, and are off to sell them to some dishonest local butcher in some town where the sheriff must also be dishonest.

CHAPTER THIRTY-SEVEN

Six-guns

THE small town of Buffalo is perhaps the prettiest town in Wyoming. Most Wyoming towns are anything but pretty except for their residence sections, tree-shaded and green with determinedly watered lawns, although, especially at dusk, their lights being turned on, they have a heart-warming quality as you come to them out of the encircling loneliness.

But Buffalo is pretty at any hour of the day or night.

Clare Sheridan, hunting her father's ranch, noticed the charm of Buffalo and put it down in her latest book, *Redskin Interlude,* which shows that prettiness has a high advertising value. Buffalo would be almost perfect if it took down the road signs littering its approaches.

Buffalo lies in a fold of the hills at the base of the Big Horns, and Clear Creek, as clear and sweet as its name, runs straight through the center of the town, a bridge spanning the sunlit water. Off to the east is the violet nakedness of the Powder River badlands, but Buffalo, surrounded by small green ranches, is embowered in big shady trees, cottonwoods and poplars, and even its main business street is not unpleasant. On the main business street is a hotel where, if you are lucky and get a bedroom to one side, you have a window that opens onto a garden and the constant chuckle of Clear Creek. If the hotel served good meals it would be famous.

Flowers do especially well in Wyoming if anyone

takes the trouble to plant them and water them. The
cool nights, the warm days, the high altitude give flowers an especial size and brilliance. Buffalo is filled with
flowers.

Buffalo has other endearing characteristics. It is a
sort of snug-harbor for retired cow persons. It is like a
New England coast village, but two thousand miles inland, its sea captains former or present ranchmen, its
horizon mountains on one side, badlands on the other.

Forty-six years ago Buffalo, at that time only about
fourteen years old, only about fourteen years away from
being Sioux and Cheyenne camping ground, was by no
means the quiet . . . well, fairly quiet . . . there're
still cowboys . . . town it is today. Everyone in it, or
who came to it, carried a gun.

On one side were the majority of its citizens, all
the surrounding small cattlemen, all the grangers, newly
come, the sheriff, "Red" Angus, and a group of mysterious former cowboys led by Nate Champion and
Nick Ray. On the other side, but greatly outnumbered,
were the owners and foremen of the scattered big outfits of the Powder River country, men like Fred Hess
the Frewens' manager, later to become a prominent cattleman in his own right. Men like Arthur Browning
Clarke of the D E and Henry Blair of the Hoe and
various other outstanding men with their cowboys.
Added to these were the stock inspectors of the state
association and above all the former sheriff and now
deputy United States marshal of the district, Frank
Canton.

Canton was a tall, fearless, arrogant fellow, a dead
shot, an Oklahoman who had a way of making himself
very popular with powerful people and extremely unpopular with the less powerful. Toward the end of his
life he wrote an autobiography in which he emphasizes

the point that without him—an innocent, peaceable man—eastern Wyoming would never have known law and order.

There are dozens of such autobiographies written by ancient far western United States marshals and sheriffs in which a similar love of quiet and peace is proclaimed. It seems strange that the authors should have chosen the life they did. Being a United States marshal or a sheriff was looking for trouble and it gave a man a wonderful opportunity to shoot and get away with it.

After Canton left Wyoming permanently he was in Alaska for a number of years as a prospector and United States marshal during the Klondike rush. He died as the adjutant general of the newly organized militia of Oklahoma.

Frank Canton and the big cattlemen were in close touch with the Wyoming Stockgrowers Association, the town of Cheyenne, and the Cheyenne Club. The small owners and the farmers of Johnson County and their allies, the mysterious cowboys, had organized a vigilante committee of fifty men, armed to the teeth, who held the town of Buffalo.

Armed men passed each other in the streets. Stepping quietly and warily like turkey cocks. They had cause to do so. There had been some mysterious deaths along the Powder, and these were getting on everybody's nerves.

This was in the early spring of 1892.

In July of the previous year, for example, a rancher named Thomas Waggoner had been lynched near Newcastle, east of the Powder and about a hundred miles from Buffalo. Three unknown men had come to Waggoner's ranch when he was alone with his wife and children, and representing themselves to be deputy sheriffs, had served upon him false papers. Waggoner disappeared. Eight days later he was found hanging to a tree up a lonely canyon, now called "Dead Man's Canyon," his hands tied behind his back, his face black, his mustache dropping from his dead face.

Waggoner was a well-liked man. Everyone, including the big cattlemen, admitted that he was honest and hard-working. He had come to Wyoming from Nebraska and was a horseman. He ran about a thousand head of horses. No one knew why he had been hanged or who the false deputy sheriffs had been. At least, no one admitted that he knew. The big cattlemen said Waggoner had been lynched by the rustlers, because he was honest and knew too much. The rustlers, well organized by now, and because of the growing feeling pretty much in temporary control of Johnson County, said Waggoner had been lynched by the big cattlemen.

Five months later four men entered at dawn the cabin of W. H. Hall on the Powder where at the moment Nate Champion and Nick Ray were living, and awakening Champion, told him to surrender. Champion, pulling his gun from under his pillow, shot so effectively that the intruders, two of them wounded, jumped on their horses and galloped away.

Joe Elliot, a stock inspector, was the only man arrested for this affair. He was put under bonds to keep the peace. No witnesses for or against him could be found.

On November 28th, four weeks after this attack on Champion and Ray, came the killings of Orley Jones —"Ranger" Jones—and J. A. Tisdale.

Jones, along with his brother, was an extremely popular young man, only twenty-three years old, a former cowboy who, since his first appearance in Wyoming five years before, had ridden for many of the big outfits of the Powder. Now he had retired and taken up a homestead—at the moment a dangerous thing to do—and was engaged to be married. A sober, hard-working, good-natured young fellow Ranger Jones, although a good many of the big cattlemen thought him a rustler. Jones had driven into Buffalo from his homestead to arrange for some lumber. On his way back he was shot from ambush just the other side of Muddy Creek, fifteen miles out of town. He was found slumped forward in his buckboard.

The killing of Tisdale was even more dramatic.

Tisdale was a married man with several small children, who had a ranch about sixty miles out of Buffalo, and he had driven in to buy his winter supplies and Christmas presents for his family. Like Ranger Jones and Waggoner, he was a quiet, hard-working man, well liked. Whoever killed Waggoner and Tisdale and Ranger Jones made a poor selection, although it is likely that Waggoner was not killed by the same people who killed Jones and Tisdale.

Jones had been shot by someone hiding under the bridge at Muddy Creek; Tisdale had been shot by someone concealed in a draw that paralleled the road that led back to his ranch. When Tisdale was found he was lying among the bloodstained toys he had bought for his children. The night before he had stopped at the Cross H ranch and had told the Cross H cowboys that he had been warned in Buffalo that his life was in danger. The Cross H cowboys said he had been very nervous. When the lamps were lit, Tisdale had pulled down the blinds.

Bad medicine to kill a man taking Christmas presents home to his children!

Nothing came of the subsequent investigation, but feeling was so high that Frank Canton and Fred Hess, both swearing that they were completely innocent, left the country for a while. Guilty or not guilty, the finger of suspicion had pointed three times, at least, at Frank Canton. Except when surrounded by their cowboys the big owners didn't have much chance; and their sympathizers, unless they kept extremely quiet, were not much better off.

Abruptly the little cattlemen also began to claim that they could obtain no justice in the courts; something the big cattlemen had been claiming for a long time. One can sympathize with the judges. Whichever way they decided was wrong. Nor could witnesses, as a rule, be found. Certainly by the New Year of 1892 the Powder River country was in a most dangerous condition.

That spring the Johnson County men struck, and the big owners and their friends in Cheyenne and in the Stockgrowers Association struck back.

The Johnson County men organized their own stock association, the Northern Wyoming Farmers and Stockgrowers Association, and this association told the state association and the local big owners that it intended to hold a separate roundup at whatever time suited it. The state association answered by instructing its inspectors at various shipping points and markets to hold all black-listed stock, with or without proper bills of sale, and sell this stock and turn the money back to the state association. The state association then proceeded to black-list most of the small owners of Johnson County.

This disregarding of proper bills of sale looks worse than it was. Out-and-out rustlers had long before fallen into the habit of using supposedly reputable farmers and small cattlemen as go-betweens so that bills of sale could be made out. It was easy. You presented some farmer or small cattleman with stolen stock—for a consideration—and he sold it with his legitimate beef.

With the end of winter the small men of Johnson County were all ready to invade the ranges of their bigger neighbors and hold their own roundup with total disregard of prior claims to range and water and mavericks. That many of these prior claims were tenuous is another matter. South of the North Platte the big cattlemen were in control and there was order; north of the North Platte, in the Powder River country, there was no order at all.

Ghosts armed with six-guns rode the ranges and phantoms followed you along the roads.

CHAPTER THIRTY-EIGHT

A Little Bloodstained Book

O<small>N</small> April 6th a mysterious train . . . a passenger car, a baggage car, three stock cars filled with
horses, a flatcar piled with camp stuff and wagons, and
a caboose . . . arrived in the railway yards at Cheyenne a little after noon. That was two days after the
annual meeting in Cheyenne of the Wyoming Stockgrowers Association—the meeting of 1892. The blinds
of the passenger car were down. That night the train
pulled out and the next morning Wyoming awoke to
the alarming fact that all telegraph wires to the north
of Douglas were cut.

We know now what was on that train, in that passenger coach with the blinds down—twenty-five expert
Texas gunmen, mostly ex-sheriffs and ex-United States
marshals with, back of them in the baggage car and the
flatcar and the stock cars, their horses, their saddles, and
their ammunition. In addition there was a complete
camp outfit and three Studebaker wagons. At Cheyenne
twenty-five Wyoming men joined the Texans. Of these
Wyoming men, six were stock inspectors or cattle detectives, three were foremen for Powder River outfits
. . . Laberteaux for Henry Blair, Parker of the Mur-
phy Cattle Company, Ford of the T A; and the remaining fifteen were owners or managers of big outfits, members of the Wyoming Stockgrowers Association. Most
of the last were Powder River men, and the total holdings of the Powder River men alone, which will give

you some idea of the values involved, were 116,905 head
of cattle; 4,657 horses; $500,000 of improvements;
86,000 acres of land.

Leading this outfit was Major Frank Wolcott, one
of the most interesting of Wyoming citizens at the time,
and Hess and Canton, coming back from the Middle
West, joined the expedition which, as soon as it struck
Johnson County, was known as the "Invasion," its
members, the "Invaders."

Wolcott was a Kentuckian, a former officer of the
northern army, now a ranchman up on Deer Creek just
south of the North Platte. An honest, stocky, mus-
tached, executive, domineering, truculent, witty little
fellow. One of his most famous retorts had been to a
Texas cowboy who, having been passed carrots at the
major's table one day, remarked, "We feed carrots to
hogs down where I come from."

"So do we," said the major. "Have some."

Wolcott had a wryneck due to the fact that an
enemy, afraid to tackle the major himself, had given a
bully in Laramie a suit of clothes to "beat the major
up."

A great many of these Invaders, like the majority
of the big cattlemen of Wyoming then as now, were
college men.

In addition to the Texans and the Wyoming men
were two young gentlemen "seeking adventure," one
the proverbial Englishman, Harry Wallace, a rancher
from Colorado, paying his own expenses; the other Dr.
Charles Penrose of Philadelphia, brother of the famous
senator, Boies, and the equally famous Colorado mining
engineer, Spencer. Young Dr. Penrose, just out of the
University of Pennsylvania Medical School, found more
"adventure" than he had bargained for. A visitor in
Cheyenne, he joined the Invaders as their surgeon.

There was also a newspaper correspondent, the city editor of the Cheyenne *Sun,* and a stray miner from Idaho. All in all, fifty-five men.

The morning after leaving Cheyenne the expedition disembarked just east of the then little town of Casper and headed north . . . up through that lovely,

wide-rolling country down which, twenty-six years before, the Oglalas from the Powder had ridden to the fight at Platte Bridge. Now it was white man against white man. The intention was to clean out as many rustlers as possible on the journey and to take possession of the town of Buffalo and hold it. Subsequently, so it is said, a list of seventy marked rustlers was found.

But the Invaders never got to Buffalo.

Of the rustlers, Champion and Ray were the principal men wanted. For some time Champion and Ray, and their closest associates, had made their headquarters at a so-called ranch, the K C, on the road between Casper and Buffalo where the Middle Fork of the Powder, coming out of the foothills of the Big Horns and the Hole-in-the-Wall country, runs across the plains to join the Powder's South Fork. Kaycee today is a tiny village on the Casper-Sheridan highway surrounded by small green ranches. There is a very pleasant woman there who dispenses Coca-Cola and other soft drinks to thirsty cowpunchers and sheepherders and tourists. But at the time Kaycee—the K C ranch—was a tumble-down log and frame cabin that at one time had been a line camp of the Frewens' and was now owned by a man named Nolan.

At dawn, two days after they had disembarked at Casper, the Invaders surrounded the K C.

It so happened that Champion and Ray were alone except for two trappers, an old man and a young one, who had pulled in the night before. Early in the morning the two trappers, the old man first, came out to wash in the creek and were captured and held prisoners by the Invaders. A little while afterwards Ray appeared to draw a bucket of water and a fusillade of bullets struck him. Mortally wounded, he managed to get back to the cabin, and Champion, now thoroughly awake, opened the door and dragged him inside.

From then on until dusk, Champion, wounded in several places, fought a singlehanded battle, and from then on he did a most remarkable thing—he kept a diary that was found afterwards. At dusk the Invaders managed to fire the cabin and Champion, forced into the open, made a dash for a near-by ravine and was killed.

Major Wolcott looking down on him said, "By God, if I had fifty men like you I could whip the whole state of Wyoming!" and on Champion's breast a sign reading "Cattle Thieves Beware!" was pinned.

Two Texans had been wounded.

But luck was against the Invaders. Early in the day, unknown to them, a neighboring rancher, Torrence Smith, had looked down, terrified and surprised, from the bluffs on the north side of the Powder and had ridden like the wind to Buffalo. A little later two other ranchers, Jack Flagg and his son, on their way to Casper for a Democratic convention, had innocently driven into the K C during a lull in the battle and, fired upon, had desperately whipped up their horses and escaped. By nightfall two hundred Johnson County men were riding.

The situation was reversed. The next day the Invaders, separated from their wagons and supplies, were galloping for the friendly T A ranch whose foreman was with them, thirty miles north on the Crazy Woman. They reached it just in time to fortify it and throw up breastworks. They were now the besieged. Leading the besiegers were Red Angus, the sheriff of Johnson County, "Arapaho" Brown, who had got his nickname from living for a while with the Arapahos, and a fighting Methodist parson by the name of Rader.

The Invaders were being invaded. Meanwhile, Cheyenne and the entire east of Wyoming was in an uproar.

Governor Baxter had just resigned, and the acting governor, the former lieutenant governor, was young Dr. Amos Barber, who had been a classmate of Dr. Penrose's at the University of Pennsylvania. Penrose had been visiting the acting governor when he made his unfortunate decision to join the Invaders. Dr. Barber, the "doctor" in Owen Wister's *Lin McLean*, had been in Wyoming only two years. He telegraphed President Harrison that Wyoming was out of hand, and down from Fort McKinney, twenty-five miles from Buffalo, came three troops of the 6th United States Cavalry.

They arrived at the T A just in time. The besiegers were completing a number of dynamite bombs with which they proposed to end definitely the two-day siege.

One Texan had been killed and one seriously wounded; both, oddly enough, by the accidental discharge of their own weapons. This made a total of one Texan killed, and three wounded, counting the two who had been wounded at the K C.

The Invaders surrendered to the soldiers and, owing to the feeling in Johnson County, Governor Barber insisted upon a change of venue to Cheyenne. For three and a half months the cattlemen and the Texans lived pleasantly in Cheyenne and for a while in Laramie, under guard, at liberty during the day to go where they pleased. They were in their own country and were local heroes. Interesting "sights." Their leading counsel, Judge Van Devanter, later became a justice of the United States Supreme Court. On August 7th an omnibus indictment was read to them and they were released on bail until the following January, the date set for their trial. The Texans went home swearing they would be back. No one ever saw them again. At the trial in January the case was dismissed on the grounds that Johnson County refused to pay any of the expenses incident to prosecution. One thousand and sixty-four veniremen had been examined and rejected before it was possible to find a jury.

Young Dr. Penrose had had a most unhappy time.

On account of illness he had left the expedition before the fight at the K C and on his way back to Cheyenne had driven into the town of Douglas to cash a check. With all due respect, young Dr. Penrose, who in later years became a prominent physician in Philadelphia and a famous hunter of big game, exhibited during his sojourn in Wyoming even more than the habitual innocence of the tenderfoot. Douglas was a bitterly hostile town, recently settled by farmers and small cattlemen. The farmers and small cattlemen immediately arrested Dr. Penrose and turned him over to the Johnson County authorities. Against the Texas gunmen Johnson County never cherished much bitterness. They were, after all, merely a lot of hard-working fellows on salary. The big cattlemen, enemies though they were, were at least citizens of Wyoming. But here, in the person of young Dr. Penrose, was an interloper. An alien—an Easterner. A mixer-up in a family quarrel. Johnson County decided to hang Dr. Penrose.

He was rescued by his friend and fellow physician, Governor Barber, who sent a United States marshal up from Laramie County with a warrant for his arrest. As soon as he arrived in Cheyenne, Dr. Barber, under cover of night, put his classmate on the cowcatcher of a Union Pacific engine and told him not to make himself visible until he was well into Nebraska.

Dr. Penrose did not come back to Wyoming for twenty years.

Nate Champion and Nick Ray were buried up in Buffalo on a warm, sunny April day. There was a silent and ominous crowd, and a wealth of flowers. Two clergymen conducted the services; a Baptist clergyman and the fire-eating Mr. Rader. In his sermon Mr. Rader said:

"These men have been sent to eternity. We do not know why. They were not criminals. They were of Christian parents." Which seems, to say the least, a *non sequitur*.

For a while along the Powder the following ballad was popular. No one seems to have the vaguest idea who wrote it or how the tune went. It is a transcription, as

it says, a condensed one, of the hour-by-hour diary Nate
Champion kept. In one place his own lines had read,
"Boys, I feel pretty lonesome, just now."

It was a little blood-stained book which a bullet had torn
    in twain
It told the fate of Nick and Nate, which is known to all of
    you;
He had the nerve to write it down while the bullets fell like
    rain.
At your request, I'll do my best to read those lines again.

"Two men stayed with us here last night, Bill Jones and
    another man,
Went to the river, took a pail, will come back if they can.
I told old Nick not to look out, there might be someone near,
He opened the door; shot to the floor, he'll never live, I fear.

Two hours since the shots began, the bullets thick as hail!
Must wait on Nick, he's awful sick, he's still alive but pale.
At stable, river, and back of me, men are sending lead.
I cannot get a shot to hit, it's nine, and Nick is dead.

Down at the stable I see a smoke, I guess they'll burn the hay.
From what I've seen they do not mean for me to get away.
It's now about noon, I see a rope thrown in and out the door.
I wish that duck would show his pluck, he'd use a gun no
    more.

I don't know what has become of the boys that stayed with
    us last night.
Just two or more boys with me and we would guard the
    cabin right.
I'm lonesome, boys, it's two o'clock, two men just come in
    view,
And riding fast, as they went past, were shot at by the crew.

I shot a man down in the barn, don't know if I hit or not.
Must look again, I see someone, it looks like." There's a blot.

"I hope they did not get those men that across the bridge
    did run.
If I had a pair of glasses here, I think I'd know someone.

They're just through shelling the house, I hear the splitting
    wood;
I guess they'll light the house tonight, and burn me out for
    good.
I'll have to leave when night comes on, they'll burn me if
    I stay;
I guess I'll make a running break and try to get away.

They've shot another volley in, but to burn me is their game,
And as I write, it's not yet night, and the house is all aflame.
So good-bye, boys, if I get shot, I got to make a run,
So on this leaf I'll sign my name, Nathan D. Champion."

The light is out, the curtain drawn, the last sad act is played.
You know the fate that met poor Nate, and of the run he
    made.
And now across the Big Divide, and at the Home Ranch door
I know he'll meet and warmly greet the boys that went
    before.

    Arapaho Brown, for a time a local hero, developed
into one of the most unpleasant badmen in the history
of the Powder. His past and future history wiped out
the momentary popularity he gained at the K C. There
was nothing gallant, dashing or charming about Arapaho. Nothing of the caballero. He was a huge, gangling
fellow, bearded and enormously strong; a Tennessean
to begin with. In the early eighties, after leaving the
Arapahos, he had wandered into the Powder River country and had settled on a small ranch on Rock Creek.
He was supposed to have murdered his partner and
possibly his partner's wife and two small children, after
gaining possession of his partner's ranch and appropri-
ating his partner's family for a while. He was finally

murdered himself by two young cowboys, who, if their object hadn't been robbery and they had been a little more frank about it, wouldn't have got into so much trouble. As it was, they were sentenced to the penitentiary for short terms. They had shot the huge old giant at dusk and then, losing their nerve, had fled.

For many minutes the enormous dying man threshed blindly about in the dusk, leaving his cabin in a dreadful state.

There was one queer thing, however, about Arapaho. He was a great reader. He left behind him a small and excellent library.

I must tell a story again. I have told it in *The Diary of a Dude Wrangler*. A friend of mine, a former Johnson County man, then a boy, was riding innocently along a swale with a companion in the deep dusk— almost dark. Suddenly on a near-by ridge, single file or by twos, outlined against the afterglow, was an army riding. Horsemen, wagons . . . black silhouettes! The two boys didn't know what this was, but it looked bad to them. They waited breathless; hidden, fortunately, by willows.

Two days later they heard about the Invaders.

CHAPTER THIRTY-NINE

Aftermath

THE T A War ended, on the surface, as abruptly as it had begun, but no war actually ends abruptly any more than it begins abruptly.

For a while the men who had been openly a part of the "Invasion" did not dare return to Johnson County. Their lives were in jeopardy, their cattle were worth nothing; most of their cattle had disappeared. The commissioners of Johnson County asked the big cattlemen to send "trustworthy and discreet persons" to look after their property, but the big cattlemen were not without reason skeptical. The Circuit Court at Cheyenne issued an injunction against the proposed independent spring roundup on the Powder, but it took place just the same.

Before the trouble was over, another man was to add his name to the already long list of victims. This was a young Canadian, George Wellman; a well-liked cowboy, who had ridden for eleven years or so in Johnson County . . . Whoever was doing the shooting on the Powder—and there is no doubt that there were different assassins, representing different sides—they certainly chose just the wrong men to shoot. In that, at least, they exhibited similar characteristics.

Wellman belonged at the time to the Blair outfit, and while its foreman, Frank Laberteaux, who had been one of the Invaders, was waiting trial at Cheyenne, Wellman had been appointed acting foreman in his

place. Wellman had the courage to return to Johnson
County and the almost insane courage to accept an ap-
pointment as deputy United States marshal. He had
been instructed to go to Buffalo to meet two other
United States marshals in order to assist them in serving
the injunction papers against the illegal roundup, and
he was riding into Buffalo when he was shot by some
men hiding in a ravine. The posse that brought his body
in found where the assassins had waited for a long while
. . . the ground was covered with cigarette butts. The
assassins had been patient but nervous.

Accompanying Wellman into Buffalo was another
Blair cowboy, Tom Hathaway, and Hathaway, galloping wildly, had brought the news to Buffalo.

Wellman's death convinced practically all the
peaceful and law-abiding men of Johnson County, no
matter on what side their sympathies lay, that it was
time to come down to earth. Cheyenne demanded mar-
tial law for Johnson County, Johnson County compro-
mised by accepting the government's proposal to send
five thousand troops into summer camp in Johnson,
Converse, and Natrona counties. Presently the troops
arrived—the 6th Cavalry and the 9th Cavalry, colored,
among them—and made considerable trouble themselves. As for the little and big cattlemen, it took awhile
longer—about fifteen years—for entire good feeling to
be restored and even now along the Powder it's just as
well to the discreet.

The T A War . . . the Invasion, the Little and
Big Cattlemen's War, the Rustlers' War, the Johnson
County War, to give it all its names . . . happened a
long while ago. Forty-six years ago. Looking back on
it, it is impossible to tell who was in the right and who
in the wrong. Even at the time it was impossible to tell,

although a great many people on both sides thought
they knew. On the one side was the old order, its back
to the wall, fighting—so it thought—for all it owned
and against ruin; cattlemen who had made the state and
on whose memories were the scars of countless hardships
and dangers. These men had survived the bonanza, the
winter of '87; were they now to be put out of business,
run off their ranges by dishonest cowboys and newcomers, many of the latter foreign emigrants who had
followed the railroads? Newcomers many of whom in
their first lean, homesteading winters the cattlemen had
befriended! For the cattleman is a generous man. He
dislikes having his cattle stolen but he will give a beef
to any starving family.

No man ever starved to death in a cattle country.

Opposed to this attitude was one equally justified.
Were the big owners, simply because they had arrived
first, entitled to hold the range and the ranching country forever? To their ranges, to their water holes and
streams, the majority had only very tenuous claims anyhow, backed more by force and custom than by law.
Was no little man ever to be given a chance to prosper?
Was eastern Wyoming to remain a closed country? Was
the stock association to be allowed to make any rules
it saw fit? Was it to be allowed to grow more and more
arbitrary, using its inspectors and detectives more and
more ruthlessly, as it became increasingly alarmed and
desperate? Was the stock association to be allowed to
run out of the country any man it wished and, if it
thought necessary, execute him?

The underlying problem is an old one. In one form
or another it has been to the front ever since that curious creature man began to inhabit the earth. Cain fought
it out with Abel. The white man had fought it out with
the Sioux, and now the white man was fighting it out

with his own kind. The big owners were in the same position the Sioux had been in fourteen years before. Their arguments were the same. Up on his reservation in Dakota, old Red Cloud must have smiled.

Philosophically, and especially in view of what we know today, it is difficult, perhaps, not to sympathize with the big cattlemen. They were fighting for a magnificent way of living, a generous and heroic and historic method of making your livelihood, and actually, as it has turned out, they were fighting on the side of common sense. Time has a way of reversing the field. Often in the end these who seem at first reactionary appear as the longer visioned and more progressive.

The great range states of the Far West are range states and not farming states. And raising range cattle means big acreage.

No one denies any honest man opportunity; but every bed holds just so many occupants. To try to squeeze eight married couples into a single bed is a mistake and a social and economic error.

But the big cattlemen need not have been so alarmed. They were not ruined. After a while, things quieting down, those who wanted to come back to the Powder came. Fred Hess's sons are still big owners on the Powder, respected and powerful men. The Senator's outfit is still there. The fourteenth son of the Scotch baronet is still there. A number of the other original owners, or their descendants, are still there. The victorious Johnson County men didn't run all their big neighbors out of the country, nor did they want to. In fact, they didn't run anybody out who had the nerve to stay or return.

Perhaps the most sensible contemporary attitude was that of one of the biggest of the Powder River owners . . . at least, this is the story.

In a tight corner this big cattleman exhibited extraordinary acumen.

His friends around Cheyenne had written him to meet the Invaders with all the cowboys and supplies he could spare. If he didn't, he would be at odds with his friends south of the North Platte; if he did, his stock and life would be worth nothing in Johnson County. For a week or so this big cattleman must have been an unhappy man. He solved his problem in the following fashion.

He sent a number of cowboys with well-stocked wagons to meet the Invaders, but the second night out —well away from the ranch—every horse, even the horse wrangler's stake horse, managed to get itself lost. An odd thing to happen to a number of experienced cowboys! For two weeks or so the big owner's cowboys were afoot; then when things were a trifle more quiet, they found their horses. Meanwhile, war had raged about them, but at a discreet distance.

The T A War happened a long while ago, but big, thinly settled countries have long memories.

Old Mr. Tarbell—that isn't his right name—from whom a few years ago I bought far to the west in Wyoming the ranch on which I now live, was on the edge of the Johnson County troubles. He wasn't a Powder River man, he lived near Ten Sleep which is on the other side of the Big Horns in the Big Horn Basin. You go up from Buffalo over Muddy Pass at an elevation of 9,666 feet, and driving for twenty miles or so through the thick forests and green mountain meadows —the summer range—of the Big Horns, drop down between the sheer walls of Ten Sleep Canyon. Ten Sleep is a brilliantly colored, painted-country. White men slipped around the southern end of the Big Horns just as the Sioux and Cheyennes and Arapahos had slipped before them.

Mr. Tarbell is a fine old fellow. Tall, white-bearded, well over eighty; a trooper with Crook before he settled down to ranching. After he sold out to me he went down to Arizona and at the age of eighty-two discovered a little gold mine. He has done well. He has made enough money to buy a beautiful shiny new car and hire a boy to drive it. Two summers ago Mr. Tarbell made a tour of his old stamping grounds and dropped in to see me. He told me that he had left the Ten Sleep country at the outbreak of the Johnson County troubles because he had received a human ear in the mail.

"Mighty nasty and dried up it was, too," he said.

The dispatch of a human ear as a warning is an ancient custom, but with the exception of Mr. Tarbell, I have never heard of its being done anywhere near the Powder, and possibly Mr. Tarbell may have been drawing on his imagination. At all events, something must have disturbed him mightily, for he left Ten Sleep in a hurry and he never went back, and he moved just as far west as he could and still remain in Wyoming.

I don't know on which side Mr. Tarbell was, I never asked him, but even now, when he talks about the T A War he looks over his shoulder to be sure no one is listening, although that, of course, is the undue wariness of age.

A friend of mine who owns a ranch near the Powder had as his cook a young married woman who was a daughter of one of the men who had been ambushed in the old troubled days. Unexpectedly, one noon a man suspected of having had a hand in the ambushing dropped in on my friend for lunch. My friend sat facing the kitchen; his guest had his back to the kitchen.

"I was awfully glad when that fellow got off the ranch," my friend said, "still walking as if there'd been nothing in his coffee."

In the doorway to the kitchen the cook had stood, staring at the back of the unsuspecting guest. Her eyes were as quiet and bright as the eyes of a rattlesnake. Her face was as white as alkali.

Cooks have an undue advantage under certain circumstances.

Shortly after the end of the T A War a printer and Democratic politician in Cheyenne published an extremely prejudiced account of the troubles in which he condemned bitterly the big cattlemen. One night his press was raided and all the copies that could be found of his book and the type for it were destroyed. Years later the book was published again. Within a short time all the copies on sale were bought up. Even today that book is difficult to come by.

Yes, big, thinly settled countries have long memories!

Last summer I was talking to an old acquaintance, a former Johnson County man; a wise, mature, humorous old-timer. He began by being good-natured, jocose, willing to admit that there are two sides to every question, but as he went on he began to wave his arms and his face grew redder and redder, and pretty soon at the top of his voice he was describing certain persons, most of them dead, in the definite language of the Far West when aroused.

CHAPTER FORTY

Pacific Creek

T HE ranch I bought from old Mr. Tarbell, although far to the west of the Powder, as far west as you can go without finding yourself in Idaho, is nonetheless intimately connected with the Powder and Frank Canton. Up the creek which borders the ranch runs the old horse trail to Cody . . . up to Two Ocean Pass, over the continental divide, and down Atlantic Creek to the headwaters of the Yellowstone, and from there across the Thorofare country and the Absorakas to the South Fork of the Shoshone, forty miles south of Cody. Beyond the Cody country, across the distance of the Big Horn Basin, so green in the spring, so yellow in the summer, so brown in the autumn, is the blue mass of the Big Horns holding the eastern horizon.

By means of the horse trail bordering my ranch, old "Teton" Jackson, my country's most famous badman, was accustomed, in the eighties, to drive east the horses he had stolen in Idaho.

Teton and his gang were in the habit of stealing horses in Idaho, holding them for a while in our valley —at the time nobody was there but Teton and his men —and then, when they had been held long enough, of running them east and selling them. Reversing the process, Teton would steal horses in the east, hold them for a while in our valley, and then sell them in Idaho. A very profitable business which is known as "playing the middle against both ends."

Frank Canton, at the time sheriff of Johnson County—this was five years before the T A War— was laying for Teton, and one night heard that he was camped in a deserted cabin back in the Big Horns west of Buffalo. Canton swore in a couple of young deputies and rode to get his man. I know one of the deputies. Between the logs of the cabin light was shining, showing that the daubing and chinking were gone.

"Stick your Winchester through the logs an inch or so," said Canton to the deputy I know, "and get a bead on Jackson. Then I'll come through the door and arrest him."

Teton was sitting before a small fire on a stool, leaning forward warming his hands. On a table five feet away was a lighted candle and his Colt and cartridge belt. Why he had been so careless he never explained.

The rifle crept noiselessly through the crack between the logs. Teton warmed his hands. Then he got up and strolled toward the table, paused, changed his mind, and came back and sat down again. Thoughtfully he warmed his hands.

Canton threw open the door, his two guns ready for action.

"You're under arrest, Teton," he said. "I've a warrant for you for robbing the mails."

Teton got leisurely to his feet, holding his hands above his head—a huge, redheaded, gangling fellow.

"Canton," he said, "I ain't afraid of you or your guns. I'd fight that out, but what's been a-bothering me is the end of that rifle that's been trained on my head for the last five minutes."

I could tell a lot more stories about Frank Canton. Canton was the man—after he left Wyoming and before he went to Alaska—who broke up the Dalton Gang down in Oklahoma . . . Bill, Bob, Grat and Emmett, and very respectable they look, along with their sister, in their family photograph. As respectable as the leaders of the Hole-in-the-Wall Gang did years later in a similar group photograph. Derby hats, high starched collars, neat suits. Western badmen loved to dress up like Sunday-school superintendents and have their photographs taken.

Canton, when he first came to Wyoming and Powder River, helped, as one of the earliest sheriffs of the newly made Johnson County, to suppress Powder River's first type of badman . . . the road agents who held up the stages that ran to the gold fields of the Black Hills and to Montana. I could tell a lot of stories about these road agents too. "Big-nosed" George— George Stevens, and "Black" Tom, and Frank Lamb, and Bill Booth. These were the most famous of that particular species of badman.

Big-nosed George, incidentally, had no connection with "Flat-nosed" George Currie of the Hole-in-the-Wall Gang who did not appear until fifteen years after Big-nosed George's sudden and bullet-filled end.

CHAPTER FORTY-ONE

Hole-in-the-Wall

IF you leave the highway at Kaycee and go east
. . . Kaycee of the T A War . . . a country road will
take you to Sussex, a tiny isolated post office on the
Powder where the Powder turns north to enter its badlands. If you leave the highway at Kaycee and go west,
another country road will take you up the shallow narrow valley of the Middle Fork until, coming abruptly
and astonishingly to a red sheer canyon just wide enough
for the Middle Fork and the road, you find yourself
about to enter the Hole-in-the-Wall country.

Sussex is about fifteen miles east of Kaycee; the
Hole-in-the-Wall country about the same distance west.

Until you get to the red canyon, the shallow narrow valley of the Middle Fork is occupied by a few
small ranches, their tiny fields of timothy and alfalfa
lying on either side of the creek. It is a very quiet and
remote valley, the sides of the road yellow with sweet-
clover which, however justly despised by ranchers, nonetheless makes a country sweet to the passing stranger's
nose. Halfway up the valley you pass the mouth of
Red Fork, which comes in from the north. It was up
the Red Fork, ten miles or so from its mouth, that in
November, 1876, Ranald Mackenzie and his troopers
wiped out Dull Knife's village of Cheyennes. Beyond
the short red canyon of the Middle Fork you emerge
into an entirely different country.

A wide, rolling country of horizons added to horizons, bounded by long low hills, a few of them covered with timber; a country even quieter and lonelier than the valley of the Middle Fork. There is nothing here except the wide rolling country, the long low hills, and a couple of hidden ranches. One of these ranches is the post office of Barnum. You wouldn't know that it was a post office unless somebody told you. Just below Barnum a prong of the Middle Fork, narrow and twisting, loses itself in blue hills miles to the south and becomes the Buffalo Fork. The country gets lonelier, wider, as you ascend into it. The red sheer cliff through which you have come bends in an enormous arc south and then west, a wall of red that follows you for miles, cutting off from you the east.

You are now in the southern foothills of the Big Horns, and the Big Horns are no longer in sight. You are in a sort of Lorna Doone country, but much bigger.

One of the immediate effects of the T A War was that it threw upon the country a certain number of rustlers, for the time being lacking occupation, to whose numbers were added the average quota of ambitious and energetic young men loathing honest work which each generation presents to a long-suffering world. In addition to this, some years before, Granville Stuart and the big cattlemen of Montana, with their cowboys, had made war on the rustlers of the Little Missouri, and had about cleaned them out and driven them south. Montana and South Dakota's gain was Wyoming and Utah and Colorado's loss.

The Lord gave dogs fleas in order, as has been recognized, that they might never forget that they are dogs and so continue to gratify mankind with an appropriately humble attitude. In the same way, no doubt, the Lord gave farmers and ranchmen constant trouble,

starting with the weather, so that there would always
be in the world one large section of the population distinguished for philosophy, patience, and a grimly
humorous point of view.

No one knows how the Hole-in-the-Wall got its
name. The red canyon, to be sure, does make a hole in
a wall . . . a sizable hole in a sizable wall . . . but the

country beyond is not a "hole" in the sense the term is
used in the West. It is not, like Jackson Hole, for instance, a deep valley entirely surrounded by mountains.
Nor is it a deep basin like Sunlight Basin north of Cody.
The Hole-in-the-Wall country is a great rolling range
country and the low hills that surround it can be easily
ridden over from the north, the west, or the south. It is
thought the Frewens named the country. There was an
eighteenth century tavern in London known as the
Hole-in-the-Wall . . . the Hole-in-the-Wall in Bald-
win's Gardens . . . and the Hole-in-the-Wall in Wyoming was part of the Frewens' range, as we have seen,
and one of their ranch houses was on the Middle Fork.

Whoever named it, and for what reason, the Hole-

in-the-Wall country became for a while in the late
nineties and early 1900's the most famous country in
Wyoming. As famous as a little while before the country of which it was a part, the Powder River country,
had been. The Hole-in-the-Wall country became not
only famous, it became infamous. More famous and
infamous, perhaps, than it deserved. There was a time
when anyone who held up a train, or robbed a bank,
or shot a man, or rustled cattle and then disappeared
for a while, was supposed to have gone into the Hole-
in-the-Wall. Almost every crime, however disconnected,
that occurred in Montana or Wyoming or western
South Dakota was attributed to a somewhat vague Hole-
in-the-Wall Gang. The most preposterous stories were
spread about. If all the badmen and their women who
at one time or another were supposed to have gone into
the Hole-in-the-Wall had been there together, even
that wide country would have been crowded.

There was an impression, among those who didn't
know it, that the Hole-in-the-Wall was a sort of
pirates' rendezvous; a Port Royal.

The most popular story described a settlement,
even a town, of badmen and their wives and children
located in a round deep valley surrounded by impassable cliffs. To this valley the single entrance was through
a canyon, much like the actual canyon, guarded day and
night by a couple of hidden outlaws with Winchesters.
Anyone who tried to enter did so at the risk of his life.
Inside their valley the badmen with their families lived
a happy and sequestered life, raising vegetables and tend-
ing milch cows, and guarding in turn the only entrance.
Every now and then they rode out in force to raid the
Powder River country to the east or the Casper country
to the south. But one day a brave sheriff—name unknown—calmly entered the Hole-in-the-Wall through

the perilous canyon, looked about him, and came out again, the outlaw sentries respecting his courage too much to shoot him.

I heard that one up in British Columbia.

As a matter of fact, the Hole-in-the-Wall needed no gilding. The men who frequented it and passed through it during its major period were hard enough citizens without exaggerating them, and the fact that the country was so easy to enter and leave aided rather than hindered its quicksilver occupants. Had the Hole-in-the-Wall been an actual "hole" it would have been easily taken. As it was, it not only afforded an excellent back-door route between Montana and southern Wyoming, but if a posse came in at one end, or on this side or the other, you could ride fast in the opposite direction. The nearest thing to a village was a deserted line-camp cabin far up the Buffalo Fork which the outlaws used as a gathering place, a headquarters for plans and intelligence, and an occasional hide-out before scattering.

The Hole-in-the-Wall Gang depended, as all such gangs must depend, upon secrecy, quickness of movement, dispersal after a crime until the hue and cry had died down, and uncertainty as to actual membership. Above all, the Hole-in-the-Wall Gang depended, as all such gangs must depend, upon the goodwill of the less clear-thinking residents of the Powder River country and the Big Horn Basin.

The Robin Hood tradition and the inherent dislike of the law on the part of law-abiding people are what save most outlaws for as long as they are saved.

The Hole-in-the-Wall Gang was careful, for example, never to rob any small rancher or steal his cattle. It was generous to the little man. After some especially impudent exploit the members would separate and lie low for a while, working as cowboys or in other positions in widely scattered parts of Montana, the Dakotas, Wyoming, Utah, and the Southwest. "Butch" Cassidy, during one of his hide-outs, was for a long while a respected bartender at Alma, New Mexico, although Alma at the time was itself a pretty tough town.

The Hole-in-the-Wall country attained its full stature slowly. It began as a rendezvous for rustlers, horse or cattle; it ended as a rendezvous for bank and train robbers, the most famous place of its kind in the history of the West. For several years prior to 1897 it had been building up a bad reputation. And deep in the records of the Powder are these two letters; the first written by Bob Devine, the C Y's—the famous brand of the Curey Brothers—doughty and bearded range foreman; the second by the men in the Hole-in-the-Wall whom Devine had accused of rustling C Y stock and of interfering with his roundup.

Devine's challenge was an open letter to the Casper *Tribune*, dated July 19, 1897. The result was a famous fight in the Hole-in-the-Wall between the cowboys of the C Y led by Bob Devine, accompanied by some United States marshals, a few representatives of other cattle outfits, "reps" they're called, and the men Devine suspected. An encounter in which several men on both sides were wounded and Al Smith, one of the leaders of the supposed rustlers, was killed.

Bob Devine's letter read as follows:

I have seen all sorts of reports bearing upon John R. Smith and the Nolan gang stopping the round-up from working in the Hole-in-the-Wall Country. They will have a hard time of it. Neither the C Y boys, the Keystone, nor the Pugsley outfits are hunting a fight. We are all working men and only want such cattle as belong to our employers and it is an indisputable fact that the Hole-in-the-Wall is a hiding place for thieves and has been for years. Thousands of dollars worth of cattle have been stolen by these outlaws, brands burned out and their own brands substituted. Their friends can help to dispose of the burned cattle. Every year I have gotten back cattle from there that were taken from their mothers and lots of cattle on which the brands were changed. I am going to work that country and have asked the sheriffs of Natrona and Johnson Counties to work with us and see that everybody is treated right. The time has come for all honest working men to declare themselves in favor of law and justice. And, if these men want to fight us, when we know we are right, I say fight.

R. M. Devine

Back at once came this anonymous reply, also an open letter to the *Tribune:*

Bob Devine you think you have played hell, you have just begun, you will get your dose, there is men enuff up here to kill you. We are going to get you, or lose twelve more men, you must stay out of this country if you want to live, we are not going to take any chances any more but will get you any way we can, we want one hair apiece out of that damned old chin of yours, you have give us the worst of it all the way through and you must stay out or die. You had better keep your damned outfit out if you want to keep them. Don't stick that damned old head of yours in this country again if you do not want it shot off, we are twelve men appointed a purpose to get you if you don't stay out of here.

Revenge Gang

Very coolly Bob Devine and his cowboys, and the officers of the law with them, rode into the Hole-in-the-Wall and very coolly started to gather their cattle. The rustlers met them only halfheartedly, and the fight already mentioned took place. Badmen, especially when boastful, as a rule don't amount to much.

But these supposed rustlers were not the famous Hole-in-the-Wall Gang, and the real Hole-in-the-Wall Gang did not come into national prominence until the robbery of the bank at Belle Fourche, South Dakota, in the same summer—1897—as the C Y fight. And with the robbery emerged "Harve" Logan, one of the deadliest and most dangerous badmen the West has ever seen; certainly Wyoming's worst badman, save, possibly, Tom Horn. And along with Harve Logan emerged Butch Cassidy, Wyoming's most charming badman. One of the few charming western badmen.

Badmen, east or west, generally speaking, are not charming—they're rattlesnakes. But Butch Cassidy, as much as anyone, came near to living up to the mythical Robin Hood tradition, and Wyoming and the Powder still remember him with tolerance and even affection.

CHAPTER FORTY-TWO

The Long Riders

THE Hole-in-the-Wall Gang, the "Wild Bunch," as it liked to call itself and was locally called, except for its inner circle was a loosely knit and misty organization and at one time or another numerous fairly innocent people touched its outer edges and a great many not so innocent cowboys and independent outlaws were temporarily connected with it. Also, as I have pointed out, a number of men were supposed to belong to it who didn't.

After the Belle Fourche robbery—there had been an earlier, fairly noteworthy robbery of the bank at Montpelier, Idaho—Harvey Logan, alias Ed Howard, alias "Kid Curry," became the acknowledged leader of the Hole-in-the-Wall Gang and his principal lieutenants seem to have been George Currie—Flat-nosed George, like Butch Cassidy an honest cowpuncher gone wrong, Butch Cassidy himself, Harry Longabaugh—the "Sundance Kid"—Tom and George Dickson, also known as the "Roberts brothers" and Tom and George "Jones," together with Bill Carver and Ben Kilpatrick, the "Tall Texan." The gang when fully organized had a series of "blind post offices" . . . crevices in the rocks, holes in trees . . . running all the way from Montana to New Mexico, where members in flight and on their own could stop to pick up any notes or orders that had been left for them, or any warnings or other news from friendly gangs or ranches. The inner circle of the gang came to be known as the Curry Gang, while the gang as a whole, the loose organization of rustlers and the nucleus of more deadly bank and train robbers, together with friendly neighboring ranchers, was called the Hole-in-the-Wall Gang.

Scattered throughout Wyoming today there are a number of highly respectable and prosperous citizens who knew a great deal about the Hole-in-the-Wall Gang in their flaming youth.

To describe accurately one of these old-time far western gangs which flourished particularly in the nineties, even so famous a one as the Hole-in-the-Wall Gang, is an almost impossible task. They lived by secrecy, by aliases, by swift movement, by equally swift evaporation after a crime, and especially by that extraordinary far western word-of-mouth communication which used to be known as the "tomato can telegraph," and which traveled then, and still travels, as swiftly and mysteriously as African talking-drums, and far more silently. The hidden post offices, the holes in rocks and trees, that extended from the Northwest to the Southwest, useful as they were, were not half so useful as ranchers and allies who talked out of the corners of their mouths, their eyes level.

When the more serious-minded of the far western badmen gave over the exciting but more youthful and less profitable pursuits of cattle and horse rustling for the big stuff of bank and train robbery, Pinkerton detectives followed them for months, and even years, all over the Northwest and Southwest, for the most part with minor results. When a member of one of these gangs died with his boots on it was usually because of accident or miscalculation, and usually at the hands of some local sheriff or United State marshal, and because the badman, forgetting himself, had offended local manners and prejudices.

They had other factors in their favor besides the ones mentioned, these western gangsters. In the first place, they were "good hands," good cowboys, good bronco twisters, good everything; they could turn to anything from bartending to dishwashing, were the latter necessary. In the second place, they didn't look like badmen, they looked like ordinary cowpunchers. In the third place, and very important, when they weren't on business bent, when they weren't back of six-guns, they were, unlike city gangsters, for the most part "nice fellows," easy to get along with, marked by the habitual far western humor and good humor. People liked them. They weren't as a rule quarrelsome. They were careful not to be. The barroom bully was usually a small-timer not connected with a gang.

There was of course a vague, far-distant liaison between these gangs; between the Hole-in-the-Wall Gang in eastern Wyoming, for instance, and the Brown's Park Gang in Colorado, and the Blue Mountain Gang, and so on, and down in Utah, in San Juan County, there was a famous general rendezvous known as Robber's Roost Mesa. The members of the various gangs knew each other and to some extent drifted from one gang to another, and the gangs sent word, when possible, of the activities of pursuing Pinkertons, sheriffs and marshals, but country-wide organization has been greatly exaggerated. There was nothing like the present close-knit organizations of city gangsters. There couldn't have been. The Far Westerner doesn't organize well. Like the Sioux chiefs, it was all the local leaders of gangs could do to keep their own men together and under orders. Besides, in those days, countries now only a few hundred miles away by automobile, were days apart by horse.

As for tracing in detail these gangs, the histories of their members, even the crimes committed, that will never be done. For every man, for every crime, there are a dozen conflicting stories. The best you can do is to follow the good old western custom of choosing the story that suits you best. It doesn't make much difference anyhow. They came, they flourished, they're gone, these "leather pounding" gangsters. Their real importance is that they expressed a certain phase of frontier history, of the history of the Far West, and, so far as we are concerned, of that part of it that lies along the Powder. With few exceptions these "sticky loop throwers," as rustlers used to be called, these cowboys turned safeblowers and train robbers, weren't individually important. The best memory they have left us is the name by which they were called . . . "long riders."

Think that over, and think what it means! The difference between that and the ordinary honest "waddie"! He, too, rode long, and many times, in pursuit of his duties, but not again and again the shining infinite ridges and valleys of the backbone of the Rockies from the Canadian Border to the Mogollons; equal shots, equal riders, men as secretive, and tireless, and as accustomed to the country, frequently in pursuit.

Harve Logan was the youngest of three brothers who had come originally from Missouri and who had worked as cowboys, but mostly as rustlers, in Montana. John, one of the brothers, was eventually killed by a Montana cattleman named Winters whose herds the Logans had been harrying. Winters was acquitted on the testimony of another cattleman, Pike Landuskey, who had been in the fight, and the remaining Logans swore to get him. They did, but having fled back to Missouri, Lonny, the second brother, was shot and killed by a pursuing detective. Harve, the only Logan left, drifted west again.

The outlaw "killers" of the West, and I stress the word "outlaw" for a reason that you will see, men like Billy the Kid, men like Harve Logan, were usually motivated by some strange twisted sense of loyalty and injury. They were always revenging what they considered a wrong, just as Harve Logan was revenging the death of his two brothers, never taking into consideration, apparently, the fact that the men they were avenging had committed the wrong in the first place. The habitual killer is, of course, a neurotic. There is a well-substantiated theory that he is a coward as well. He shoots easily and nervously because, having shot once, he is from then on afraid of being shot. Killers aren't brave men. Bravery consists in doing what you have to do and in never shooting until the last minute. The real heroes of the West saved their cartridges.

It is fairly certain that Harve Logan killed nine men before he was through. Tradition credits him with having killed forty, but that, of course, is an exaggeration. He was a silent neurotic, however. His manners were as softly velvet as the movements of a coral snake. Harve Logan was one of those steel-wire neurotics. He hardly ever said anything but "Yes, sir," and "No, sir." Not a bad-looking fellow, either, with a firm chin, a black mustache, but with deadly, somewhat staring, cold eyes.

For a couple of years after the Belle Fourche robbery the Curry Gang contented itself with sporadic, if numerous, bank robberies, store robberies, and a general business in horse and cattle stealing. The last was more recreation than anything else. The gang's operations took it far west in Wyoming, north into Montana, east into South Dakota, but it was not until 1899 that it pulled its second grand coup, nerve-shaking and country-wide in its reverberations. This was the robbery of a Union Pacific train at Wilcox in southern Wyoming. The gang, however, had overreached itself and the Wilcox robbery proved to be the beginning of the end. Railway detectives, United States marshals, sheriffs with their local posses, even bloodhounds, close upon its heels, the Curry Gang fled across the Hole-in-the-Wall country and up along the western shadows of the Big Horns into one of the most inaccessible countries of the West; the great canyon country of the Big Horn River where the Big Horn leaves Wyoming to enter Montana. Here to some extent the gang disintegrated.

Flat-nosed George was killed by sheriffs a year later in Grand County, Utah, for cattle stealing. The fate of Logan himself is less accurately known. On July 3, 1901, he and some of his men held up a Great Northern train at Warner in Montana and got away with $40,000 in bank notes. A few months later Logan was recognized and, after a gun fight with the police, was arrested in Knoxville, Tennessee, but escaped. On June 7, 1904, a Denver and Rio Grande train was held up at Parachute, Colorado, by three men, and in the subsequent chase one of these men was badly wounded and, unable to ride any longer, was left behind and committed suicide. A great many people think this was Harve Logan. But there is in contradiction a Wyoming story, probably apocryphal but worth telling.

After his escape from Knoxville, rumor has it that Harve Logan was seen at Kaycee with a companion, both men on foot, and that night horses, saddles, and six-shooters were stolen from a neighboring ranch. A couple of deputy sheriffs, following the trail, overtook, but at a distance, the two men, and fired on them with rifles, wounding, so they thought, one of them. A couple of nights later a doctor at Thermopolis was awakened from sleep by two masked men who took him blind-folded for miles into the Owl Creek Mountains. Here in a log cabin, its walls hung with blankets so that the doctor would not recognize the room, was a masked patient, a terrible wound in his groin. A week later the doctor was summoned once more under exactly the same circumstances. By this time his patient' was deliri-ous, dying of gangrene. After that, the doctor was never called again.

At all events, Harve Logan disappeared for good, and so pretty soon rumors were abroad that he hadn't died at all, but had gone farther east and had settled down and become a "prosperous businessman." Some authorities believe that he made his way to South America, as so many other far western badmen did, and was eventually killed in an attempted holdup.

You can take your choice. As for the history of Harve Logan as I have given it and the history of the Hole-in-the-Wall Gang, I foresee immediately a score of fierce contradictions.

The rest of the Hole-in-the-Wall Gang, those who had either been closely connected with the gang or at times had flirted with it, met various fates. Here is what befell a few of them.

"Driftwood Jim" McCloud, a minor member, was sentenced in 1904 and sent to Leavenworth for robbing the post office at Leavenworth. After his release he dis-appeared. "Black Dick" Hale—"Stuttering Dick"—fought a gun battle with Johnson County sheriffs in 1901 and, escaping, was never heard from again. Tom O'Day, Powder River's most notorious horse thief, ac-

tually did settle down and become "prosperous." He
served six years in the penitentiary and retired to Iowa
and bought a farm. Tom O'Day was with the Hole-in-
the-Wall Gang only at odd moments, most of the time
he operated on his own with his own small gang.

Harry Longabaugh escaped to South America with
Butch Cassidy and was shot several years later by Boliv-
ian police after the robbery of a pay train at the
Aramayo Mines. Several historians believe that Butch
Cassidy was killed at the same time, or a little later.
Ben Kilpatrick, the Tall Texan, after serving a term
in the Atlanta penitentiary, was killed by a railway
express messenger with an ice mallet in 1912 while
attempting to hold up a western train. Bill Carver was
killed by a Texas sheriff in 1900.

At all events, enough has been said to prove that
crime in the Far West doesn't pay; or at least, didn't;
not in the long run.

One of the most curious of Powder River's un-
wanted residents was a certain Otto Chenoweth, known
as the "Gentleman Horse Thief." Chenoweth was a
charming young man of excellent family in the East,
an artist, who came west in 1884 to paint the Powder
River country. For a while he worked as a cowboy
apprentice with a cattle outfit on the Cheyenne River,
but pretty soon was hand in glove with two horse
thieves, "Dad" Young and "Kid" Anderson. From then
on he went from bad to worse, finally forming a part-
nership in the Kaycee country with Stuttering Dick
Hale. Several times he was overtaken by posses and several times he engaged in gun fights with them, and on
one occasion being arrested, and having lunch with the
arresting sheriff in the back room of a small restaurant
at Lost Cabin, he escaped through the front room, the
sheriff after him. Recaptured, he apologized in the most
winning fashion to the men and women who had been

lunching in the front room for his own intrusive flight and for the bad manners of the pursuing sheriff.

Both he and the sheriff had run through the room without any explanation and with their hats on, and the sheriff had been shooting.

Perhaps the oddest thing about Chenoweth was that every now and then he went east and visited his mother at her quiet and handsome home in Massachusetts, where he behaved in the most circumspect manner.

The West ever since its beginning has been used to Otto Chenoweths. A few of them arrive every year, and the innocent rancher continues to wonder what it is that produces them. Very often, if the innocent rancher is an Easterner to begin with or has eastern connections, these Otto Chenoweths are sons of old friends whose characters have not been indicated prior to their dispatch. The West has always been regarded as an excellent place to send dangerous or impossible relatives. It is, of course, the worst place in the world, for almost everybody minds his or her own business until the final desperate and irritated moment.

Otto Chenoweth was fortunate. He was adjudged insane and his mother came to take him east, where she put him in a sanitarium.

One of the most interesting and curious threads in the tapestry of far western folklore, is the belief in the indestructibility of the badman, provided he has been bad enough to be famous. Famous far western badmen never die. Even when there have been witnesses to the demise, even when the badman has been positively identified, even when he has been legally executed, the far western badman, according to popular tradition, invariably "reforms," and goes east, or farther west, or south, and settles down, and becomes a "prosperous citizen," for some strange reason usually a banker. A final embellishment which you can take or leave according to what you think of bankers. Wall Street is especially requested to take notice.

Teton Jackson, for example, is credited with having become a banker after he had served his term of fifteen years in the penitentiary, although he could barely read or write, if at all. Harve Logan, as you have seen, although he did not become a banker, is still supposed by numerous people to be alive. I knew the sheriff who said he hanged Tom Horn in the fall of 1903, but Tom Horn "isn't dead." He was "seen around Buffalo" a couple of years ago, although why he should be seen around Buffalo when he never operated in the Powder River country, but only in the south and center of Wyoming, is difficult to imagine. However, he was "seen around Buffalo."

A little while ago I heard an elderly gentleman announce from the stage of a motion-picture theater that he was Jesse James. He had a good story too. At any moment, especially when cashing a check, I expect to look up into the ancient but clearly recognized face of Billy the Kid.

But there is one famous member of the Hole-in-the-Wall Gang who I, for one, am sure is still alive. The tradition in his case, too, is that he has become a banker; a prosperous banker in the state of Washington. As for that, I don't know, but I'm certain he's alive. There are too many people who ought to know who are equally certain; including a most trustworthy neighbor of mine, a prosperous and highly respected cattleman.

If George Leroy Parker, alias Butch Cassidy, is still alive he is an old gentleman somewhere between seventy and seventy-five years of age.

I wonder if he'll read these paragraphs.

CHAPTER FORTY-THREE

I'm Leading Old Dan

Perhaps you remember "old Bill" Jones who was
blithe no matter what happened to him. In case you've
forgotten, I'll repeat two verses of his song:

> I'm riding old Paint, and I'm leading old Dan,
> And I'm off for Montan' for to throw the hoolihan;
> Feeding in the coulees and a-watering in the draw,
> Their tails are all matted and their backs are all raw.
>
> Ride around the little dogies, O ride around 'em slow,
> For the fieries and the snuffies are a-raring to go.
>
> Old Bill Jones had two daughters and a son,
> One went to Denver and the other went wrong,
> One got killed in a pool room fight,
> But still Bill goes singing from morning to night,
>
> Ride around the little dogies, O ride around 'em slow,
> For the fieries and the snuffies are a-raring to go.

And since I've started, I might as well set down
the third and final verse:

> When I am dead, take my saddle from the wall,
> Bridle up my pony and lead him from the stall.
> Tie my bones to the cantle, and head us t'ward the west,
> And we'll take the trails that we love best.

As to the "fieries" and the "snuffies," you know
enough about them already.

Bill was perhaps a little too blithe, but insouciance and debonairness are nonetheless fine qualities, and especially needed just at present. It is lopsided, of course, to dwell too much on badmen, or upon obvious drama, or melodrama, when describing a country, no matter how dramatic the history of that country has been. A coun-

try is not made by badmen or obvious drama. Drama is an emanation; the surface of a pool; and it is what lies at the bottom of the pool that counts. While as for badmen, it is not they who give a country its character but what good men do to the badmen, and themselves, and to circumstances and environment.

Powder River was made by quiet, peaceable, and desperately hard-working people about whom we seldom hear, although they, too, had a gift for adventure or they would never have been where they were. Furthermore, so that the earnest economic Zeitgeist of the present may be satisfied, enough of the drama of these quiet, desperately hard-working men and women was economic and some of it, because of poverty, was sufficiently sordid and grim. A whole book—several of them —could be written about what happened to the majority of homesteaders. About—to come back to it again —the cruel and disingenuous land policy of the United States government. About the land swindles, political or private, that marked the nineteen-tens and twenties. The people who fooled the ignorant homeseekers were Hole-in-the-Wall gangs, differently dressed.

All over the Far West are great and beautiful valleys scarred by deserted homesteads and broken fences. It will take fifty years for the range to come back. The people who left those homesteads were just as surely robbed as if Harve Logan had raided their ranches.

But, on the other hand, there is this to be said about the Far West, especially about such countries as Powder River, and such states as Wyoming, where the basic life is the inevitably hardy, and at times not to be evaded heroic, life of the out-of-doors. Such countries and such a life attracted, and still attract, hardy and fairly heroic people, bad or good. There is space, there is fresh air, and there is always, as I have said so often in this book, a touch of the caballero. A hint of color. Of lithe movement. To repeat the word, insouciance.

Altitude has a lot to do with it, air like wine. Half the time out west you are walking six inches or so above the earth. About most far western badmen and women, at least those of the stock country, there has been, anyway, a certain exhilaration, a certain highheartedness, even when the highheartedness has been evil. At least, these men and women took an interest in what they were doing. They were neither glazed with drugs nor merely bored gangster "businessmen." They were bad, and they enjoyed it, and they admitted that they were bad, and in this age of warless wars and "economic victims," and girls who "just can't resist" this, that, and the other, there are times when it seems as if what the world needed more than anything else was a few badmen and women who admit they are bad.

You can do something about them then.

The Hole-in-the-Wall Gang turned to train robbery, the holding up of banks, because the cattle rustling which had occupied its members during their youth was "too tame and not exciting enough." As they matured they became more serious-minded and ambitious; less "trifling." Tom Horn, on the scaffold, shrugged his shoulders and said, "Well—a man has to die sometime."

In all fairness, there are other things to remember about the Far West. In a big, lonely country badmen are hard to catch and it is difficult to detect them at their work; in a big, lonely country it takes some time for the law to function, and even then the law is often a personal matter. Most of the badmen shot or hanged in the West, legally or otherwise, were shot or hanged on general principles. And I'm not a bit sure that isn't the best way of shooting or hanging a man. A single act, unless an egregious one, frequently doesn't mean much. A long-continued record means a lot.

At all events, the Far Westerner is very much the repository of the original American Idea, of the favorite American method of procedure. The bona fide American is a queer fellow—Kipling perceived that— bewildering to the average foreign observer. He is incredibly patient and long-suffering, too much so; apparently indifferent; walking past with his eyes averted, lest he find trouble, and then suddenly he bursts into flame, fierce and terrible and searing. You have to realize that about Americans—at least the authentic ones—if you wish to remain safe.

As to the legal killers of the West, the peace officers, they were puzzling people. I have already hinted that if you had a homicidal predilection, getting yourself sworn in wasn't a bad idea. The law backed you up and excused any nervousness you might exhibit with your trigger finger. A number of the most deadly, cold-blooded men in far western history wore shields on their chests.

Remember this at all events: different sections of the Far West exhibited different characteristics, but by and large, especially for a frontier, the Far West had no more than its natural share of disorder, and as Theodore Roosevelt pointed out in his autobiography, the quiet man who minded his own business, but at the same time firmly resented intrusion, usually got along fairly well.

The Far West—that is, the range country—is still a country of pretty "direct action," and will always remain so. The quiet man who minds his own business remains, as always, fairly safe.

Like "rustling," "orneriness" is another excellent, commonly used far western word that has several definitions, directly opposed. Orneriness is a good old American expression now, unfortunately, mostly lost east of the Mississippi. In the case of orneriness, the diversity of implication is more a question of intonation and facial expression than of anything else. In its primary sense orneriness means distinguished meanness. Not just plain meanness, but inherent and cultivated meanness; meanness indulged in for meanness' sake. If you say a man is "ornery," and frown about it, you describe him as an artist in meanness; if you say he's an "ornery sort of cuss" and smile, you mean he's a hard man to keep down. Used in this sense orneriness is about as high a compliment as you can pay. It means a refusal to go under; a refusal to stay down; it means the little spark at the back of a man's spirit that the winds of Fate can never quite blow out.

The phoenix, arising from its ashes, is an "ornery bird." John Colter's flight from the Blackfeet was an epic example of orneriness.

The badmen and women of the Powder had plenty of orneriness in its primary meaning; the good men and women of the Powder were equally distinguished by orneriness in its secondary usage. Neither Indians, nor badmen, nor range wars, nor bonanzas, nor winters of '87, nor anything else could drive the best of them out. They knew why they were there, and they stayed.

Two summers ago Powder River and all of eastern Wyoming suffered from the worst drought in their history. Old Colonel Jones—I'll call him that—smiled when I asked him what he was going to do. This was the seventh time he had been wiped out.

"I'm getting together quite a nice little bunch of yearlings," he said. "I'll get along."

Colonel Jones was eighty-two.

I suppose the big difference is that the Far West lives by the weather, and the Northeast by the stock market. The Far Westerner gets up in the morning and looks at the sky and not the market reports. That's why the Far West is constantly fooling the East, politically and otherwise. To the Far Westerner a cloud is more important than a headline. The Far Westerner is all the time smelling earth, and he is interested in it. And he wouldn't be half as interested in his earth if it was soft, easy earth. When the Far West is up it can wear evening clothes, when it's down it can go back to overalls and sowbelly. Neither overalls nor sowbelly depresses nor mortifies it.

There is another meaning to orneriness . . . a sort of halfway meaning. Every far western country cherishes the sagas of certain local bad goodmen who seem to have been bad merely because they were too healthy, in the manner of cowboys who come into town once a month and drink too much simply because they can't stand being in such splendid condition.

Powder River, like every other far western country, has had its quota of these harmless, if at times annoying, trolls. Such a bad goodman was George W. Pike, a gay and careless young man who flourished in Converse County, just south of the Powder, in the 1890's and early 1900's, and who was often in the Powder River country. Everybody loved George, even those he stole from, which was the entire community. He was generous. Having been accused one day by a neighbor of stealing his horses, George waved an indulgent hand and said, "All right! Go on down to my corral and pick out any horses you like—they're all stolen!" On another occasion, having removed the entire contents of a neighbor's kitchen, newly bought, when the neighbor came over to identify his stove, George said sorrowfully, "You're not honest. Your stove was new, wasn't it? New stoves have legs. Look at this stove—it only has bricks under it." Which was true, but George had removed the legs.

When George died the entire countryside mourned him, and his friend, Lee Moore, an honest and prominent cattleman, erected to his memory a florid and deeply scrolled tombstone in the cemetery at Douglas. On the tombstone was this verse:

Underneath this stone in eternal rest
Sleeps the wildest one of the wayward west.
He was gambler and sport and cowboy too,
And he led the pace in an outlaw crew.
He was sure on the trigger and stayed to the end,
But he never was known to quit on a friend.
In the relations of death all mankind is alike,
But in life there was only one George W. Pike.

I rode all over the Hole-in-the-Wall country again, lately. In through the red canyon and then south and west along the Buffalo Fork, the high red wall riding beside me. High up in the low hills to the west I looked down upon the Hole-in-the-Wall cabin. All that day I had seen only three people: two small boys—a woman—at a ranch halfway up the Buffalo Fork.

It was a blue, cloudless day. The red wall rimmed the day with geranium scarlet. High on the hill opposite the Hole-in-the-Wall cabin was the skeleton of an ancient Ford. Just beyond it were the skeletons of a winter-killed team of white horses, bits of hair still clinging to the bones.

CHAPTER FORTY-FOUR

Tom Horn's Gun

GEORGE LEROY PARKER was his name, but when, for obvious reasons, he chose an alias, he showed a genius for selection. Butch Cassidy suited him perfectly. He was typically Irish both in appearance and in behavior; the way he cocked his sombrero over his left eyebrow, his blue, wrinkled lidded eyes, his short red mustache, his red hair, the deep Celtic lines that ran from the corners of his nose to the corners of his mouth, his square Hibernian chin. Furthermore, he was swaggering, laughing, unexpected and extremely lazy, but when necessary could put forward long-continued bursts of activity, ingenuity and endurance.

The most remarkable thing about him was that, a dead shot, a boon companion of a cold-blooded killer, Harve Logan, and of other men like Harry Longabaugh, the Sundance Kid, who were not unknown to shoot with mortal intent, a leader of the Hole-in-the-Wall Gang, he was never known to kill a man or even to hurt one. That's a strange record for a man often in danger from the guns of others. It is also a sign that perhaps this is the best way to preserve your own life, for of all those outlaw leaders Butch Cassidy is the only one who by any possible chance may be alive today. No one ever wanted to kill Butch Cassidy.

He was born in Utah somewhere between 1865 and 1870 of a respectable Mormon family and for a while worked as an ordinary young cowpuncher; then, his imagination getting the better of him, he took to stealing cattle.

There is a tradition that he participated in a holdup —a petty one—down in Utah when he was only fifteen. About 1890 he drifted north into southwestern Wyoming, homesteaded with a partner near the Owl Creek Mountains, and presently was arrested for rustling horses and convicted. When he came out of the Laramie penitentiary he had evidently thought things over. He had given up childish ways and had become a big-time badman. Pretty soon he had met Harve Logan, the Montpelier bank robbery in Idaho had been pulled off, and the Hole-in-the-Wall Gang was forming.

Stories of Butch Cassidy's generosity, laughter, and love of practical jokes are still part of Powder River and Wyoming folklore. On one occasion, entering a saloon, he saw the local drunkard asleep in a chair tipped against the wall, and first shot the rungs out of the chair one by one, and then the tips of its legs until it collapsed with its still slumbering occupant. On another occasion he neatly clipped the tassel off a Negro cook's hat. And so on and so on. When he offended anyone he gave the victim a twenty-dollar gold piece.

Finally captured and standing trial, he made a compact with the state of Wyoming. He was released on condition that he would never again disturb the state or rob anyone in it. He never did, but he immediately went up to Montana and robbed a bank in order to pay the expenses of his trial in Wyoming. Then he fled, as we have seen, along with Harry Longabaugh, to South America where he was a member of that curious colony of far western badmen—road agents, train robbers, bank robbers, rustlers—which flourished for a while in the mountains of Ecuador and Bolivia.

There's a curious note about these badmen just before they fled, the now thoroughly aroused railroads and state governments hot upon their trails with Pinkerton detectives and United States marshals. The Spanish-American War had just been declared and most of the leading badmen of the West at once wanted to enlist in the United States Army. Well-wishers persuaded them that discretion is often the better part of patriotism, but some minor hard characters did get to Cuba. Possibly you remember the famous story told by Colonel Theodore Roosevelt in his autobiography of a friend of his in New Mexico who wrote as follows:

Dear Colonel:
I'm sure sorry I can't join you and the other boys in your Rough Riders. But, Colonel, I'm in jail. I shot a lady in the eye. It was a mistake, I meant to shoot my wife.

I have seen the same sort of uncanny shooting myself as the shooting characteristic of Butch Cassidy. A friend of mine, now dead, an ex-cowboy and railway detective who ran a general crossroads store, in his lighter moods was fond of clipping cigarettes and cigars out of surprised mouths, and hats off unsuspecting heads. He never missed, and it's a good joke, but slightly eerie. And despite my friend's often spoken-of "kind heart" and the equally kind heart of Butch Cassidy, I think there must be a somewhat cool objective attitude somewhere in case by one chance out of a hundred your hand trembles.

Tom Horn wasn't a bit like Butch Cassidy. No one could have been more different. Tom Horn, at least, if the stories told about him and generally believed are true, was a businessman pure and simple. He killed for money, at a distance, with a rifle, and well concealed.

Ordinarily he was a secretive, close-mouthed man, but when he was drinking he boasted and explained himself, some people think deliberately in order to create a figure of terror in the popular imagination . . . at least, once more, that is what you hear about him. You must take the phrases "at least" and "hearsay" for granted all through these paragraphs concerning Tom Horn. He was a mysterious man, he operated mysteriously in Wyoming, and he met a mysterious fate. Perhaps he created too successful a figure of terror in the popular imagination. Maybe that was what hanged him.

He was hanged in 1903 for the alleged murder of a fourteen-year-old boy. A neighborhood story is that he made the mistake of shooting the fourteen-year-old boy instead of his father. The story goes, this neighborhood version, that the father, suspected of being a rustler, suddenly felt ill at breakfast and so sent his son down to the corrals instead of going himself. Carelessly the boy put on his father's coat and hat, and Tom, lying out on a hillside with a rifle, and seeing the boy at a distance, shot him thinking he was shooting the father. A justifiable mistake under the circumstances, but thought-provoking.

But this version was not the one brought out at the trial and contained in Tom Horn's famous supposed "confession." In that, Horn is supposed to have confessed that he killed the fourteen-year-old boy because the boy came across him while he, Tom, was waiting to ambush the father.

At all events, with Tom Horn's trial in Cheyenne

in 1902 a controversy broke out the embers of which are still smoldering. With Horn's hanging a year later, fresh fuel was added. His numerous friends claimed that he was being thrown to the dogs by men higher up . . . his employers, some of the big cattlemen. His enemies asserted that he was the coldest of methodical cold-blooded killers that had ever appeared on the western ranges. And once more the "indestructibility" of the western badman appeared.

Many people believed that Tom Horn was never hanged; that he was bribed to hold his tongue on the promise that a dummy would be used in his place. Certainly if he wasn't bribed in this fashion he deserved what happened to him, unless . . . a sinister thought . . . he was bribed and then, at the last moment, the bribe withdrawn.

I don't believe this story, and, like most people in Wyoming, I believe that Tom Horn, despite his former record and all his charm, was no more than the killer he was supposed to be; to all intents and purposes, like most of his kind, a homicidal maniac. I know too many men who knew him or who worked alongside of him as cowboys when, ostensibly a cowboy, he was in reality investigating the adjacent range. I know one old gentleman who lived alone with Tom Horn for five winter months in a line camp of one of the big outfits. Tom explained himself. He was "no barroom brawler," although he always wore two ivory-handled, beautifully carved guns at his waist. He was a "quiet businessman," who, since he was a businessman, killed with a rifle and took no more chances than he had to.

But don't make the mistake of thinking that this particular killer wasn't brave. He was an exception; he was exceedingly brave. His record before he came to Wyoming had proved it. This handsome Missourian—

he had left Missouri as a boy—with probably some Indian and Spanish blood in his veins, had a magnificent record before, as a man of forty, in 1900, he drifted quietly into Wyoming and went to work as a stock inspector. He had served splendidly with the army down in Arizona as a scout in the Apache campaigns; he had served equally well as an army packmaster during the Spanish War. He was a famous cowboy; a champion rodeo roper. He had been a Pinkerton detective. He had made a name for himself in the Southwest as a relentless enemy of rustlers and other evildoers. How many men he killed after he came to Wyoming, no one will ever know. How many crimes were credited to him he did not commit, no one will ever know. It is said that after he killed a man he put two stones under his head, then, when those who employed him heard of this they sent him a check for five hundred dollars. Letters, which are always dangerous, were thus obviated.

In any case, shortly after Tom Horn's arrival in Wyoming, something unseen and deadly—a new ghost —was abroad on the ranges.

Tom Horn was trapped into making . . . in order to satisfy everybody, let's say again . . . a "supposed" confession while drunk in a room in Cheyenne. In the next room, listening, were some United States marshals and a stenographer. The man who extracted the confession was Joe Le Fors, a United States marshal who, five years before, had been with Bob Devine, the C Y range foreman, at the cowboy-rustler fight in the Hole-in-the-Wall. Joe Le Fors is still living in Buffalo; a hale old gentleman. Could somebody get hold of his autobiography, the world would have a valuable far western document.

Tom Horn never operated in the Powder River country, but solely in the south and center of Wyoming, mostly the southeast; it is impossible, however, to mention the cattle history of Wyoming without referring to Horn. To Wyoming ears his name is as familiar, and has much the same ring, as the name Billy the Kid to southwestern ears. Rightly or wrongly, he shares honors with Harve Logan as Wyoming's most notorious badman, and he is a far more mysterious, far more interesting figure than Logan.

The evidence upon which he was convicted was bad. The boy he had killed, Willy Nickell, was the son of Kels Nickell, a sheepman, and at the time the enmity between sheepman and cattleman was at its height, and several of Kels Nickell's cattle-ranging neighbors had it in for this intruder. Tom Horn flatly denied the confession supposed to have been extracted from him in Cheyenne, but, on the other hand, he didn't put up a very good defense. There had been a good many mysterious deaths in southern Wyoming just as, ten years before, there had been a good many mysterious deaths up on the Powder. Wyoming was jittery. An atonement of some kind seemed necessary. The West hangs slowly, but, as I say, it usually hangs on general principles. It looks as if Tom Horn was hanged on general principles and for good reasons.

The train was sliding through the dusk of southern Wyoming; a warm August night, with a big planet and a few stars out over the Red Desert. The old gentleman on the observation platform beside me—the only other occupant beside myself—wore a neat small sombrero and had the look of an old-timer, but I didn't know what part of the West he came from. He smoked. I smoked. We both wanted to talk, but didn't know how to begin.

Finally I said: "You know this part of Wyoming?"

He smiled. "I punched cows all through here when I was a kid. I worked for so-and-so" . . . he mentioned a famous old Wyoming outfit. Finally he said, "Tom Horn was with that outfit for a while. I liked him, but I quit because of him. I and my side-kick." And he told me a story of how he and the cowboy who was his especial friend were out looking for horses one morning and came upon Tom Horn, who had been absent from the ranch for a few days, riding blithely down a draw in the warm sunshine, homeward bound. He borrowed a cigarette, talked, rode on. Also, but very casually, he had misdirected them about the horses so that they wouldn't continue up the narrow long valley in which they were. After a while, however, they had circled back to the head of the valley and there they had come upon the small ranch of a suspected rustler and the suspected rustler's wife and small children.

At dawn the suspected rustler had gone down to his corral and someone at a distance had shot him. Under his dead head had been found two stones.

The young cowboys looked at each other, after helping the widow as best they could, and rode back to the ranch and handed in their time. The next day they started the long ride to the railway. Looking back they saw a man galloping. It was Tom Horn.

"Here's where we fight it out," they said to each other, and, knowing Tom's deadliness, "We're out of luck!"

But not at all. Tom caught up with them and smiling his charming smile, took one of his beautiful, ivory-handled guns from his waist and handed it across his saddle horn.

"Here," he said to my acquaintance of the observation platform. "I want you to have this. You and I have worked pretty close together, and I like you. I

want you to keep it. . . . Don't think too hard of me."
And then he turned and rode back to the ranch. In the
distance, he halted his horse and waved.

That's the last those two cowboys ever saw of him.

The old gentleman in the sombrero paused and
looked at the dusk; the big, quiet, yellow dusk of the
desert.

"I'll show it to you," he said, and was gone, and
presently came back with Tom Horn's gun.

This was in 1929, the last year of extravagant pros-
perity, and the city of Chicago was holding a rodeo. I
was going back as a guest of the city and the Chamber
of Commerce, and I discovered that the old gentleman,
who was a sheriff of a Nevada town and who had been
a well-known sheriff up in Montana, and was a famous
far western figure, was also a guest.

"Tex" Austin had got the rodeo together and was
managing it. Tex Austin, at least at that time, often
carried a .22 revolver and was an expert shot from the
hip. The Chicago Chamber of Commerce, with the
Babylonian spirit then prevalent, had asked some thirty
men from all over the West to be its guests. These men
were either far western characters, like the sheriff, or
else cowboys turned illustrators or writers. Will James
was there. So was Ross Santee, the man who illustrated
this book. It cost the Chicago Chamber of Commerce
six hundred dollars to transport me from my Wyoming
range and get me back, and I was just a suburban visitor
compared with some of the rest—nor had I lost any
weight in shipping. All the guests had to do was wear
sombreros and cowboots in addition to their ordinary
clothes, and ride around the arena at Soldiers' Field
twice a day, and when the loud-speaker announced their
names and residences, arise and bow. It was lovely!

In Chicago the rodeo stopped at the "biggest hotel

in the world," which had been open only a week. This hotel advertised, if I remember correctly, that you could sleep in it for seven years and never in the same room, which didn't seem to me a particular recommendation. The hotel was very nice, however, to us in the beginning. We had two floors; a clubroom; a private breakfast room.

The second night of the rodeo the Chicago Chamber of Commerce, not satisfied with what they had already done for us, gave us a banquet in the brand-new state dining room of the hotel, never used before; a Louis XIV dining room; crystal chandeliers and all. There must have been about three hundred people present—cowboys, cowgirls, far western guests, the Chicago Chamber of Commerce; everyone in fact but the Brahma steers and the bucking horses. Somewhere around the end of the dinner the ex-sheriff from Nevada produced Tom Horn's gun and it was passed around the table. All the Far Westerners were justly excited. Finally the gun came to Tex Austin. Sitting on his left was a Chicago cartoonist. Austin looked at the gun, threw it open, closed it, tried the hammer. He passed it to the cartoonist. "That's a wonderful old gun," he said. "It's action is still just like velvet. Try it."

The cartoonist was doubtful.

"It's empty," said Tex. "You saw me break it. Try it! Stand up and point it at that chandelier, and try it."

Still slightly doubtful, the cartoonist obeyed. He pulled the trigger and there was an instantaneous report. A piece of the crystal chandelier fell to the table. The cartoonist stood with his mouth open, horror on his face. Everyone present who knew guns, knew that the report was that of a .22 and not a Frontier-model, and those who knew Tex Austin knew of his skill. But the cartoonist didn't know either of these things, nor did the majority of the Chicago Chamber of Commerce.

The shooting seemed to excite a number of the gentlemen present—inside of five minutes there was hardly a light left.

The Chicago Chamber of Commerce took it, I must say, like men. They looked a little pale and didn't move their heads much, but not a man left his seat. One member asked a trifle faintly, "I suppose all these men are good shots, aren't they?"

"Wonderful!" he was told.

The next day our breakfast room was closed to us. We could get no service at all. The biggest hotel in the world was angry.

Just opposite the biggest hotel in the world is one of the best hotels in the world. The then owner knew the West well and was an old friend of mine. He called me on the telephone and asked me to have lunch with him.

"What a strange idea of publicity!" he reflected. "To get angry! Why, if that had happened to a new hotel of mine the news would have been in Tokyo by now. Thousands of dollars' worth of free advertising! I have two floors ready for the rodeo. Tell them to come over!"

So all that afternoon across the narrow street between the two hotels there moved a small and curious procession, men in sombreros and high-heeled boots, girls in sombreros and high-heeled boots. Accompanying them were bellboys carrying luggage.

CHAPTER FORTY-FIVE

Dead Line

J̲OEL J. HURT, and for a while his name was appropriate, according to tradition, was the first man to trail sheep in any large quantity into the cattle country of eastern Wyoming. In 1888 Joel Hurt trailed three thousand sheep into Natrona County.

Natrona County is the county just south of Johnson County and the Powder, and it lies almost in the exact center of the state. Natrona County is the county of the old Platte Bridge, and the county where the Sweetwater joins the North Platte as the latter, after its long journey north from the Sierra Madres, swings east. Natrona County is the county where Robert Stuart built the first house in Wyoming, and it is where the Buffalo Fork, the South Fork, and the Salt Fork of the Powder head. On the northern rim of Natrona County is the Teapot Dome Divide.

Joel Hurt trailed his sheep into the very heart of the cattle kingdom. He was either an extremely courageous man or else an obstinate one.

Nowadays in most parts of the West the sheepman and the cattleman, owing largely to the allocation of range on the part of the government and the Forest Service, manage to get along together fairly well. Nowadays a good many of the big ranches run both cattle and sheep—in good years sheep are extremely profitable —but the man who runs both sheep and cattle is very careful to divide off and take care of his own range. He establishes his own dead lines.

There is nothing, of course, the matter with sheep if they are properly handled; something that has hardly ever happened in the United States, and something that never seems to occur to most sheepmen. Sheep in small bands help a range just as they help a lawn or a pasture, but in large bands, carelessly and selfishly run, they are death. And you won't get that idea out of the head of the cattleman, or the horseman, no matter what you tell him.

Sheep in too-large bands, allowed to graze too long on a range, leave behind nothing but desolation. They feed the grass down to the roots, and then, having done that, they cut the roots to pieces with their thousands of sharp little hoofs. Meanwhile, they have polluted water holes and streams so that other stock will not drink after them, and when they have nothing else to eat they browse. That means they tear the bark off trees and kill all underbrush.

Sheep, improperly run, destroy all ground cover and vegetation; ruin water; start erosion; and make a pleasant land look like the craters of the moon. There is a far western phrase, a "sheeped-off country," which conveys immediately to the minds of all Far Westerners a picture of ruin. The West is filled with sheeped-off countries that once were lovely valleys and uplands. In addition, sheep in large bands smell abominable, keep up a constant, nerve-destroying blatting, and are curiously ugly on the landscape. "Maggots" are what they are called by those who don't like them, and the ugly simile is correct.

Finally, sheep carry the Rocky Mountain tick, so named incorrectly—the dreaded spotted-fever tick—into localities where it never was before.

All of which has nothing to do with a business that is a good business when properly run, and an animal that is a good animal, and essential, and not unpleasant properly ranged and properly handled, which means with some regard to the rights of other men. Australia is the biggest sheep country in the world. In Australia you buy land from the government for a song and you run your sheep inside your own fences. The best sheep ranches in the West today do the same. Nothing is more illuminating than to see a sheep range leased by some sheepman and a range owned by that same man. The former is likely to look like a desert; the latter is usually well taken care of.

But there was something else, too, that brought the cowboy and the herder into immediate conflict; a curious and antagonistic difference in character. It is still a mortal insult in the Far West to call a cowboy a "sheep-herder," unless you know him well and smile when you say it, although as things are now lots of cowboys, temporarily thrown upon a cruel world, have at various times, with grave distaste, herded sheep.

The cowboy is gregarious and works in company with his fellows; also he works with fast horses and fast and running stock. Both his life and his inclinations are hard-riding, a trifle reckless, a trifle flamboyant, although as a rule on the surface quietly so. The sheep-herder is usually mounted too, but he has an ambling nag. He seldom rides except at a walk, and he is a solitary fellow; often sullen, sometimes a poet and dreamer, frequently a Mexican, often a Basque . . . they're the best of the lot. If an American, likely to be a queer sort of dick. A man has to be queer to be willing to live for months with no other companions but sheep and dogs. The blatting alone drives most normal men crazy in a month.

Lots of herders during the summer months see no one except when their camp mover with his supply wagon comes around, or, if it is a rough country, the camp mover with his pack outfit. Some of the far western states have passed laws making it obligatory to send herders out in pairs; but that doesn't do much good. They go queer together and often murder each other.

A big owner I know two summers ago paid off one of his herders, giving him a check for over two years' work; somewhere around fifteen hundred dollars. For two years the herder had taken no holiday and had drawn no wages except a few dollars for tobacco and clothes. Now he was going to have a holiday and so he set off for town with the check in his pocket. He got no farther than the nearest post office, a tiny collection of houses, including a saloon, thirty miles down the valley. The next day the owner received a telephone call asking for money. The herder said he would come right back and go to work. In one night he had spent fifteen hundred dollars; his earnings for over two years.

If you add the large carelessness and unconscious—or conscious—selfishness of the average American to the large carelessness and often deliberate selfishness of the United States government where free land, the range, and the Far West are concerned, you have among other things sheep and cattle wars.

In the Far West the government frequently created, or permitted, situations in which men, made desperate, had no recourse except to their own sense of justice. We have seen how accurately the government created such situations when the Sioux owned the Powder. Joel Hurt started something that lasted for two decades and isn't altogether over yet. Adjudication between sheep and cattle interests, between sheep and cattle range, is still a delicate matter.

Here are a few of the things that Joel Hurt
started . ... just a few out of scores of similar occur-
rences throughout the length and breadth of Wyoming,
throughout the length and breadth of the Far West.
During the nineties, during the first decade of the nineteen hundreds, well into the second decade, underneath
all other troubles, local or state, was this constant ani-
mosity between the cattleman and the sheepman, likely
to flare into flame at any moment.

On the 24th of August, 1905, for instance, ten
masked men rode down on the sheep camp of Louis
Gantz, fifty miles or so out from the town of Basin in
the Big Horn valley, shot or knocked over the head four
thousand head of sheep, shot a valuable team of horses,
burned all the camp wagons, grain, provisions, and
everything else in the camp, and even tied the sheep
dogs to the burning wagons and burned them too. The
Gantz sheep were on their way to the high summer pastures of the Big Horns and it was claimed that, despite
warnings, they were being trailed with unnecessary
slowness and were destroying the range as they passed
along.

Gantz's herders were warned to leave the country
and never come back.

Four years later, in the same general locality, an
even more drastic raid took place. On No Water Creek
in the Ten Sleep country, Joe Allemand, a sheepman,
his camp mover, and one of his herders were overtaken
by masked men and shot. All of Allemand's sheep were
killed and his camp was burned to the ground.

I relate these stories merely to show what happened
again and again. There is no use duplicating them. They
are not especially pleasant. But if you realize that with
the then lack of control of the range it was often a
question of life or death for both the cattleman and the

sheepman, such outrages, on the one hand, and such obstinate recklessness, on the other, can at least be understood. Back of it all, responsible for it all, more deadly
than any machine gun ever invented, was the land policy of the United States government, of the various
states. Back of it all was politics. I don't know, but I
would hazard the guess that politics in the United States
has killed as many men, directly or indirectly, as all our
wars put together. Often the murder has been merely
the slow one of starvation. This would be a wonderful country if senators, congressmen, and governors—
usually honest men and intelligent men, outstanding—
would just keep on being honest, I mean intellectually,
and did what they thought best. The average senator to
begin with is even a modest man, although you may
not believe it. It takes at least two years to change him
into a combination of dictaphone, fourth-class post
office, prima donna, and motion-picture character
actor.

Because of the land policy of the government and
the various states, cattleman and cowboy murdered
sheepman and herder, nor were the sheepmen slow to
retaliate if they saw a chance. Plenty of cowboys were
"dry-gulched."

All through the Far West sheep camps were raided
at intervals, sheep were wiped out, herders were
whipped, or warned out of the country. If they were
obdurate, or put up a fight, they were killed. In many
countries, sheepmen lived for a while in constant danger.

A favorite method of destroying sheep was to saltpeter the range. You rode across it, spreading a narrow
trail of saltpeter behind you, and as the sheep fed across
this trail, the saltpeter killed them. Another method was
to drive the sheep over a precipice. Once the leaders
started, the whole band would follow. Sheep are fa-

mous for following their leaders, even to death. In this respect no other animal equals them, except man.

Where sheep and cattle were concerned the Powder River country was quieter than its neighbors to the east, south, and west. Apparently the Powder River men, because of the troubled eighties and nineties, had learned patience and self-control. And today along the Powder the sheep and cattle range in quiet. A number of the big cattlemen are also sheepmen, a number of the sheepmen run cattle, but there are still a number of cattlemen who will have nothing to do with sheep.

The "Senator" felt that way.

I remember the look in his eyes when by mistake I once asked him if he also ran sheep.

Many countries in the Far West still maintain absolute dead lines; that is, they will not permit sheep at all, an attitude backed up by the Forest Service which has made such decisions local rulings. With all due respect, countries like this are blessed. They are also becoming rare. The sheepmen are now pretty much in control in most far western states. The woolgrowers' associations tell the stockgrowers' associations where to head in.

There was a great drought over most of Wyoming in 1935; a dreadful drought. The summer pasture went; the winter pasture. Men saw their sheep and cattle starve, weaken, die. The markets were overstocked. Yearlings, seed cattle, everything, sold for what a man could get. Drought is like a dying woman, wide-eyed, staring, never moving, fever on her lips. It is slow. It is never for an instant to be forgotten. It is like the droning of a fly on a breathless summer afternoon. You go to sleep with it, you wake up to it, you dream of it. It is a band about your head and a hollowness in your stomach. It is a nightmare you cannot wake from. A dusty, rattling corpse.

All to the east the cattle and the sheep had come down from the mountains where no feed was and were along the roads gaunt-ribbed, wandering, sick-eyed.

I happened to be in a mountain valley that was untouched by the drought; a cattle country where there was a strict dead line. There were rumors that the sheepmen to the east and the west had their eye on that valley; on its water and grass; and that they were petitioning Washington for a temporary summer permit. If the permit were given, the valley knew that the marching, starving sheep would mean destruction, at least for the time being. Perhaps for good. Once you let sheep into a country, they are hard to get out.

On my way up the valley one afternoon I stopped in at a ranch to see its foreman about some business. It was a hot July dusk. The foreman and one of his cowboys and myself were sitting on our heels near a corral talking. A man rode in and said: "Well, they're coming! Washington's given permission. The Forest Service is on the long distance, trying to stop them!"

He meant that sixty thousand sheep were on their way through the mountain pass to the southeast and about forty thousand sheep on their way through the mountain pass to the west.

The foreman looked at the man who had just come in, and then at the cowboy, and then at me. "All right!" he said. "Let's go!" He went over to his house and came back with rifles and revolvers. The three of us climbed into a car and started down the valley.

When we got to the little town at the foot of the valley, it was crowded. The whole valley was there; milling about, talking, waiting. The bars were doing a big business. Men had come in from ranches miles away.

A lot of them hadn't seen each other for years. All the local supply of saltpeter had been bought up. In some casual way or other organization seemed to be complete. Certain men were to hold one pass and saltpeter it and stop the herders; certain men were to do the same with the other pass.

It was all very quiet and arranged and decided. There was no discussion about the propriety of the extralegal proceeding.

Meanwhile, the Forest Service had an open wire to Washington.

At ten o'clock word came that Washington had changed its mind and that forest rangers over in the sheep countries were turning the sheep back.

The gathering turned into an impromptu party; one of the best imaginable.

CHAPTER FORTY-SIX

Ladies in Pants

A<small>ND</small> now we come to the last invasion of the Powder, an extremely benign and peaceable one, not to say at moments humorous. On the whole, though, say useful; say fine. Sometimes on Saturday nights it isn't altogether peaceable, but, along with the cattle business, it seems to me one of the best things that has ever happened to the West. The West has always been recruited by some of the fine blood of the East; the East has always been recruited, ever since there was a West, by some of the fine blood of the West. A number of the best ranchers and citizens of the Powder came out first as "dudes."

Howard Eaton and his two brothers, Willis and Alden, started it—the dude business, and they started it by accident, the way all the original dude wranglers started. And they had no idea at the time what they were starting. The business just happened to them, and it grew like Topsy; strong and exuberant, and because it couldn't help itself.

Howard and Willis and Alden Eaton were three young men from Pittsburgh, Pennsylvania, who had a big horse ranch up in the Dakotas. Howard, the oldest, came out first . . . he came in the seventies . . . and Willis and Alden joined him later. The Eaton brothers were extremely popular. That's the main secret of the dude business. You have to be popular to be a successful

dude wrangler. If you're not, you'd better go back to cattle, or horses, or sheep. Personality doesn't make so much
difference to them. But the Eaton brothers were so popular that a number of their friends wanted to come out
to the Dakota ranch for the summer and for the autumn hunting, and pretty soon the Eaton brothers, like
a good many other popular and hospitable people, found
they were spending more money on their friends than
they were making from their horses. One of the friends
made a brilliant suggestion . . . he suggested that the
visitors to the Eaton ranch help pay expenses. A little
later, another friend made an even more brilliant suggestion; he suggested that the visitors pay more than
their expenses.

And that's the way the dude business started.

The soil, however, was ripe, and the dude business
has about as solid a foundation as any business I know.
The demand was there before the supply. The original
dude wranglers became dude wranglers willy-nilly.
They just had to. The demand was too much for them.
All good businesses, like all useful inventions, come into
being willy-nilly, because the demand is there first.

As a matter of fact, the demand for the dude business started not long after John Colter discovered Wyoming. From the very beginning adventurous people
"wanted to see the West"; tourists, and hunters, and
writers, and young men who wanted to dig for gold or,
later on, to become cowboys. And in the wake of the
young men came, naturally, young women anxious to
find out what the young men were doing and to marry
gold miners and ranchers and cowboys. Even at its
most dangerous the West had plenty of tourists, exploring or hunting, and as soon as it was possible to go
west without much danger of being scalped, the dude
business formally began.

Strange things happen to men and women when they go touristing; the West and Powder River cherish a portfolio of stories. All through history numerous tourists, and now not a few dudes, have preferred to die, figuratively speaking, rather than be right.

But, by and large, big hats, loud shirts, and everything else, the West in the last thirty years has gained much from the East, and the East has gained much from the West. The East has even taught western girls to wear overalls and "riding pants," something never dreamed of when I first went west. In those days if a lady wanted to mount a horse, and didn't have a divided skirt, she mounted regardless of the scenery. But not riding pants! Those were immodest.

Pretty soon the Eaton brothers, up to their neck in the dude business, moved from the flat Dakota country over to the base of the Big Horns where their famous ranch is today, at Wolf, Wyoming. Their sons and nephews carry on the ranch.

Howard Eaton was one of the great characters of the West and of the Powder. A big, square, charming, humorous man; a wonderful storyteller. In all his long, exceedingly useful and exceedingly picturesque life he did only one rash thing and that was to give the business that had been wished upon him and his brothers its name. Howard Eaton invented the word "dude," or rather he gave to the old word a new meaning.

Most dude wranglers wish that the name had never been thought of. It has been a constant source of misunderstanding and trouble, giving to a bona fide and dignified business, and to dignified ranchmen and visitors, an undignified twist. Nor did Howard Eaton mean the term to have any of the implications that sometimes mistakenly it carries today.

The word "dude" does not necessarily mean tenderfoot. It has no social or class connotations. There is no contempt intended. It simply means someone, usually a stranger, who pays his way on a far western ranch or pays someone to cook and guide for him out in camp. The oldest cattleman in the world, the most experienced citizen of a far western state, is a dude while he is doing that. Naturally, however, it has been difficult to keep

tenderfoot out of the minds of those who misuse the term.

The Eaton brothers showed the world and, having shown it, the dude business grew by leaps and bounds. Pretty soon almost every ranch in the West, whatever else it did . . . cattle, horses, sheep . . . was a dude ranch. That is, it threw up a few log cabins, got out a circular, and hired a bad cook, if it hadn't already. Often if it had a nice, nonblurring brand to begin with, it added as its trade-mark, not to be used on stock, something fancy like Quarter Circle Full Moon W, or whatever else the owner thought would appeal to the romantic imagination of the East. To the contrary, sometimes in despair, the owner, being himself an unimaginative man, just waved his hand and called his place "Smith Dude Ranch" or "Jack Pine Lodge." During the dear dead decade that followed the war, when everybody made money, even cattlemen, and three dollars was worth six dollars and three cents, it began to look as if a new bonanza had struck the Rocky Mountains.

Just as in the cattle bonanza, or the gold bonanza before it, or before that the beaver bonanza, the dude business seemed to present a wonderful opportunity for those who couldn't do anything else to fail at that too. And a number of them did. They still have their buildings.

Young man after young man, coming west with the intention of curing his passion for alcohol, opened a dude ranch. And young women, not so alcoholic but equally irresponsible, did the same. The mountain fastnesses are still filled with them, and in their ignorant and not-so-tender keeping the dude is still breaking bones and getting lost. Strange that you would trust yourself in a lonely, and always potentially dangerous, country, if you don't know what you are doing, with anyone but an expert! It all looks so simple, but it isn't. Surgery looks simple too. And the more a man knows, the more easy it looks. But don't fool yourself by thinking that because the West has big roads it isn't still the West. And my advice is that if you want to go to a dude ranch, find out first the history of the man who runs it. A college education doesn't necessarily make you good in the mountains.

Nowadays there are signs that the bonanza is slowly approaching its end. There are more dude ranches than ever, hundreds of them; all through Colorado, Arizona, New Mexico, Wyoming, Montana, and even Idaho, that curious and suspicious state whose gorgeous wildernesses are inhabited by ancient mountainmen who don't like strangers. But any number of these dude ranches have within the last two years folded up, or else have settled down to the fairly lucrative but less glamorous business of being roadhouses and gasoline stations.

There are, as you probably know, dude ranches on
the outskirts of New York and Philadelphia, and various
other eastern cities, whose brands are particularly eso-
teric when they aren't the stolen brand of some well-
known ranch in the West. A famous dude wrangler of
my acquaintance who goes east each winter to remind
Easterners there's a West, as most dude wranglers have
to, tells me he is immensely bothered by telephone calls
on the part of slightly foreign-sounding ladies and gentlemen who want to run out over Sunday to his dude
ranch in New Jersey. There happens to be a "ranch"
half an hour from Times Square using his brand.

In New York and Atlantic City, and for all I
know in dozens of other cities, there are Dude Ranch
restaurants. The waiters pack guns and wear sombreros,
and the waitresses wear overalls. Recently a club has
been started in Paris, known as "Le Cercle de Wild
West," whose members wear cowboy clothes, when
around Le Cercle, and are taught roping, branding and
bronco twisting.

As a matter of fact, of course, there is nothing that
requires more experience and more character, if sometimes a peculiar one, than the running of a successful
dude ranch. In the first place, you have to be a ranchman; that is, you have to know all about stock and agriculture. In the second place, you have to be a good advertising man. In the third place, you have to be a psy-
chologist. In the fourth place, you have to cultivate, at
least during the season, the disposition of an angel. In
the fifth place, you have to be a big-game hunter and a
mountain and pack-outfit man. Not to mention also
having to be something of a hotel man and chef, and a
county and state and national politician. Frequently you
even have to be a psychiatrist. These are just a few of
the things you have to be.

High altitude, breath-taking scenery, comparative loneliness, the candor and simplicity of ranch life, at times have queer effects, often curative, but by no means always, upon spoiled and softened people. Ladies ask you about their husbands; gentlemen consult you about their wives and their businesses; and old ladies and young ladies fall upon your breast and weep. As I have frequently remarked before in print, a good dude wrangler is a combination of a doctor, an older brother, a son, a parent, a father confessor, a riding instructor, a fishing guide, a chaperon; a storyteller, a crooner, a cowhand, a horse wrangler and the United States Weather Bureau. Frequently he is also a big-league umpire.

In the winter you come upon dude wranglers taking a couple of months off just to be bad-tempered.

But it's worth it. The dude wrangler achieves the most useful bit of knowledge possible; especially useful nowadays, and for the most part denied. Like the "Senator," the dude wrangler gets to know people, and getting really to know them, comes to the conclusion that most people, uncrowded, are curiously nice. Strangely nice—nice against all odds and for no especial reason. That changes his point of view about everything. Some people think this ingenuous. It is, of course, the height of wisdom; so mature as to be beyond the reach of cynicism.

As soon as you decide that, terrible as most people are, it is marvelous how fine they are under the circumstances—the circumstances being life—you've grown up.

Along the Big Horns are many of the oldest and finest dude ranches in the West, and the men who run them are among the Powder's most useful citizens. I don't think what the dude ranch and the dude wrangler has done for the West has as yet ever been properly assessed. The dude wrangler and the dude ranch came just in the nick of time.

Ideas run away with people. If men and countries could only maintain an even keel and go forward sensibly, retaining what is good of the past and adding what is good of the present, everything would be well. But countries, like men, suddenly become ashamed of their youth and think that growing up consists of putting on a derby hat and looking as ugly and determinedly uninteresting as possible. There was a time, about twenty years ago, when the Far West sold itself to what it called "progress," and the idea is still knocking about. That meant land speculation, destruction of natural resources, a passion for hydroelectric power, although what you were going to do with so much and so remote hydroelectric power when you had it was another question, and a hankering for skyscrapers, still considered a good way to make money and a sign of civilization. All this implied an earnest determination to forget that the stock business had made the Far West and was still its most valuable asset, and that the scenery and the life of the West were the only things that differentiated it from Hoboken.

The dude wrangler has steadily fought all that, and it is beginning to be recognized that far from being a reactionary, he may have some sense after all. Nor has he had to fight his battle along aesthetic and imaginative lines, even if often he may have wished that perhaps he could. Scenery is good business. Honest color and atmosphere is good business. Beauty and cleanness is good business. A sufficient amount of wilderness is good business. Game is good business. So are fish. The cowboy costume is the only native American costume ever invented, and a beautiful one. It is also as useful a working outfit as a man can wear.

In addition to this, the dude wrangler saved the cattle business and the horse business just when the folly of men had about wrecked them. The dude wrangler brought round hard money into the country. If he was a cattleman, he found himself able to continue in his profession. If he was a horseman, he could do the same. The dude business has changed the face of the West. When I first saw the West, half the population was starving to death because of homesteading, and the chances for a permanently submerged population, such as there is in the South, were growing. The dude wrangler created all kinds of new jobs.

People often wonder what is back of the dude business. What the primary springs are that first made this curious business, that made it grow, that made it into the regular and steady business it now is, to the astonishment of most of those who originally found themselves in it? The answer, it seems to me, lies deep in the nature of the American.

There are, of course, the obvious answers, and they do well enough for the majority. But the obvious answers fail to take into account the imaginative and the passionate man and woman—passionate in the sense of feeling life deeply. Why do people have such a deep and inarticulate love of the West that they cannot express it? Why do so many people year after year return to the West with a poignant twist in their hearts that is almost like a physical tightening? Why is such a country more home to them than their own homes?

The clear air? The clear skies? The warm great sunshine? The quiet hours and nights? The outdoors with all kinds of sports, easily come by and informal?

Horses? Cowboys? Simple food, plenty of sleep, an absence of telephones and engagements? Those are the surface explanations, with a dozen others there's no time for, but underneath there are more fundamental reasons. Racial memories, I would hazard the guess. Wide, and so far undefined, national and individual dissatisfactions and aspirations.

Americans are descendants of adventurers; of men and women who made one of the greatest leaps-in-the-dark of history. That's in their blood, even if they don't know it and no matter how much they may foolishly deny it. And most northern Europeans, and their descendants, are lonely and solitary folk, too, who like to walk by themselves and meditate, and look slowly about them. They are dreamers, most of them.

A paradox has arisen. The adventurers, the forest people, the mountain people, found a great continent that only the machine could develop. But I don't think they're happy, and I don't think they actually love crowds. Nor do I think most of them like fat, crowded countrysides. And I don't know anybody who really likes a suburb. Everything in places like that interferes with the dawns and the trees and the grass and the horizons and the dusks, and a chance to really look at things.

Dawn along the Powder is as slow and uncrowded as creation. You understand why there is color in the world. And you start the day with a sense of space. The day rises and has a climax, and descends. The hours are round like orbs and seem to have some sequence and reason, containing, each one, at the center of the roundness, something sensible and important. And always, to give a sense of permanence there are mountains in the distance. And at night when you fall asleep there is a cool contentment deep down, deeper than sleep.

The West is essential. It satisfies some American desire. It is simple, it is stark, it is dignified, and yet it is lovely. I think, incidentally, that is also a definition of real democracy. The West gives the American, and those like him, a feeling that perhaps there's some rational explanation, after all, for life and for his point of view.

And then there is, of course, just the niceness and simplicity of the way you meet and see people.

I don't think Americans are a "fashionable" people, the way the Latins are. Nor the English either; nor any northern nations. I think Americans when they try to be fashionable are silly, uncomfortable and disagreeable. I think they like old clothes, the country, quiet meditation, and a few friends easily come by. The other thing makes them nervous and unhappy. That's why they drink too much at parties; just as the more released and fashionable English do.

The northern races have none of the French or Italian love of crowds just for the crowd's sake; of "causerie." They can't talk about a timetable for hours the way the French can . . . wittily, pleasantly, and easily.

Years ago a very distinguished Frenchman, but a tall, blue-eyed Breton, who, as a Breton, would understand these things better than most of his nation, spent the summer with me.

All day we rode or fished or worked. He was an editor and novelist. At night we ate quietly and then sat around a fire and talked. The nights were still with hundreds of miles of country not too much occupied; of forests not occupied at all. One night the Breton, staring into the fire, raised his head and slapped his knee.

"I have it!" he said. "I understand! I've been wondering why all this seemed to make me feel so good and happy inside; as if I had recaptured the past, and were able to give the past, and present, and future some continuity. It's because this place is like one of those medieval gatherings at some quiet country house we read about. It's like the *Decameron* with the plague and other unpleasant things left out."

CHAPTER FORTY-SEVEN

Tally

THERE is so much to say! So many stories to tell! One has a sense of inadequacy, more even than when finishing most books. One longs for the gift of a wand that with a single encircling gesture would make people perceive without the halting imperfection of words what he has been trying to say. The passion he feels. The memories that are part of him. The visions he has pursued, most of them never caught up with. The sounds. The scents. A wand that would give the color he has been trying to catch. The atmosphere. The character. These are such subtle things. So hard to loop with the mind. So difficult to confine within the narrow compass of a sentence. And especially when the history of a country has been dramatic, one feels, as I have said, that one has emphasized too much the drama; too little the quiet solid facts. Too little the solid quiet people.

There is so much to say! So many stories to tell!

I would like, for instance, to talk about a man I know who has a gift of inverted stabbing aphorism. Something as sudden and illuminating as summer lightning. You come across this often in the West. One day he said of another man, "He's so crazy about himself that if anyone else likes him he gets jealous." Again, speaking of a certain dangerous acquaintance, he remarked that he "was the best man to be an enemy to he had ever met." And I would like to analyze in loving detail the type of mind that makes cowboys and Far Westerners in general the heroes of such stories as the following.

The hero in this instance is a cowboy who worked for a friend of mine.

It seems that the cowboy had also worked for a very arrogant and very famous old ranchman . . . very arrogant . . . but as the cowboy told my friend, he "worked only half a day."

The morning after he had signed on, he happened to be near the ranch house when out came the arrogant old ranchman, his hair sticking up straight with the frost of dawn.

"Hey! Come over here, Bill!" he called.

Bill came.

"Bill, I want to explain something to you."

"Yes, sir—Mr. Trompee." We'll call the ancient ranchman Mr. Trompee.

"Bill, you're new around here, and I've got my own system, and anybody who wants to work for me has to learn that system. The point is, I'm a man of very few words and I don't like to waste 'em, see?—A man of very few words. Now, any time you're around and I whistle, you come running, and I'll tell you what I want. Understand? Don't call, and don't just stand and look at me. When I whistle, you come running. I'm a man of very few words, and I don't like to waste 'em."

"And what did you say, Bill?" my friend inquired.

"Well, sir, I looked at him, and I said, 'Mr. Trompee, that's mighty interesting! Yes, sir, mighty interesting! I got exactly the same nature as you, Mr. Trompee. I'm a man of very few words, and I don't like to waste 'em. And when you whistle, Mr. Trompee, and I shake my head thisaway . . . why, that means, Mr. Trompee, I'm not coming.' "

When I first settled in the West, all along the Powder River and everywhere else there was another distinct type of Far Westerner, now almost gone. Just a few survivors left—very old men. This was the old soldier. The men who had served with Crook and Miles and Custer and Howard, and some even with Connor, and the majority of whom had also served in the Civil War. Most of them had turned rancher, some of them were peace officers, a few were small-town businessmen.

Straight-backed, gray-headed, interesting old fellows, with the underlying gravity of men who have seen a lot of sudden death. I wish that for most of them there had been a stenographer to take down exactly what they said. History can carry the facts—sometimes; it can carry the atmosphere; it can even carry the feeling; but it can't carry smells and intimate sights. It can't, for instance, describe a battlefield knee-deep in blue July lupine.

There was old "Uncle Jimmy" Curtis, for example. The last time I saw Uncle Jimmy, only a couple of years ago, he was ninety-three and when he walked away from me, his back was that of a strong man of forty. Broad-shouldered, narrow-hipped, young. He had complained that he couldn't remember his reading glasses—"The doctor tells me to use 'em," he said, "but I just somehow can't remember them!" Uncle Jimmy had served with Miles and before that with Sherman on his march through Georgia. After leaving the army, he had been a scout, and later a sheriff. A gentle, amused old man, Uncle Jimmy. He described one Indian fight where, at dawn, the cavalry had charged down from the top of some hills. In the cool July morning you could smell the smoke of the Indian village in the valley. That's where the lupine came in, too . . . History doesn't tell you those things.

Uncle Jimmy had helped to chase Chief Joseph—
Thunder-Strikes-out-from-the-Water—and been present at his surrender. He told how surprised most of the
soldiers had been when a Nez Percé in the robes of a
Roman Catholic priest had buried the Nez Percé dead,
reading the Roman Catholic burial service, and he described the chagrin of his commanding officer when
Chief Joseph, during a truce to discuss surrender, had
gently rebuked the somewhat pompous colonel in these
terms:

"My warriors, colonel, do not mutilate the dead.
The Nez Percés are Christians. I am sorry, colonel, that
your men scalped and mutilated my dead."

There was, also, old Mr. Hendricks who had served
with Grant, and with Custer, and who had been in all
sorts of fighting. The gentlest and kindest old man
imaginable. His hatred of bloodshed amounted to an
obsession. He talked about it constantly. He hated death.
Wouldn't even kill a ground squirrel. And then one
day, out of a perfectly clear sky, he ran out of his house
and shot and killed an innocent neighbor who had come
to see him on some ordinary business.

Just like that! Laughing and shooting!

Old soldiers gone; stagecoach drivers; bullwhackers
and mule skinners; but cattleman and sheepman, and
cowboy, and mountainman, and prospector, and sheriff
left! And added to these some new far western figures
with plenty of action about them and color. The forest
ranger, for instance. And the national park ranger. And
the game warden. And the dude wrangler and his
charges.

I would like, too, to devote an entire chapter to far
western place names, those round, bright, unworn coins
flung in the poet's lap! They seem to me among the
most indigenous of native products. They could occur

nowhere except in the United States. Strange that only one American poet, Stephen Benét, has had the good sense to use them!

Take, for instance, the names of far western creeks! Lodge Pole and Lightning. Cow Creek, Wild Cow Creek. Old Woman, Young Woman. Black Thunder. Squaw. Raven, Little Bear, Rawhide, Porcupine. Big Bear, Lost Cabin, Separation, Wagonhound, Box Elder, Bluegrass, Dry. Crying Water. Hanging Woman. Crazy Woman. No Wood. No Water. Tragic names, those last two! Skull. A hundred more! Like the crack of a whip they lash out at you, telling you plainly what they mean.

And then, as you come to the mountains, to living water and green dusks: Big Piney and Little Piney. Columbine. Boulder. Beaver. Clear. Black Rock. Soda Fork . . . white water bubbling like soda! Lynx and Wolverine and Fox. Swan, Salmon, Tepee, Elk, Moose, Spread. With always, of course, repeated a thousand times, in the arid as in the forested country, Cottonwood and Horse and Buffalo and Bear, and a score of others.

There is so much to say! So many stories to tell! Language is an extraordinary thing; it makes men and unmakes them. Men make it and unmake it. It is as close to a man as his blood. Action and reaction! A man is no more than the words he uses, and all words, to begin with, were symbols—pictures—of course. White is no more than wheat, and when a man says "white" he should always have at the back of his head the picture of a wheat field bending in the breeze. That is important, if no more than to remind a man in winter of the summer, and to impress upon him the close connection of everything. But the trouble with words is

that, like life, they lose their power and virtue and become corrupt and careless and greasy with usage.

Western place names are still as strong as the day
they were given.

When the Sioux came to the Powder the grass was
tall, at least it was up to a pony's shoulders and waved
endlessly in the wind. When the first cattlemen came to
the Powder the grass was still tall. A man could turn
a steer loose on that grass and, at the end of four years,
sell the steer in competition with the grain-fed, fat-
tened cattle of the Middle West. You can't do that now.

No nation in all history has had a land so kind, so
rich as ours; so willing, so patient, so aptly arranged;
so laid out for wealth and comfort and happiness. Even
all the big rivers run the right way. When the grass on
the Powder is as high once more as a horse's knees, it
will be a sign that we have discovered what we should
have known in the beginning.

Powder River is a buckaroo; a broken-nosed, insouciant, slightly swaggering old waddie. Powder River
is the shadowy figure of a rustler, hawk-eyed and cruel.
Powder River is a cavalryman in dusty blue, a fatigue
cap pulled down over one eye. Powder River is a Sioux,
naked and painted for war. Powder River is a Crow,
looking down from the summits of the Big Horns.
Powder River is a man of a dim prehistoric race who
has left only a few undecipherable signs behind him.
For all we know, Powder River may also be a "tall man
in shining clothes, feathers on his head." A ghost, speaking Spanish.

If you will get off your horse in the late afternoon,
and sit on some shoulder of the Big Horns looking east,
you will see, until your eyes lose themselves in the dis-

tance, the great and shining country. First the pines and firs and aspens about you and at your feet; then the wide fringe of green ranches; then, beyond those, the tawny yellow and browns of the Powder River valley, with the thin, twisting light-green and dark-green ribbon of the cottonwoods. And beyond that are the Pumpkin Buttes and the strange colors and shapes of the badlands. Mile after mile the country goes to the immensely distant horizon and below its edge you know the tawny, the burnt amber, the gray, the brown, the rose continue.

The sky of the horizon is a clear air washed blue, darkening a little with the late afternoon. It is immensely quiet; a tiny sound of murmuring in the pines. Far off, to the northeast, is the blue shadow of the Black Hills. And if you wait long enough, and have imagination, and will turn your eyes back to the base of the Big Horns, down there where just below you the old Bozeman ran, you will see a procession; slow moving, impalpable, shimmering with the haze of dusk.

Hunters on spotted ponies following the buffalo. Ponies dragging travois. Warriors riding, the women following them in their blankets. Carrington and his marching infantrymen. Crook and his cavalry. The Cheyennes, naked and with torn feet. Red Cloud and his armies. The wagons and horsemen of the Invaders. The scattered, quick-trotting figures of the Hole-in-the-Wall men. A hundred thousand cattle, horns tossing, dust rising like powdered gold. Then, like a ground fog moving slowly over the vast natural grazing ground, thousands of gray sheep striking their sharp feet into the grass.

Around you evening suddenly rustles in the forests and in the peaks and the mountain meadows of the Big Horns, and then is still.

You think of the great greenness of the forests, and the sharp smell of glacier streams at dusk, and how, in the dusk, you make camp, and gather together a few sticks to begin with, and some dried pine branches, and touch a match to them, and there is a small warm yellow light.

> The conchas and the saddles shine,
> The horses nod, and wake and stare;
> How many a green unknown mile
> Of forest and of tangled fern,
> Of meadows with an aspened isle,
> Before the hills with sunset burn!
> My lips are forming all the while
> A little song, a riding song,
> A song that has a swaying rhyme,
> That hangs together like a thong
> That's linked of lupine and of thyme.
> The music does not reach to sound;
> I would not break the hush around.

You remember, perhaps, this line from Job: "Or speak to the earth and it shall teach thee."

Bibliography

THIS is not a history. I could not write a history if I would. I have none of the qualifications of a historian, honorable as that profession is. The historian is interested only in the purity of his crop; the novelist, or storyteller, to which category I belong, is just as much interested in the tares and thistles as in the wheat.

Even if I were a historian I wouldn't dare write a history of the Far West, or any part of it. Far western history is the most difficult history imaginable. Not only are there a myriad lacunae, to use a fine, big, scholarly word, but the Far West was explored and settled by men and women who not only had as a rule little time to write history while they were making it, but who also knew their own minds, and whose descendants still know theirs. My state, as I have said, boasts somewhere around two hundred and twenty-five thousand inhabitants. It has at least two hundred and twenty-five thousand different opinions, firmly held, and at moments one is inclined to think even more. That's one reason why it is such an interesting state.

A friend of mine trapping in the mountains came down at dusk to the cabin of an old bachelor whom he knew. The cabin was blazing with light and he heard many voices—in turn—indulging in earnest debate. Looking through the window he saw that the old man was alone. He was holding court, taking the part of judge, witnesses, criminal, and counsel for the defense and for the state.

Well, that's the Far West. When a man can't find someone else to argue with, when he's "argument hungry," he splits himself into halves, or quarters, and argues with halves or quarters. We're amoebas when it comes to argument.

The Far Westerner thinks deeply, thinks long, and when

377

at length he has decided, well, all you can say is that he has decided.

To spend an evening with an old-timer is a treat, intellectual and aesthetic. Invariably old-timers tell their stories beautifully, passionately and convincingly, but being men of conviction, you must be prepared for entire contradiction when you spend the following evening with the next old-timer.

At all events, if, in these pages, you have come upon what you consider to be errors in fact or opinion or deduction don't tell me about them. Probably you are right, and probably I'll admit that you are, but that won't change my opinion. I'm a Far Westerner too . . . an adopted one.

The bibliography of the Northwest is voluminous and steadily increasing, but if you wish to read just a few volumes that will tell you practically all you want to know, I cannot recommend too highly the following: *Journals and Letters of La Vérendrye and His Sons,* edited by Lawrence J. Burpee (Champlain Society, Toronto, 1927); *The Cowboy,* Philip Ashton Rollins (Chas. Scribner's Sons); *Red Cloud's Folk,* the definitive history of the Oglala Sioux by George E. Hyde (Univ. of Oklahoma Press); I am indebted to Mr. Hyde for the various Indian names of the Sioux in Chapter III; *The Day of the Cattleman,* Ernest Staples Osgood (Univ. of Minnesota Press); *The Fighting Cheyennes,* George Bird Grinnell (Chas. Scribner's Sons); Granville Stuart's two volumes of *Recollections;* and, of course, *Astoria* and *The Adventures of Captain Bonneville,* by Washington Irving. These are only a few of the books on a long list.

If you wish a clear and dramatic picture of the Sioux, Stanley Vestal's *Sitting Bull* is excellent, and if you wish a clear picture of the trapper, his *Kit Carson* is equally good. Paul I. Wellman's *Death on the Prairie* is an exciting, concise description of the fighting along the Powder. Eugene Cunningham's *Triggerometry* gives you excellent pictures of the most famous badmen of the West.

Mr. George Hyde has recently sent to me the following:

Powder River news item: Colonel F. W. Brabson, 18th U. S. Infantry, commanding Fort Hamilton in New York harbor, wrote me August 9th requesting information on an old picture of Red Cloud, who fought his regiment on Powder River in 1866-67. He intends to have the portrait painted on the wall in the Officers' Mess. This mess is in a casement of the old fort, where Robert E. Lee and Stonewall Jackson served as junior officers. I sent the colonel a very old picture of Red Cloud and he is going to have the painting based on that.

And that is about all you will need, although having read those you will want to read more.

For western atmosphere, of course, nothing has ever beaten, or ever will beat, that classic, *The Virginian*, which is still selling, and which is one of the few books in the past four decades that has sold well over a million copies. Every American boy and girl should be given a copy of *The Virginian* on his, or her, tenth birthday and then be told to read it again when he and she reach twenty. As I write these words, I have just learned of the death of Owen Wister, author of *The Virginian*. He was one of my first guests, years ago—away back in 1910—on the old J Y Ranch when, altogether unexpectedly, I found myself in the dude business, and there an odd thing happened.

Owen Wister had married his cousin and his father-in-law's name was the same as his. While at my ranch, the elder Owen Wister died in an out-of-the-way part of Maine, and I well remember getting Mr. and Mrs. Wister to the railway station, then a hundred and ten miles distant. When Owen Wister emerged into civilization, he found that the world thought that it was he who had died, and he was one of the few men in literature—Mark Twain was another—who possessed columns of obituaries years before his actual death. Curiously enough, these premature obituaries truncated and seriously hampered his subsequent career.

In conclusion, I wish especially to thank Dan Greenburg, Director of Wyoming's State Planning Board, as unselfish a friend as a man can have, with both his time and his information. Wyoming has no more intelligent and devoted son than this adopted Idahoan. I also wish to thank Mrs. Carl Arnold (Olga Moore), wife of the Dean of the University of Wyoming's Law School, and Wyoming's first, homebred, range-raised woman novelist, and a good one too. Powder River is where she came from. Then there is Miss Nina Moran, State Librarian, Miss Mary Marks, Librarian of the University of Wyoming, and Miss Nina Schloredt, kindest and most intelligent of secretaries. In addition to these I wish to thank the Wyoming Stockgrowers Association, and its Secretary, Russell Thorpe, together with the Sheridan *Press* for permission to use the letters from old-timers. I am also indebted to Wyomingana, Inc., Casper, Wyoming, for permission to quote from that excellent book, *Malcolm Campbell, Sheriff*, compiled by Robert B. David. And to W. J. Ghent for his *Early Far West* (Longmans, Green & Co.) and for his article on John Colter in *Wyoming Annals*. Nor am I forgetting dozens of old-timers whose names I could not mention without embarrassing them.

The untitled verse at the end of the last chapter is from a book of poems of mine called *When I Grew Up to Middle Age* (Chas. Scribner's Sons).

Index

INDEX

RIVERS AND AMERICAN FOLK

By

CONSTANCE LINDSAY SKINNER

PUBLISHERS' NOTE

Miss Skinner's essay, "Rivers and American Folk," is included at the end of this volume for the benefit of those readers who are most interested in our American heritage, and who may want to know more of the idea responsible for the Rivers of America.

WHEN American folk have troubles which do not end swiftly, they begin presently to examine their own sources as a nation and their own story as a people. They forget about these in good times. But when they are hit they remember that a new story, like no other in the world, was carried in chapters and cantos across the American wilderness on a strong rhythm and they catch at phrases to console and encourage themselves.

From Maine to New Mexico and from Texas to Oregon, old phrases are being spoken and then newly turned. There is in a number of states a very keen interest in the earlier life of those sections and efforts are being made to interpret it, or at least to make some new record of it, in literature and art. A new record, that is, which shall bring the vital past into the living present, unite them; so that it can be said "this we were and are, and there is beauty in it."

The first necessity of our times, as they relate to letters, would seem to be the retelling of the American story as a Folk Saga; if only to make the parts luminous by shedding on them the light of the whole.

There are, of course, several ways of doing it. Forms came into being for such material long ago.

The two most familiar are the epic poem, such as the Iliad in which a great poet blended fragments of history and myth, and the prose chronicle like the Icelandic Sagas told by several bards who could speak in prose as well as verse. We are conscious of rhythm as we read the Icelandic Sagas, as if thought sounded as it flowed, and the land the Saga-tellers lived in seems to rise visibly and move about the characters in the stories. The American Indians were aware—at least, their poets and dancers were—that rhythm flowed out of their beautiful land to them, bringing them thoughts, helping them to interpret Nature, their past history and their present experience.

The natural rhythm moving the pioneer life of America forward was the rhythm of flowing water. It is as the story of American rivers that the folk sagas will be told.

There are several reasons for telling the great saga along the rivers. We began to be Americans on the rivers. By the rivers the explorers and fur traders entered America. The pioneers, who followed them, built their homes and raised their grain and stock generally at, or near, the mouths of rivers. As their numbers increased they spread up the valleys, keeping close to the streams, since water is an indispensable element of the sustenance of the soil and all animal life. The rivers were the only highways of communication and commerce between solitary hamlets. Settlement expanded from the rivers. To repeat, the first foreigners on these shores began their transition from Europeans to Americans as River Folk.

Naturally enough, the effort to make a whole interpretation of a few American folk in localities has played its part in opening up the greater adventure, namely a composite study of the American Folk as a nation. This interpretative study will be issued in twenty-four volumes by Messrs. Farrar & Rinehart under the general title of *Rivers of America*.

This is to be a literary and not an historical series. The authors of these books will be novelists and poets. On them, now in America, as in all lands and times, rests the real responsibility of interpretation. If the average American is less informed about his country than any other national, knows and cares less about its past and about its present in all sections but the one where he resides and does business, it is because the books prepared for his instruction were not written by artists. Few artists have displayed to him the colors and textures of the original stuff of American life; or made him a comrade of the folk who came from the crowded civilizations of the old world and entered the vast wilderness of the new by all its shining rivers; or thrust him, as one of them, into the clash of spirit with circumstance, under the green arches of beauty, from which emerged the democratic ideal and American individuality—"rugged" truly, in its loyal strength, sacrifice and self-dependence. He has not been led to feel himself a neighbor and brother in the foreign groups which developed into separate Little Americas; evolving their own lore by blending old memories with fancies kindled by the new experience and, as the groups enlarged and mingled and occupied wide sections of river-pathed territory, spreading their imaginative compound of pioneer and Indian folkways, stories, songs and myths like a rich loam over all the seeding-ground of this present nation.

The average American has been prevented from a profound self-knowledge, as a descendant and a citizen, and deprived as an individual of the thrill and inspiration of a dramatic experience, because the epic material of America has been formulated by the scholastics instead of by the artists. This is said with full realization that we can hardly give adequate thanks for the patient researches of the scholars, and may properly say a word in censure of those budding writers who went to colleges and drowsed through the history hours without hearing even a few phrases of the great rhythm pulsing under the berceuse.

What has caused the tardy awakening? Partly, of course, the depression, and the present war of soap boxes beneath the artist's window. But the deeper reason for it is found in the recent self-assertion of the American spirit as expressed in sectional fiction and verse. There is something new in the approach which indicates that the American writer's reliance on traditional forms and methods is coming to an end. The spade striking to the root today seems to be sharper (if also wielded with less concern for surrounding growths): the horizon is often no farther off than the farm fence, the foundry wall, the end of Main Street; and there is an intensive, meticulous, and on occasions tediously thorough, searching of the particular spot and of the minds of the few characters; for the aim, whether it hit true or not, is such spiritual interrelationship of folk and scene that the ground itself shall sound under their footsteps and the shadow of their bodies never pass from the meadow or the forge where they labor.

The historical part played by rivers in the folk

life is evident but it may be a new idea to many that geography itself determined that Americans should first live on and by the rivers.

Here the map of North America unrolls, and comes into the discussion; hinting that Nature foresaw the day when old world folk would feel the need of a new world, and the new world call for inhabitants, and therefore set about her topographical modeling of the major part of the continent, between the Rio Grande and the Arctic sea, with accessibility as her chief aim. She traced large rivers in deep long lines north and south, such as Mississippi and Mackenzie, and east and west, as Rio Grande and Missouri. Others she drew with a fanciful touch; like Ohio and Columbia, which mark the map in large, irregular loops with an angle or two. There seems to be little logic in their designs yet, on their careless rambles—Columbia is more erratic than careless—they make contact with scores of smaller streams and so gather huge territories about them. The modern map is too crowded to do justice to the free beauty of the watercourses. They should be studied from the early pen-and-ink maps of the fur traders, who set down little else; since beauty wherever found is significant, and nothing is more so, and these charts show all the land traversed, and its remotest bounds linked, with rhythm, power, and grace. Philip Turnor's map, the first ever drawn of the beaver-hunters' canoe trails in the Northwest, is before me. The slender curving lines of the rivers, with the lakes set in like jewels, make a design a master goldsmith might choose for an empress's necklace.

In the heyday of the beaver trade, rivers opened

most of the territory between the Arctic coast and the Mexican border to the daring, singing voyageurs of the fur fleets. There was the famous Canadian route, traveled yearly from Montreal by the St. Lawrence, Ottawa, Great Lakes, and Lake Winnipeg to the Saskatchewan, which is commonly said to empty into Lake Winnipeg, but which, in reality, flows through its northern end and continues under the name of Nelson to Hudson Bay. From New Orleans the voyageurs went by the Mississippi and the Missouri, the true Upper Mississippi, to Montana: or ascended the Mississippi to its Minnesota headwaters, crossed into Canada by Rainy River, turned west through Lake of the Woods and English and Red rivers into Lake Winnipeg, and out again by either the Nelson, or the Hayes, thus following the whole of the water chain which connects New Orleans, La., with York Factory on Hudson Bay.

Mackenzie opened two new trails whereby traders in canoes could go from Montreal to the Pacific coast, having entered British Columbia by Peace River and to the polar ocean by Slave River, Slave Lake, and the Mackenzie. If they had a mind to go to the mouth of the Mackenzie from the mouth of the Mississippi they could do so, by water and the portages which were a part of all canoe travel.

When the trade was carried west of the Rockies, the favorite route led through the mountains from the headwaters of the Saskatchewan to that bizarre but navigable north angle of the Columbia River thrust up into British Columbia. From this point the voyageurs might choose to follow the river to Astoria at its mouth; or to swing eastward again by the passes, coming out in time on the Missouri at Three Forks and going on from there to St. Louis or New Orleans.

These were the routes of the great journeys, but the singing voyageurs found many other water trails, branching off from Ohio and Mississippi—the Arkansas, Illinois, Red, Canadian (named for them)—and all the smaller rivers lacing the western lands. They had no thought of settlement, their aims were fur and freedom, as they flashed their paddles in every navigable stream and loosed more than a thousand new songs on the air to the rhythms of new waters. Yet little as they thought it (and how much less would they have desired it!) they were opening a continent to the Folk. By the shining, running rivers, which had inspired men to sing in the wilderness, entered "a great number of weake and distressed soules, scattered, poor and persecuted," to grow strong and confident upon their banks. In which connection, let us recall that long before voyageurs caroled of "good wind and swift water," an Indian poet sang prophetically:—

Bright with flashing light the distant line
Runs before us, swiftly runs,
River runs, winding, flowing through the land . . .
Water brings to us the gift of strength.

Good reasons are found then, in geography and history, for telling the American Folk Saga beside the rivers. In this literary series, however, and it should be emphasized that the *Rivers of America* is literary, as distinct from historical, other reasons are paramount.

The special function of literature is to diffuse enchantment without which men's minds become shrunken and cold. There is a magic in rivers, beyond their gleaming beauty. They are unending rhythm; even when winter closes over them, in the mind, like remembered verse, they are still flowing. They are the motion in the still land, the vital fluid coursing through the clay body. To the first American, the Red Man, seeing them ever flowing away, yet ever there, they were mystery and wonder and beckoning—"That broad water, that flowing water! My mind wanders across it." Rivers symbolized life to him, as they have to other primitive poets in other lands. Our rivers typify for us our living link with the pioneers, who received "the gift of strength" on the banks of American rivers; who there became American Folk "naturalized" not by artificial processes of law and politics but by fearless submission of their hearts, and by honest putting of their hands to work.

The American nation came to birth upon the rivers. Has the fact colored our temperament? Are we a restless people because motion flowed by us continuously in our youth? Are we optimistic, eager, imaginative, daring, and even recklessly experimental, because of the beckoning of the tides "bright with flashing light" which ran swiftly past our known shores into domains beyond our vision? Are we in any part what we are, because of rivers? Possibly only a poet would answer yes. Poets have written of rivers and men, blending the spiritual over-tones of both: Spoon River in our time, Kubla Khan and Sorab and Rustum of an earlier period. Poets had discerned the power of Nature to influence thought and character long before the geographers of our day—more power to them!— began to contend with the economists for the soul of man. The *Rivers of America* offers a new and stirring appeal to the imagination of authors and readers. It is like a light slanted down into the depths of the American consciousness, which have become obscured from us by confusion in the shallows.

It is, of course, impossible to tell the complete story of America in any one series of books. The *Rivers of America,* also, is selective, conceived within definite limits set by the basic idea, namely the rivers and the folk. People are supreme; events are secondary. This is natural and right, because past events in America have been peculiarly an expression of the Folk of America, in striking contrast to the determining events in European history, which have been more often set afoot by monarchs and ruling classes from motives that took small account of the masses. The folk groups have increased mightily since they first planted themselves by the rivers; they occupy large sections and these various sectional groups now need a new introduction to one another. These volumes will make the inhabitants of the Columbia River country, for instance, acquainted with those who live in the Connecticut valley, the people along the Gila with the people beside the Hudson, on the basis of their common origin as River Folk.

The idea of the *Rivers of America* is original, and the plan it dictates breaks with both the old systems used thus far in American literary and historical series; i.e., the chronological plan, which divides material into periods, and the topical plan which arranges it by subjects. The periods will appear in these volumes as the intimate setting in which the folk of the times lived out their lives. The topics will be there, too, treated as larger expressions of the folk's energy, initiative, and will to life and power; which is what they were, in reality.

Instead of volumes on shipping, cattle, the fur trade, etc., stressing their economic importance, fur traders, cowboys, farmers, lumberjacks, fishermen, shipbuilders, will be shown as pioneer folk being cast in new molds by their occupations; for these labors and trades were natural and primitive, indigenous to the folk life, the soil, and the times. The church, the school, and the assembly have their place in these volumes. Civil rights, God, and the primer were held in honor on the banks of American rivers. How many state buildings, besides the Capitol, how many universities, agricultural colleges, how many temples, today lift their domes and towers above running water? A large number. We can still find some of their modest forerunners—on the Connecticut River at East Haddam, for instance, where Nathan Hale's schoolhouse remains and the chaste spire of the old church rises, radiant under the sun and, in the dusk, cloud-white. Religion, arts, crafts, and folklore will be treated in these volumes as characteristic expressions of the folk mind. Religious sects will be handled in the manner of good neighbors who show courtesy to other folks' opinions whether they agree with them or not. The plan will be carried out by the Editor, who has selected the rivers and outlined the material, i.e., the special folk stories for the several books. Each volume will be fully illustrated. The series has two purposes, to kindle imagination and to reveal American Folk to one another. Its authors, illustrators, editor, and publishers are also "folks," absorbed in issuing the story they have discovered which has been, thus far, a lost version of a great saga.

Everyone, apparently, has his "revolution" today —the word makes nice large mouthing, anyway—and American writers and illustrators are entitled to theirs against the "economic interpreters" with their foolish notion that the belly is the hub of the universe and America's own bright and morning star. If, as we hear shouted from the soap boxes, the old America with its customs and ideals is on the way out, we can march to intercept it and seize its baggage for our own purposes. Before the citizen, who flees history books, and is justified, agrees to exchange the American system for some other he should at least know what he is parting with. He really has no idea: he has not met "the folks." To be sure, philosophies change and systems fall; and the present is wiser to forbid nothing to the future since the past, heady too in its time, sought to picket the present and is proved foolish. To the creative imagination, the poet—and all artists are poets whether they use words or paint—the impermanency of structures is relatively unimportant. The significant thing is the beauty they have recorded and the inspirations of that beauty which flowed by many brooks into the long river of human thought.